The Unknown Cultural Revolution

THE UNKNOWN CULTURAL REVOLUTION

Life and Change in a Chinese Village

Dongping Han

MONTHLY REVIEW PRESS

New York

Originally published as *The Unknown Cultural Revolution: Educational Reforms and Their Impact on China's Rural Development* by Garland Publishing, Inc.
Library of Congress Cataloging-in-Publication Data
Han, Dongping.
The unknown cultural revolution : educational reforms and their impact on
China's rural development.
    p. cm.
Author: Dongping Han.
Originally published: Garland Pub. : New York, 2008.
ISBN 978-1-58367-180-1 (pbk.)
    1. Rural development--China. 2. Education, Rural--China. 3. Educational
change--China. 4. Rural children--Education--China. 5. China--Social
conditions. 6. China--Politics and government. 7. China--History--Cultural
Revolution, 1966-1976. I. Title.
    HN740.Z9C6377 2008
    307.1'4120951--dc22

                          2008050563

Monthly Review Press
146 West 29th Street, Suite 6W
New York, NY 10001

5 4 3 2 1

CONTENTS

TABLES

PREFACE

The experiences of the attempts to build socialism in the Soviet Union and China have made it clear that the class struggle continues even after power has been seized in a revolution. They also teach that path to socialism is a long one along an uncertain route. As Mao Zedong wrote:

> Marxism-Leninism and the practice of the Soviet Union, China and other socialist countries all teach us that socialist society covers a very, very long historical stage. Throughout this stage, the class struggle between the bourgeoisie and the proletariat goes on and the question of "who will win" between the roads of capitalism and socialism remains, as does the danger of restoration of capitalism. (Mao Zedong, "On Khrushchev's Phony Communism and Its Historical Lessons for the World: Comment on the Open Letter of the Central Committee of the CPSU," 1964)

Mao's purpose for initiating the Cultural Revolution (1966–1976) was to mobilize and engage millions and millions from all sectors of society—workers and peasants as well as students and intellectuals—in a struggle against the forces within the Party that favored the restoration of capitalism. Among most intellectuals in China and the United States, the Cultural Revolution has been viewed as an era of inhumane chaos. And it is true that the Cultural Revolution was chaotic, with various Red Guard factions (some were even sham Red Guards, possibly organized by those under attack to confuse the masses) and many instances of exaggerated and inhumane treatment of people, including some killings.

Most of the writings about the Cultural Revolution have emphasized the problems, especially of intellectuals. However, in the rural areas of the country this period is still viewed in a much more positive light—an era when much infrastructure was built, agriculture advanced markedly, and attention was paid to problems of the people living in the countryside. Thus the lives of the rural population—in other words, the great mass of the people—during this period has received little attention.

Few people are aware of the visit to China in the summer of 1974, during the Cultural Revolution, by a delegation of U.S. agronomists. They traveled widely and were amazed by what they observed, as described in an article in the *New York Times* (September 24, 1974). The delegation was composed of ten scientists who were "experienced crop observers with wide experience in Asia." As Nobel Prize winner Norman Borlaug put it, "You had to look hard to find a bad field. Everything was green and nice everywhere we traveled. I felt the progress had been much more remarkable than what I expected." The head of the delegation, Sterling Wortman, a vice president of the Rockefeller Foundation described the rice crop as ". . . really first rate. There was just field after field that was as good as anything you can see." They were also impressed with the increased skill levels of the farmers on the communes. Wortman said "They're all being brought up to the level of skills of the best people. They all share the available inputs." A detailed description of their observations on agriculture in China was published in prestigious journal *Science* in 1975 (vol. 188:549-555) by Dr. Sprague. Much of the progress in China's agriculture after the Cultural Revolution was made possible by the advances during that period. Even the increase in fertilizer use that occurred in the late 1970s and early 1980s was made possible by factories that were contracted for by China in 1973.

During prolonged discussions in the 1990s with a former village leader from another province during the Cultural Revolution, I heard a remarkably similar description of events to the one described in this book. The importance of this work by Han Dongping is that it brings into focus the lives of villagers during a dynamic period of great positive change in the countryside. This is a very significant work—a counterweight to the conventional writings about the Cultural Revolution.

Fred Magdoff
University of Vermont
Burlington, Vermont

Preface and Acknowledgments

I grew up in a Chinese village during the Cultural Revolution. In 1966, when the Cultural Revolution started, there were many illiterate people in my village. My mother never went to school and my father had learned how to read and write simple words by attending night school in his factory. My elder sister had only three years of primary school education. In my neighborhood, many children who were a few years older than I either never went to school or dropped out after one or two years of primary school. Not many people finished primary school, and only a few went as far as junior high school in my village.

During the educational reforms of the Cultural Revolution, my village set up its own primary school, and hired its own teachers. Every child in the village could go to the village school free of charge. My village also set up a junior middle school with six other villages. Every child could go to this joint village middle school free of charge and without passing any examinations. The commune that included my village set up two high schools. About 70 percent of school-age children in the commune went to these high schools free of charge and without passing any screening tests. All my siblings except my elder sister, who was four years older than I, were able to finish high school. At the time we did not feel this was extraordinary at all. Most people took going to high school for granted. Upon graduation from high school, I went back to my village like everybody else, and worked on the collective farm for one year and then worked in the village factory for three and one half more years before going to college in the spring of 1978.

While I was in college, the Cultural Revolution, together with its educational reform, was denounced by the government. Deng Xiaoping, the paramount Chinese leader then, said that schools should be like schools. The implication was: the rural schools set up during the Cultural Revolution educational reforms were not like real schools. At the time I felt there was some truth in his comment. The rural middle school I attended engaged in too many things. It had several workshops, a farm and a lab. Students had to work in the workshops and on the farm regularly one afternoon a week. Students also engaged in other money-making activities, transporting gravel to construction sites, cutting grass for animals,

xi

and gleaning wheat and sweet potatoes to help finance the school. I enjoyed these activities at the time, but I did not appreciate their usefulness as educational activities.

In 1986, while teaching at Zhengzhou University, I was involved in a research project in rural Henan with a group of American historians and political scientists. The presence of foreigners in a rural village attracted a big crowd of children of different ages. Out of curiosity I asked some children to read some newspaper headlines. One after another they shook their heads. I thought they were simply shy, but other children explained that they were not in school. To my dismay, it was the same story everywhere that we went. I talked with people about why this happened. They told me that since the collectives were broken up, and land was divided among individual households, village schools were no longer free of charge. Some families could not afford to send their children to school. Others needed their children to help in the fields. Girls were among the first to be sacrificed, as they were assigned to household chores and to take care of their younger siblings. Their parents were more reluctant to invest in their futures than in those of their brothers.

Rural children's loss of educational opportunities shocked me and forced me to think. The government attributed the lack of educational opportunities to the poverty of Chinese rural areas. However, I reached a different conclusion. It was not poverty that deprived the rural children of educational opportunities. Poverty is only a relative term. Why were the children of villagers able to finish high school during the Cultural Revolution? China's rural areas were poorer then than now. Cautiously, and skeptically, I began to appreciate the significance of rural educational reforms during the Cultural Revolution. I myself am a product of these reforms. As an educator I found it hard to remain indifferent to the sad consequences of the condemnation of the rural educational reform of the Cultural Revolution years. I asked myself many questions and decided to study the issue. However, I could not do the research in China then because the Chinese government did not allow research related to the Cultural Revolution.

In 1990, 1 came to study in the History Department at the University of Vermont for my master's degree. I decided to write my thesis on the Cultural Revolution. I felt that there was a need to go beneath the surface structure of the events that occurred at that time. After I entered the doctoral program in political science at Brandeis University I was able to return to China a number of times to research in depth the evolution and consequences of educational policy in the country where I grew up.

I decided to study the impact of the Cultural Revolution of educational reforms on the educational expansion in the rural areas and its relation to the economic development during that period as well. As I began to investigate the education reforms of the Cultural Revolution, I came to understand that they were integrally linked with a comprehensive program of rural development. I broadened the scope of my study to include the changes in rural political culture and efforts to advance agriculture and develop rural industry that were initiated during the Cultural Revolution decade. I conclude, based on the evidence I present in this book, that educational reform, changes in political culture and rural economic development were closely linked.

I received much encouragement from professors and friends for the research I did for both my master's thesis and my doctoral dissertation. I also received institutional support that enabled me to make five field trips to China's rural areas and conduct substantive research on rural educational reforms. I received a summer research grant from the University of Vermont, two Sacher Summer Research grants from Brandeis University, and finally a Spencer Foundation Dissertation Fellowship.

During the course of the research and writing of this study, I have accumulated intellectual debts to numerous professors, colleagues and friends. Professor Peter Seybolt advised my master thesis. He gave me valuable guidance and tremendous encouragement both at the master thesis stage and during the writing of the dissertation. I feel very indebted to him and his wife who read my master thesis as well. Professor Ralph A. Thaxton Jr. guided me through the research and writing of the dissertation. He read the manuscript several times, giving advice for improvement each time. Professor Thaxton and I have fought many friendly battles over this thesis on rural educational reform and my own interpretation of the Cultural Revolution in the countryside. I am enriched for his advice and challenges. The Spencer Foundation asked Professor Stanley Rosen to be one of my critical mentors. He gave me very important suggestions for improving my work. I am also indebted to Professor Ruth Morgenthau and Professor Gary Jefferson for their advice and suggestions while on my dissertation committee. Professor Keith Boeckelman, my colleague at Western Illinois University, read and commented my dissertation extensively. Finally I am greatly indebted to my friend Joel Andreas and his mom Carol Andreas They spend more than one week helping me overhaul the dissertation into a book format.

I want to express my special thanks to many farmers and former rebel leaders in rural Shandong and Henan who spent time sharing with me their thoughts and experiences related to the Cultural Revolution, then a for bidden topic in China. Because they did not want me to use their real names in my work, I can only express my indebtedness to them in a very general way. Without their willingness to share with me their experiences, this book would not have been possible. Since it is in large part an attempt to tell their stories and experiences regarding the educational reforms of the Cultural Revolution, it is only proper that it be dedicated to them.

I also want to thank my editors Mark Henderson, Nicole Ellis, and Becca Murphy for their meticulous attention to the details of the book. I am responsible for all its mistakes.

Dongping Han

Maps

Jimo county is in Shandong province of PR China

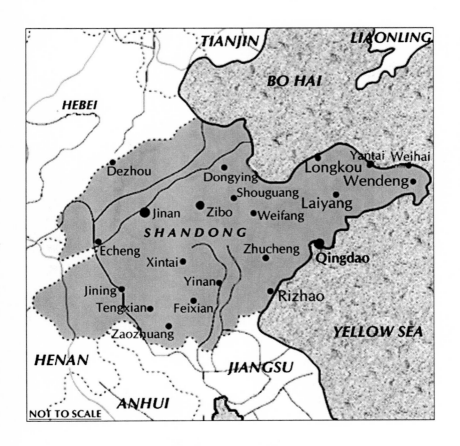

Shandong province

NOT TO SCALE

Jimo county is near Qingdao City

Introduction

Are efforts to attain social equality and efforts to attain economic development contradictory? This is one of the conclusions often drawn from the collapse of the great socialist experiments of the 20th century. Political utopianism, it is reasoned, had to give way to economic pragmatism. In China this view has been strongly promoted by the government for the last two decades. The radical egalitarianism of the Cultural Revolution decade (1966-76), official history maintains, led to economic disaster. The official assessment is widely endorsed by Chinese intellectuals and echoed by Western academics. Indeed, in many accounts the Cultural Revolution has become symbolic of the disastrous economic consequences of the pursuit of egalitarian goals.

This book challenges this view by re-assessing the impact of the Cultural Revolution on rural development. Carefully examining the history of a rural county in Shandong Province, this study contends that the political convulsions of the Cultural Revolution democratized village political culture and spurred the growth of rural education, leading to substantial and rapid economic development. Each of these claims is contentious. The Chinese government maintains that the Cultural Revolution trampled individual rights, devastated the education system and led to economic catastrophe. The reader is invited to examine the evidence from Jimo County, gathered from local interviews and county records, presented in the following chapters.

The first chapter recounts the relationship between Jimo peasants and the Communist Party during the Civil War, the promises the Party made to the peasantry and the betrayal of these promises as communist cadres gradually assumed the traditional autocratic political culture of rural officials, their power over villagers augmented by the collective structure. Chapter Two describes the perpetuation of the urban/rural education gap during the first two decades of communist power and how the rural education system, instead of educating the rural population, acted as effective siphon, draining talent from rural areas. The third chapter describes the successes and failures of the first years of collective economic organization and points to obstacles to rural economic development, including the lack of democratic participation and education.

Chapter Four presents an account of how the Cultural Revolution in Jimo began to change the political culture by enabling villagers to challenge local officials and opening up possibilities for institutionalizing mass participation in decision making. Chapter Five documents the massive expansion of rural education during the Cultural Revolution decade, which allowed virtually all Jimo children to attend primary school and lower middle school, and over two-thirds to attend upper middle school. Despite obvious shortcomings, these new schools, it is shown, produced the first cohorts of educated youth who remained in the village. Chapter Six documents the rapid growth of agricultural production and rural industry in Jimo during the Cultural Revolution decade, highlighting the foundations provided by the development of infrastructure, experimentation, and mechanization. The expansion of rural education, local initiative and mass participation, it is argued, were crucial to these advances.

Chapter Seven outlines some of the consequences of the reversal of Cultural Revolution reforms and the dismantling of rural collectives, including the growth of official abuse and corruption and the collapse of rural education, health care and social welfare systems that depended on the collective economy. While Jimo's economy has continued to grow rapidly during the period of market reforms, aided by Jimo's advantageous geographic position, questions are raised about the threats to future development that long-term deterioration of productive infrastructure and rural education present.

This study, thus, presents evidence that the egalitarian policies of the Cultural Revolution not only did not hinder economic development, they actually played an important role in advancing the rural economy in Jimo County. National statistical evidence is cited to show that the advances in both education and production in Jimo were not unique.

The sharp contrast between the assessment advanced here and the official government assessment undoubtedly results, in part, from a difference in perspective. The official assessment is largely the work of officials and scholars who, because of their social positions, were subject to attack during the Cultural Revolution. Almost all published accounts are written from the perspective of urban elites. This book presents a rural perspective, one rarely found in the current literature on the Cultural Revolution. From different perspectives you see different things and see the same things differently. Radical efforts during the Cultural Revolution to level the social hierarchy of education, for instance, had very different impacts on urban universities and rural middle schools.

INTRODUCING JIMO COUNTY

Jimo County is where I grew up. I decided to study the history of a single county in depth in an effort to ground social science theory in the reality of people in a small place over time. I chose Jimo because I felt that I could get at local knowledge best by going back into the local society of which I have been a part, and where I have an intimate connection with the local people.

Jimo County is on the eastern part of the Shandong Peninsula near the port city of Qingdao. It covers an area of 1,780 square kilometers, and is composed of 30 townships (formerly communes). Within these townships there are 1,033 villages. The county seat is the town of Jimo, with a population of 61,327. Today over 1,000,000 people live in Jimo County; the population has steadily increased since 1949 when there were 656,634 people. When the first national census took place in 1952, population density in Jimo was 341 people per square kilometer; by 1987, the population density had reached 560 people per square kilometer.[1]

With changes in the developmental philosophy of the Central Government over the years, jurisdiction over Jimo County has changed several times. When the Central Government stressed agriculture, Jimo was shifted to either Laizhou or Yantai prefectures. When industrialization was stressed, Jimo was shifted to the jurisdiction of Qingdao City. The frequent changes in jurisdiction made the Qingdao City and Laizhou and Yantai prefectures feel insecure about Jimo County and they all tended to withhold capital investment in the county.

In 1981, Jimo County had a total of 2,670,000 mu[2] land, of which 1,626,900 mu, over 60 percent, was farmland, and nearly 8% per cent was forest and orchards. Wasteland, bare mountain surface, roads, rivers, reservoirs and residences took up the rest. On the national land quality scale of one to eight, Jimo had no first grade land. About 197,000 mu was classified as second grade, 1,172,600 mu as third grade; 326,100 mu as forth grade; 217,700 mu as fifth grade land; 52,100 mu as sixth grade; and 2,050 mu as eighth grade.[3]

Historically, Jimo was a poor place. Before 1949, Jimo's economy was almost entirely agricultural. The northwest third of the county is a lowland area about 20 meters below sea level. The land in this region long had a high level of salt and alkaline and was vulnerable to frequent floods.[4] Jimo people frequently had to flee their hometowns and go to Northeast China during difficult times. Local people called this journey *"chuang guandong"* (venture into the northeast). However, the last of this kind of population exodus in contemporary Jimo occurred during 1959 and 1961, when three years of consecutive droughts and floods plus mismanagement during the Great Leap Forward led to a severe food shortage. About 77,900 people left Jimo for the Northeast during these three years.[5]

From 1961 to 1978, when Jimo County was one of the seventeen counties under the jurisdiction of Yantai Prefecture, it ranked sixteenth among them in wealth. Since 1978, Jimo County has been one of the six counties under the jurisdiction of Qingdao City, and it ranks as a poor county among them. However, compared with the rest of the country, Jimo's productivity is relatively high today.

Much of the data gathered for this study was gathered in South River and neighboring villages in Chengguan Township. There are 50 villages (formally productive brigades) in this township. South River is the village where my family lives. In 1956, the village was organized into *Liming she* (Liming cooperative) and became part of Chenguan commune during the Great Leap Forward. At height of the Great Leap Forward, the village was divided into four teams, two teams in the eastern part of the village and two teams in the western part of the village. My family belonged to the second team in the eastern part of the village. Following the failure of the Great Leap Forward, the size of the production teams was reduced by splitting each team into two. First team became team one and two, and second team became team three and team eight in the eastern part of the village. While the old team three became team four and team five and old team four became team six and team seven. Each team managed its own production with a team committee including a team head, a deputy head, an accountant, a store keeper, work points recorder and woman team head.

Of these eight teams, production team one was the best, and important village leaders were from this team. Their land was better and closer to the village. The value of work points in this production team was generally a few cents higher than other teams. Team members got more grain and cash at the end of the year. Jiang Zhichuan served as the head of the production team throughout the collective period. Team two had about the same amount land of similar quality. It did pretty well but not as good as team one. The team's leadership changed a few times Over the years. Team three and team eight had poorer land. Their land was also furthest away from the village. But team three did better than team eight during the collective period. During the Cultural Revolution years, team eight had to change its leadership almost every year, and the team was highly divided. In 1967, the team was actually divided into two groups, one lead by Liu Chengrui and the other by Guan Dunlin. However, the village and the commune leadership did not sanction the splitting. They had to merge again half a year later. Of the four teams in the western part of the village, team four and five did better than team six and seven. Team seven was the worst among the four teams.

In 1976 with the improvement of collective economy, the eight teams merged into four teams again, to increase the relative equality among the teams. My family fell into the second team again in the eastern parts of the village.

Among the 50 villages in the commune, South River's performance was far below average. It was nicknamed a *lao da nan* (an old headache case), and the commune constantly sent its representatives to the village to help it improve performance. It did poorly not because its land was particularly poor. Villages like Yaotao had worse land and did much better than South river. Many villagers believed that their leaders had too much infighting among themselves.

While this is a case study of only one county, there is no reason to think that the experience of its people is not similar to that of people in many other rural counties. In fact, I have also done interviews in rural Henan Province and have found through preliminary research involving forty randomly chosen local county records striking similarities to my findings in Jimo.[6]

METHODOLOGY AND SOURCES

For quantitative research on Jimo County, I relied on the *difangzhi* (local records) that have become available in the last few years. These records were edited by local historians under official auspices, as is the tradition in Chinese historiography. Although tending to reflect the current official political culture, they nevertheless contain valuable information that can help reconstruct the landscape of recent Chinese political history and help us understand the events of the Cultural Revolution. It should be noted that because of official condemnation of the Cultural Revolution, if there is a bias in the accounts presented in these records, it is not towards presenting Cultural Revolution endeavors in a positive light.

For qualitative research, I have conducted more than 200 interviews with farmers, workers, schoolteachers, students, parents and local leaders in the rural areas of Jimo County. These interviews were conducted over a number of years. Oral histories by rural people are valuable sources for social science research. Often unsophisticated, rural people reveal their feelings, emotions and political attitudes through conversations focused on the subtle details of their daily life experiences. It is important to emphasize that Chinese farmers, like other people in Chinese society, have their own way of conforming to the political correctness of the time. Some of them do not want people to see them as being unsophisticated and unacquainted with what is politically correct or what is incorrect. Sometimes, they will guess or try to pick up hints of interviewers' political biases, and try to adjust their answers to questions posed to them. This would lead to distortion of the truth the interviewers seek.

Rather than either claim neutrality or declare my own political biases when approaching interviewees, I have sought to make my own research agenda insignificant to them. Before interviewing, I prepare a questionnaire for myself in order to structure my questions, but interviewees never see this questionnaire. Instead of asking farmers to answer direct questions, I want my interviewees to tell me their life stories with a natural flow of memories without interruption. I start by inquiring about a farmer's experience during a particular period or event in a very casual manner. Questions are asked only according to the logical flow of the farmers' memories. Even when a farmer started to ramble, I did not interrupt him, playing the role of a mere recorder of the farmer's story. I believe even this kind of rambling — the rambling has an order and significance of its own — can provide me important information I may not be able to get otherwise. My conversations with farmers always take place in a casual and relaxed home environment. This approach reduces the interviewees' burden of seeking political correctness. I eat with interviewees, sleep in their homes, and sometimes work with them in their fields and do household chores, helping create an atmosphere of trust. I was treated as a trusted friend more than a researcher or scholar.

Apart from these major sources, I also used materials from the Chinese press. During and after the Cultural Revolution, there were heated debates in the Chinese press regarding the direction and philosophy of education. Often one-sided, these press articles nonetheless reveal a lot about the role of the Cultural Revolution in the process of educating Chinese society.

Between 1990 and 1997, 1 also corresponded with a broad spectrum of people in China regarding my research topic, including correspondence with former teachers, former classmates, farmers, workers and soldiers who participated in running schools and compiling textbooks and other activities. These informal letters, several dozen in all, are another important complement to the information I gathered from interviews. They were produced with careful thought on the part of the writers.

Notes

1. *Jimo Xianzhi*, 145-147.
2. A mu is about one sixth of an acre.
3. *Jimo Xianzhi*, 129.
4. *Jimo Xianzhi*, 107.
5. *Jimo Xianzhi*, 149.
6. I purchased and asked my friends in China to purchase for me these County Records without any preference. We simply bought whatever we could.

CHAPTER 1

Communist Power and Rural Political Culture

The Chinese Communist Party owed its survival and eventual victory to the rural poor[1] In face of Chiang Kai-shek's slaughter in 1927, a small and defeated Chinese Communist force was able to survive and grow quickly in the Jinggang Mountain region and other remote places because of the support of the rural poor. Overwhelmed by Chiang Kai-shek's superior forces[2] and forced onto the "Long March" in 1934, the defeated Communist forces did not have much else to depend on except the support they got from rural people. They would have perished without that support.

JIMO VILLAGERS' CONTRIBUTION TO THE COMMUNIST VICTORY

In Jimo, Shandong, as elsewhere, it was the support and protection from the rural poor, sometimes at the risk of their own lives, that enabled the weak and scattered Communist forces to fight and grow behind the enemy lines of the Japanese invaders.[3] Some people argue that the common people had supported the warlords and anyone who had a gun.[4] However, there is a big difference between passive (often coerced) and active support. It has been well documented in China that the Nationalist army had to tie up their conscripts for fear of their running away.[5] The Communist forces, on the other hand, were composed of peasant volunteers. That was why the poorly equipped Communist forces could eventually defeat the much better armed Nationalist forces during the Civil War of 1946-1949. Elderly Jimo peasants said that they had risked their own lives to hide the Communist solders pursued by the Nationalists during the Civil War. The support the Communist Party got from the rural people was very different from the passive support the warlords and the Nationalists had extracted from the common people through the use of force.[6]

In 1946, in order to mobilize the rural poor to join the Communist war effort against the Nationalists during the Chinese Civil War, the CCP sponsored the land reform in part of rural Jimo that was under its control. The majority of the rural poor benefited from the land reform at the expense of landlords. With the help of CCP activists, poor farmers organized themselves and struggled against the powerful landlords. They confiscated landlords land and properties and distributed them to the villagers. While the rural poor benefited tremendously from the land reform, landlords lost their land and properties. Some Jimo landlords were treated very badly by the poor

7

and landless at the beginning of the land reform. Some poor farmers took advantage of the opportunities provided by the land reform and took vengeance against landlords who had abused their positions of authority and wealth in their villages. Many landlords had to flee their homes.[7]

The pre-1949 land reform in Jimo was carried out while the CCP was dominant at a particular moment and a particular location. But as the military situation shifted in favor of the Nationalists during the course of the Civil War, CCP forces retreated, and landlords who had fled returned to their hometowns with the Nationalist forces. With the support of the Nationalist forces, some Jimo landlords organized small military groups, which villagers called *"huan xiangtuan"* or "returning home regiments."

When landlords came back to their hometowns in Jimo after CCP forces departed in the face of Nationalist attack, they retaliated against their poor challengers. On April 28, 1946, one group of *huan xiangtuan* led by landlord Huang Xiangcui killed 25 leaders of the Poor Peasant Association and the village militia in Diaoyuzui village. Nie Yinhua, the head of the village Women's Association, was only eighteen years old at the time. The landlords tortured her, then buried her alive. They sawed her palm with a string, and burned her breast with a gasoline lamp. In addition, Nie's parents, grandfather, and two younger brothers were all killed.[8]

On September 12, 1947, landlords Yu Chenfeng and Xin Ziyu, together with their 18 associates, killed more than two dozen people in Dongwa Village. They killed Gu Xiuzhong, the head of the village Women's Association, first. Then they killed her mother and three younger brothers and threw their bodies into a well. Her youngest brother was only eight years old at the time. The landlords held his legs and tore him apart before they threw him into the well. They also killed CCP village head Xin Zegeng's family—his wife, two sons and two daughters. They forced them to kneel beside a well, and struck them with a big shovel and then threw the bodies into the well. Xin's wife was eight months pregnant at the time. In the same night, they also killed Xin Leigeng's family—his wife, his thirteen year old daughter, his nine and five year old sons—in the same way. The next day, the same group of landlords killed Li Xifa, the head of the village Workers' Association, and his wife. They also killed Sun Sifa's mother, two sisters and two brothers because Sun Sifa was a soldier in the Communist-led People's Liberation Army.[9]

On February 21, 1946, Landlord Liu Hengzun, Xu Zhengkai, and Li Qingshan, together with their associates, captured CCP village leaders Ji Qijian, Ji Zhentong, Ji Liangtong and Ji Tongqi from Beihuangfu Village. They tied these people onto trees and sliced them alive. Afterwards, they killed all the family members of these village leaders, old and young. Following that, the same group of *huan xiangtuan* carried out a series of slaughters in Nanbeihang, Dahainan, and Shesheng villages.[10] Many villages in Jimo experienced this kind of violent bloodletting during the Civil War. In Ligou Village and Dun Polan Village more than one hundred people were slaughtered by *huan xiangtuan* during the Civil War. After the CCP won the war, it used these villages as sites of historical education for young people before and during the Cultural Revolution. Schoolteachers, students and farmers traveled to these places to see the bones and skeletons left from the slaughtering.[11]

To the former landlords, these brutalities were justified because the poor and landless had taken their land and properties and jeopardized their way of life. On the other hand, the rural poor and the landless, who were influenced by the communist ideology of class struggle, felt justified in taking the land and properties of the landlords and rich peasants who had been exploiting them. After the Communists won the Civil War, the poor often settled scores with elements of *huan xiangtuan* by executing them. Villagers from Beihuangfu stoned to death Liu Hengzu, head of the *huan xiangtuan*.[12] On January 14, 1948 the *huan xiangtuan* killed the head of the Peasant Association Yu Chenggan and his son in Xiwa Village. The next day, angry villagers killed two *huan xiangtuan* family members in retaliation. They threatened to kill two *huan xiangtuan* family members for every CCP village leader the landlords were going to kill.[13]

In the final confrontation between the Communists and the Nationalists, the Communists were outnumbered, and their weaponry was inferior. The Nationalist army was armed with American weapons and had logistical support from U.S. Support of the rural people for the Communists changed the equation. They rushed to fill the ranks of the People's Liberation Army (PLA). They pushed wheelbarrows to transport supplies for the PLA and carried stretchers to take the wounded PLA soldiers to safety. In Shandong Province alone, several million peasants were on the road transporting supplies with wheelbarrows for the PLA during the Civil War. Ninety thousand peasants from Jimo armed with 3,500 stretchers and 7,600 wheelbarrows participated in the Civil War on the Communist side. Peasants contributed to the war in many other ways. Rural women in Jimo made 5,000 pairs of shoes and ground 650,000 *jin* [14] of grain for the PLA during the Civil War.[15] Such popular contributions and sacrifices helped decide the outcome of the Civil War. It is no exaggeration to say that without the rural people's support there would have been no Communist victory at all.

The Communist policy of land to the tiller and of eliminating entrenched injustices in Chinese society, undoubtedly appealed to the rural poor. The Communists also proposed free universal education throughout China. The talk of free universal education was no doubt very appealing to the rural poor, who were largely denied educational opportunities. In the poor peasant's mind, the lack of access to education was an important factor contributing to their being exploited and oppressed by the rich and powerful in China.

The Communists' wartime strength also came from their willingness to share hardship with the rural poor. The Communist practice of forsaking special privileges fired the imagination of the rural poor who were so accustomed to being bullied and oppressed by state officials and by the rich and powerful. To a significant extent, the Communists derived their strength from the support of the rural dwellers and their legitimacy resided in their commitment to fight for the interest of the rural poor.[16]

REVOLUTIONARIES BECOME RULERS

After the victory of 1949, the Communist revolutionaries became Communist rulers. In this new role and new social context it was no easy task for the CCP to uphold the previous practice, which had been dictated by wartime necessity, of its cadres sharing hardships with the people in general. Entering the cities, the Communists, who previously had been living and fighting in a rural environment, saw a different world. They saw the luxurious apparel, sumptuous five course meals, shiny cars, and special schools and clinics catering to the urban elites. Inevitably, some of them began to be envious of the life style of wealthy urbanites.[17] In this new social context, the rural poor, like the rural spouses of many veteran Communist leaders, became dispensable. Just as many Communist Party leaders divorced their former rural wives after they entered cities, so the Communist Party divorced itself from its former allies in the rural areas.[18]

This is not to say that the rural poor did not benefit from the Communist revolution. They got land, farm implements, houses and furniture through participating in the Communist-sponsored land reform. Through agricultural collectivization, the Communists sought to promote production and improve the living standards of the rural residents through better organization and institution building. But these efforts were not enough to change the peasants' relative position vis-a-vis the urban population. Compared to urban residents, rural residents were still second class citizens in China. The peasantry was still treated as stupid and ignorant *xiangbalao* (a derogatory term for rural residents) under Communist rule. Rural people's incomes lagged behind those of the urban residents.

In Jimo, in the early 1960s the state bought grain from farmers at a price of eight cents a jin for corn, 10 cents a jin for wheat, while farmers had to pay 80 cents a jin for fertilizers and three yuan for a shovel. Farmers in Jimo produced wheat, but they could not afford to eat wheat bread except on special occasions, and they ate sweet potatoes most of the time. In contrast, urban residents in Shandong Province enjoyed a much better diet than their neighbors in rural Jimo — seventy percent of their grain supply was composed of wheat flour, while the other thirty percent was composed of rice, millet, beans and corn flour. Farmers raised pigs and poultry, but they could only afford to have meat on rare occasions such as the Chinese New Year.[19] Urban workers enjoyed free medical care, and their family members could get a fifty percent refund for their medical expenses from the state. Farmers had to pay for their medical bills. There was no medical insurance in China's rural areas and little access to modern medical care before the Cultural Revolution. Urban workers had paid holidays, weekends, paid sick days, insurance against injury and retirement pensions. Farmers had none of these benefits. The government rapidly expanded educational opportunities in urban areas. But in the rural areas like Jimo many rural children were denied a formal education for lack of space in schools.[20]

In 1953, Liang Shuming, a conservative social reformer, protested that "peasants were in the ninth hell, while the urban workers were in the ninth heaven" His protest aroused the fury of Mao Zedong who lashed out at Liang with ruthless sarcasm.[21] It was tragic that Mao, as a great revolutionary leader who fought for the interests of peasants for so long, did not take Liang Shuming's thought-provoking criticism as a warning and use it as an opportunity to make some policy amendments. Mao might have been *too concerned about Communist legitimacy* because Liang's criticisms had revealed a crack in one of the main pillars of this legitimacy — the communist claim to represent the peasants' interests. Whatever the reason, Mao's personal attack on Liang Shuming confused the real issue at hand, and as a result Mao missed a good opportunity to address Liang's concern about CCP's rural policies.

RURAL COMMUNIST CADRES IN POWER

The CCP had very high standards for its new recruits. When the CCP was fighting underground only those who were ready to risk their lives for the cause joined the party. In the villages, those who had the courage to oppose the landlords and rich peasants and support the PLA's war effort joined the CCP.[22] After the CCP's victory, joining the party involved less risk but more benefit. Certain positions were reserved for party members. In order to have an official career, party membership was often indispensable. Naturally, some people joined the party with an official career in mind. But as the benefits associated with party membership increased, it also became harder to acquire party membership in the rural areas. Between the land reform in the early 1950s and the Cultural Revolution in 1966, many rural party branches did not accept new members.[23] The party branch in South River village in Jimo, for example, did not accept anyone into the party during this period. Of the four party members in South River, three were Korean War veterans who joined the party during the war.[24] Jiang Zhiming, the first party member of the village, came from Laiyang County. He came to Jimo with the PLA and was sent to South River to organize the land reform.[25] In the neighboring Guo Jiaxiang and Yaotao villages, the new additions to the party had also joined while serving in the PLA.[26]

The increased difficulty in joining the Communist Party in rural China certainly reduced the chance of opportunists entering the party. But this measure also had negative ramifications. Without new blood, the old party members were able to monopolize village power. The Communist political structure in the rural areas gave the village party secretary supreme authority. Membership in the CCP was an important condition for holding offices in the village. Of the three party members in South River village before the Cultural Revolution, one served as party secretary, one as deputy party secretary, and the third as the security officer of the village. Their control of the village seemed complete. By refusing to let any other villagers into the party, they effectively eliminated any serious competition in the village. Ma Yutong, the security officer of South River village, was illiterate and was frequently drunk. His incompetence was a private joke among villagers. The CCP branch as a whole was supposed to supervise and monitor party members' behavior in the village. But that supervision and monitoring was not effective. Since the two other party members had their own shortcomings to worry about, they had to weigh the possible repercussions for themselves if they were to criticize Ma seriously. As a result, Ma was very secure in his position. Villagers said that he was a very loyal and brave soldier during the war. In fact, Ma often used his wartime performance to justify his drinking and non-participation in physical labor.[27] This feeling of "earned privilege" was not very much different from that of the landlord class who believed that their superior education and wealth entitled them to power in the village.

Corruption and abuse of power became widespread among the rural Communist leaders soon after the CCP came to power. Of the 625 CCP cadres in Jidong (the eastern part Of Jimo),[28] 404, more than 64 percent, were found guilty of corruption charges during *sanfan yundong* (the campaign to oppose corruption, waste and bureaucracy) in 1951.[29] In January 1953, Ji Chuanfu, the deputy militia chief of Jidong, beat up 288 people, forced 107 people to kneel down, and caused four suicides in 14 villages.[30] Perhaps this was an extreme case. The question is how could this kind of outrageous case happen at all? After all, CCP cadres were supposed to be different from the old type of officials, they were supposed to be servants of the people.

One explanation is the continuity of China's political culture. By political culture, I refer to the official code of conduct of a given time period in a given country. This official code of conduct is not necessarily written but is established through a long period of interactions between officials and ordinary people. In old China, the wealthy and powerful landlord gentry who ruled the countryside were known to be arbitrary in dealing with poor peasants, and they were known to have used their political control to advance their economic interests.[31] The *Wen shi ziliao* (culture and history materials) and *difang zhi* (local records) published in recent years in China record the tax farming and abuses of power by the gentry class before the Communists came to power. There is abundant evidence of gentry corruption in the countryside. The long history of the landlord gentry rule in China had set the tone of traditional political culture. It was relatively easy to eradicate the power base of the landlord gentry class by dividing their land and wealth among the poor villagers. But it takes time to build up a new political culture in the place of the old one. In a sense, the Communists built a new house on the ruins of the old with the Revolution, but the air of the old society still permeated this new house. With the old culture largely intact, the new communist leaders who replaced the old oppressors of the village, "slide into certain habits well known to traditional upholders of 'law and order.'"[32]

During the War of Resistance against Japan and the Civil War, many Communist leaders risked their lives. Some sustained serious wounds and injuries. Their sacrifices were tremendous. In the traditional way of thinking, these Communist cadres were *gongchen* (people of great merit) for the new government and were entitled to some special privileges. Naturally, some Communist leaders felt that they earned their right to enjoy the luxuries of the old elite.[33] Zhang Shaofeng, Chief of the *Wu Zhuangbu* (Military Department) in Jimo, for example, liked to show the wounds he sustained during the war years as proof of his merit.[34] According to the traditional political culture, there was nothing wrong with their enjoying these luxuries and privileges. Throughout Chinese history, every time a dynasty was overthrown, people who contributed to the establishment of the new dynasty would take the place of the old elite. This was a natural part of a given cycle of China's dynastic history, and of the restoration that followed a successful rebellion.

ABUSE OF POWER AND CORRUPTION

In 1946, attracted by reports of Yanan's unique political climate, six democratic personages *(minzhu rensbi)* from Chongqing, the wartime capital of the Nationalist State, traveled to Yanan to inspect what was going on in the communist-controlled areas. Huang Yanpei, one of the six visitors, made some remarkable observations to Mao. He said that it was relatively easy to uphold morality and integrity before winning victory. But it would be difficult to maintain the same integrity once in power. Eventually corruption would set in and the system would collapse. And as far as he knew, no organization and no government in China had ever avoided this fate. Mao answered Huang's challenge with confidence that the Chinese Communist Party had already found a new way to transcend that cycle. The new way was *minzhu* (democracy).[35] Only by placing the government leaders under the supervision of the people, Mao said, would government leaders maintain their integrity.[36]

After the Communists took power, Mao Zedong was a curse to corrupt officials in his government. To fight official abuses and maintain a clean government, Mao launched numerous campaigns. The *sanfan* (anti-corruption campaign) in 1951-1952 was the first such movement. *Xin sanfan yundong* (a new campaign to oppose bureaucracy, commandism and violation of disciplines and law) followed in 1953. In the same year, there was also *wufan yundong* (campaign to oppose corruption, speculation, waste, fragmentism and bureaucracy). In 1954, *ganbu zhengfeng yundong* (the rectification campaign among the cadres) was conducted. In 1955, there was *shuiwu bumen fantanwu yundong* (anti-corruption campaign among tax collectors). Another *zhengfeng yundong* (rectification campaign) was introduced in 1957. After the Great Leap Forward, *nongcun sanfan yundong* (rural campaign to oppose corruption, waste and bureaucracy) was initiated in 1960. Finally the *siqing yundong* (the socialist education campaign) took place in 1964-65.[37] Before the Cultural Revolution, there was an anti-corruption campaign almost every other year. Still, without a radical change of the political culture which would empower ordinary people, all of Mao's efforts to curb official abuse fell short.

As was the case with oppression, corruption, and abuses of power before the Communist victory, lack of political control by villagers was a major cause behind the abuse of power among village leaders in the Communist era. Mao Zedong stressed that it was the Chinese people who gave the Communist Party power, and that the CCP had to be accountable to the Chinese people.[38] But this was true only in the abstract. That power, which originally came from the people, was lost in the real world of everyday political operations. The CCP cadres who ruled rural areas after 1949 did not derive their power from villagers. They were not elected by the villagers. Further, their political fortunes were dependent on their superiors, not on the people they governed. Consequently, commune and village leaders were more inclined to please their patrons than respond to villagers' needs and aspirations.

Theoretically, with the collectivization of the means of production in the rural areas in the mid-1950s, farmers were supposed to become the real masters of the collectives, and should have been able to participate in decision-making processes as owners of the collective enterprises. As everybody was economically equal and had an equal economic stake in the collective, ordinary members of the collective should have been empowered both politically and economically, thus providing conditions for democratically managing the collective. In reality, the collectivization of the means of production did not transform everybody into equal owners of the collective, and did not empower the farmers politically or economically to the extent expected. Instead, it turned farmers into dependents of the collectives the same way it turned factory workers into dependents of modern industry. This, of course, is a common trend in the process of modernizing production. But without institutionalized popular supervision and democratic mechanisms in the newly organized agricultural cooperatives, village party leaders acquired even greater power over villagers through collectivization. This made farmers more vulnerable than before to potential abuse of power in the village.

Prior to collectivization, village leaders' power was limited. They were essentially managers of the public affairs in the village. Their basic functions were those of tax collectors and arbitrators of disputes among villagers. Collectivization gave village leaders more tantalizing power. The grain production of the collective was under their management. Their management of this grain, which Chinese called *kouliang* (the life-sustaining grain), meant control of villagers' lives. Thus, though unintended, collectivization often placed ordinary villagers at the mercy of village power holders.

The concentration of power in the hands of party officials who were not responsible to ordinary villagers had tragic consequences during the Great Leap Forward (1958-9).[39] Bent on pleasing their superiors and on achieving quick results, village and commune officials became slave drivers in some cases.[40] Many leaders forced villagers to work twenty hours a day. Frequently, it was no longer possible for rural people to meet the officials' ever-increasing demand for quick results.[41] The commune and county leaders' irrational planning, in disregard of villagers' conventional wisdom, and their tendency to inflate production figures during the Great Leap Forward caused the break-down of effective communication.

Many commune and village leaders in Jimo ignored the food shortages in their communes and villages, and sold more grain to the state to please their superiors. Consequently serious food shortages occurred in some areas.[42]

A rural investigation conducted jointly by the Shandong Provincial Government and Qingdao Municipal Government illustrates this point. In September 1959, upon receiving an anonymous letter protesting the miserable living conditions in northwest Jimo County, the Shandong Provincial Government and Qingdao Municipal Government sent eight officials to investigate the case.[43] The investigation covered several villages of three communes in the northwest of Jimo County. The investigation team found that village party leaders in these villages were corrupt. They did not participate in productive labor as required by the CCP. Because they had access to collective grain, the leaders often ate and drank at the expense of the collectives. In some cases, they had illegally divided collective grain among themselves without the knowledge of ordinary villagers. When ordinary villagers who worked in the fields did not have enough to eat during the years of grain shortage following the Great Leap Forward, village leaders and their families were well-fed.[44] The party secretary in Xiaobu village, Lingshan Commune, for example, still had rice to feed his family when ordinary villagers had to feed themselves with wild vegetables and tree leaves.[45]

Leaders in these Jimo villages were frequently arbitrary and ruthless in managing village affairs. To protect their authority, they made and enforced harsh and arbitrary rules and regulations in the villages. During the food shortage of 1959-1960, when villagers were hungry, village leaders stipulated that anybody caught stealing collective crops would be fined ten times the quantity he or she stole. Of the 268 households in Xiaobu village, 84 households had been fined. Of the 84 households that were fined, 30 percent were reduced to begging outside of the village.[46] The Communist Party secretary of Xiaobu Village proclaimed in a village mass meeting: *"Shengchan you ni, shenghuo you wo"*. (You do the work in the field, and leave the management of grain to me.).[47] As there was no popular supervision in the village, village leaders were intolerant of criticism from villagers. In the spring of 1959, amid the campaign to air opinions and grievances *(daming dafang yundong)*, common villagers—encouraged by the campaign—aired their grievances against village leaders. When the campaign was over, the village party secretary said: *"jin chun nimen zheng wo yi ge yue, wo zheng nimen yi nian* (This spring you gave me a hard time for a month. I will give you a hard time for a whole year).[48]

Subjected to official abuse, some villagers even chose suicide as a way out. Yu Jiushu, a villager from Henan Village, Lingshan

Commune, Jimo county, was recruited as a worker by a state enterprise during the Great Leap Forward. When the Leap failed, he lost his job and had to return to his former village. But the leaders in his village refused to give him his share of grain on the ground that he did not bring his grain ration papers back with him to the village.[49] Yu Jiushu was forced to share with his mother what was only one person's grain ration. A full share of grain ration was hardly enough during the time of grain shortage; a half share of grain ration made life literally intolerable. In the end, Yu Jiushu's mother committed suicide to avoid starvation of both her son and herself.[50]

No doubt the village party leaders' behavior was outrageous, and should be condemned. But should not Yu Jiushu be partly responsible for what had happened? He and his mother did not have to put themselves through such suffering in the first place. They could have fought for their legal rights, but their ignorance of the law and their culture of submissiveness failed them.

Another villager from the same village went out to steal green crops with his friend.[51] However, his friend was caught in the action by the village crop watchers. Even though he managed to escape, he knew they would soon discover his involvement. The more he thought about the humiliation and the fines, the more scared he became. In the end, he took his own life.[52] Stealing and eating green crops was a conventional practice and an important strategy for fending off starvation in time of grain shortage. To be fair, the consequence of wide spread stealing and eating green crops could be suicidal. At the best, eating green crops led to a poorer harvest. At the worst it could cause total crop failure which meant even worse grain shortages for the next season, as actually happened in some parts of Jimo County during the grain shortage following the Great Leap Forward. Any responsible village leaders would have to do something to monitor the practice if not stop it completely. But at the same time, the punishment did not need to be so harsh as to frighten people to commit suicide. Eating grain crops was, after all, understandable in conditions of hunger. The villager did not have to commit suicide for such an offense. He and his friend could have fought for their legal rights in a court of justice. But again his ignorance of the available legal resources and his acceptance of the culture of submission led him to a tragic course of action.

The suicides mentioned above were no doubt extreme cases, and could not be considered typical. However, minor abuse and corruption among the lower level government officials in those years were typical. Of a dozen villages I have studied during my fields trips, virtually every one of them had problems of corruption and abuse of power prior to the Cultural Revolution.

VILLAGERS' CULTURE OF SUBMISSIVENESS

The old political culture of officials that underlay the abuse of power in the rural areas was only part of the problem. The culture of ordinary villagers contributed to the problem as well. At the very bottom of the Chinese social hierarchy, ordinary villagers had become accustomed to oppression and abuse. As a result, official abuse was normal for them.

The submissive culture of the abused was formed over a long time, and it was started in the family, in the upbringing of children. Rural children often get the following advice from parents: *laoshi changchang zai, gangqiang shifei duo* (submission ensures a safe life, courage leads to trouble and risk).[53] In a way, this culture of the abused was a factor contributing to the problem of official abuse of power. In the final analysis, officials abused their power in part because the abused let them get away with it time and time again.

In South River, for instance, villagers often tried to please the village leaders. During the Great Leap Forward, every woman was mobilized to work either in the public dining halls or in the fields. Every morning, the women in the public dining hall got up early to prepare breakfast for the whole village. Some women would prepare some special breakfast to bring to the house of Liu Mengxun, head cook of the village dining hall, so that Liu and his wife could eat in their bed. There was absolutely no need for them to do this for the head cook and his wife. They did it because they wanted to cultivate some special relations with their superiors.[54] By doing this extra service for their superiors, however, they were actually reinforcing the tendency for leaders to demand special privileges and to abuse their power and authority. Head cook Liu, originally a timid person, grew bolder and bolder in his abuse of power. He began to pilfer public money and public grain.[55] Following the failure of the Great Leap Forward, Liu Mengxun's superiors threatened to look into his records. Liu was very scared, and he committed suicide.[56]

The high-handed political style of many village leaders was unacceptable according to CCP rules and state legal codes. If villagers knew how to fight these kinds of official abuses, they often could have won the fight. However, the timid and illiterate villagers used a familiar strategy to deal with oppressive village leaders: *nilai shunshou* (put up with the oppression submissively). Villagers did not know of the law and the CCPs internal rules, much less how to use the law and CCP rules to fight the illegal activities. What villagers saw from experience was the traditional practice: *guan guan xiang hu* (officials look after each other). As a result, instead of confronting the illegal village party leaders openly, many chose to accept the oppression submissively.

Abuse of power in China is often attributed to the lack of an adequate legal code. Of course, the existence of such a legal system is important. But legal codes alone cannot solve any problem if the political culture and mentality of the ordinary people remains unchanged. Here education to empower the ordinary rural residents is key. If the ordinary people do not know how to use legal codes to defend themselves and fight those who are abusing their power, the existence of legal codes accomplishes nothing.

Abuse and corruption took place in rural China not only because the laws and regulations banning abuses of power and corruption were insufficient. These abuses occurred also because the common people did not know how, or were not predisposed, to use the existing laws and regulations to fight corrupt and abusive officials. In order to empower ordinary villagers it was necessary to transform their political culture of submissiveness and to increase both literacy and political awareness.

Notes

1. Mark Selden in his *The Yenan Way in Revolutionary China* (Cambridge: Harvard University Press, 1971); Ralph Thaxton in his *China Turned Rightside up: Revolutionary Legitimacy in the Peasant World* (New Haven: Yale University Press, 1983) and many others have shown the role the rural people played in the Communist success.

2. In the early 1930s, Chiang Kai-shek's National Government organized five wiping out campaigns with the aim to eliminate the communist forces. The Communist was able to-defeat the first four. Chalmers A. Johnson attributes CCPs defeat in Jiangxi Period to its failure to mobilize the peasants with a viable program. See Chalmers Johnson, *Peasant Nationalism and Communist Power* (Stanford: Stanford University Press, 1962) 2. 1 think the military factors played a more decisive role in CCPs defeat then.

3. Interview with former communist officials in Jimo, Shandong, Summer 1997.

4. One of the readers of my dissertation raised this question. I feel that he overlooked the different styles of Communist army and other armed forces in Chinese history.

5. See Barbara Tuchman, *Stilwell and American Experience in China,* 1911-1945 (New York: The Macmillan Company, 1971), and John Service, *The Lost Chance in China,* (New York: Random House, 1974).

6. Interview with villagers in Jimo, summer, 1995. In the first two decades after the CCP came to power, many Chinese films and literary works centered on the theme of special relation between the Communists and Chinese rural people. Films and literary works with this theme include "*Ku Caihua,* (The Bitter Flowers) *Chao Yanghua* (The Flowers that Orient to the Sun), *Ying Chunhua* (The Winter Jasmine Flower), by Feng Deying; *Lie Huo jin Gang* (Warriors of Fire), *Pingyuan You Jidui* (Guerrilla Fighters on the Plain), *Di Hou Wu Gong Dui* (Armed Worker Team Behind the

Enemy Line).
7.   *Jimo xianzhi*, 225.
8.   Fan Qilong, "The Death of Ni Yinhua," *Jimo Wenshi Ziliao (Jimo Cultural and Historical Materials) Vol. 11, 101-106.*
9.   Xin Shuying, "Dongwa Tragedy," *Jimo Wenshi Ziliao,* (Jimo Cultural and Historical Materials) Vol. 3, 157-164.
10. Wenquan Township Local History Committee, "Beihuangfu Tragedy," jimo *Wenshi Ziliao,* (jimo *Cultural and Historical Materials) Vol. 2,* 165-173.
11. Interview with school teachers in Jimo, summer, 1997.
12. Wenquan Township Local History Committee, "Beihuangfu Tragedy," *Jimo Wenshi Ziliao, (Jimo Cultural and Historical Materials),* Vol. 3, 165-173.
13. Xin Shuying, "Dongwa Tragedy," *Jimo Wenshi Ziliao, (Jimo Cultural and Historical Materials), Vol. 3,* 157-163.
14. Jin is the Chinese unit of weight, about 1.1 pounds.
15. *Jimo xianzhi*, 613. See also Ralph Thaxton, *China Turned Rightside Up* (New Haven: Yale University Press, 1983).
16. See Mark Selden, *The Yenan Way in Revolutionary China* (New Haven: Yale University Press, 1971) and Ralph Thaxton, Jr., *Salt of Earth* (Berkeley: University of California Press, 1997).
17. Mao Zedong, *Mao Zedong Xuanji (The Selected Works of Mao Zedong)* (Beijing: People's Publishing House, 1977) Vol. 5, 329. Mao mentioned in his speech at the second meeting of the eighth CCP central committee on Nov. 15, 1956, that in 1949, many CCP leaders demanded to raise salaries because the Capitalists had five dishes at their meals.
18. There are no statistics regarding Communist officials divorcing their former rural wives, but it appears to have been a very common phenomenon. I know of several cases. There is a film, *Niheng Dongxia de Shaobing (Sentry Under Niheng Lights),* which is a story about the PLA in the first few weeks after entering Shanghai. Chen Xi, one of the main characters of the film, began to compare his rural wife with the urban young woman and began to despise her. It is symbolic of the mentality of the victorious army.
19. Interview with villagers in Shandong and Henan, 1990.
20. Interview with rural residents in Jimo, summer, 1997.
21. Mao Zedong, *"Pipan Liang Shuming de Fandong Sixiang,"* ("Criticizing Liang Shuming's Reactionary Thought") *Mao Zedong Xuanji (Selected Works of Mao Zedong) Vol. V, p 107.* In this article, Mao did not answer Liang Shuming's criticism of the Communist rural policy directly. Instead he attacked Liang's history and integrity. Mao's attack was highhanded and unreasonably harsh.
22. Interviews with farmers in Jimo, summer 1997.
23. Mao ordered a moratorium on admitting new members in rural areas in early 1950s in order to reduce the chance of admitting opportunists. See Mao, *"Wei Zhengqu Guojia Caizheng Jingii Zbuangkuang de Jiban Haozbuan er Douzheng,"* (Strive for a

Fundamental Improvement of the National Economic and Financial Situation) *Mao Zedong Xuanji (Selected Works of Mao Zedong) Vol. V,* 20.

24. Interview with villagers in Jimo, 1986.
25. Jiang committed suicide when found guilty of corruption during the *sanfan yundong* in 1951-1952. Interview with villagers in Jimo, 1989.
26. Interviews with farmers in Jimo, summer 1989.
27. Interview with villagers in Jimo, 1989.
28. Jidong County comprised of the eastern part of the Jimo County. It was an administrative entity set up by the underground CCP during the war of resistance against the Japanese and lasted until 1956. In March 1956, it merged with Jimo County.
29. *Jimo xianzhi,* 33:39.
30. *Jimo xianzhi,* 35.
31. William Hinton discusses the gentry's rule in Zhangzhuang in his book *Fanshen,* 58-95.
32. Hinton, *Fanshen,* 225.
33. Mao talked about this phenomenon in his "Report to the Second Meeting of the Seventh Central Committee of the Chinese Communist Party," Selected Works of Mao Zedong, Vol. IV.
34. Interviews with farmers in Jimo, 1993.
35. "Minzhu" is somewhat different from democracy. The Chinese term literally means letting the people decide, or let the people govern. It indicates a kind of decision making power on the part of the people. Therefore the Chinese term has somewhat different connotation.
36. Xuo Jianhua, " *Women nong Tiaochu Zhege Zhouqi lu, Mao Zedong Yu Minzhu Renshi Huang Yanpei,"* Mao Zedong and His Rightist Friends (Chengdu: Sichuan People's Publishing House, 1992) 114.
37. Jimo dashi ji (Chronology of Events in Jimo), 39-67.
38. *Mao zhuxi yulu,* (Quotation of Chairman), 76.
39. During the Great Leap Forward (1958-9), some local government officials pushed for extremely rapid economic development. The movement led to severe economic disruptions that, combined with poor weather conditions, resulted in widespread food shortage in some parts of rural areas.
40. Several recently published local records, such as Jimo xianzhi, Shandong Province, and Shanglin County Records, Guangxi Zhuang Nationality Autonomous Region, reveal the extent of cruelty of local officials in their treatment of common people in their effort to achieve quick result. See also, Ding Renpu, *"Huoyang Zhengsheng de Wuwei Gongchan Meng,"*(Wuwei Communist Dream and its Disastrous Consequence") *Gong Heguo Yishi (Anecdotes of the Republic)* (Beijing: Economy Publishing House, 1997) Vol. 11, 462-475.
41. Interview with farmers in Jimo, Shandong Province, summer, 1997.
42. To be sure, Mao and other top leaders were responsible for the

failure of the Great Leap Forward, but the arrogance, arbitrariness and mismanagement on the part of lower level officials greatly exacerbated the consequences.

43. *Jimo Xianzhi* 34:50.
44. *Jimo Xianzhi* 34:35.
45. Ibid. 34:55.
46. Ibid. 34:54.
67. Ibid. 34:56.
48. Ibid. 34:56.
49. During the Great Leap Forward, many urban factories came to the rural areas to recruit new workers. Faced with economic difficulties caused by the natural disasters and Russian withdrawal of technicians and the Russian pressure for China to pay back the loans and debts, many factories had to cut back their work forces. Some of the rural workers had to go back to their former villages. When a rural worker left his village, he had to get his grain ration paper from his village government and bring it to the city where he was going to work. The village would then stop providing him with grain, and the city would upon the receipt of his grain ration paper start providing him with grain. When he came back to the village, he was supposed to get his grain ration paper from the city and gave it back to the village. Transfer from rural to urban areas was hard and required full documentation. Transfer from urban areas to rural areas was relatively easy and usually did not require strict documentation.
50. *Jimo xianzhi, 34:56.*
51. Green crops refer to unripe crops, such as wheat, corn and sweet potatoes. Because they were unripe, eating them often involved a lot of waste.
52. *Jimo xianzbi 34:56.*
53. Interview with villagers in Jimo, summer, 1990.
54. Interview with villagers in Jimo, summer, 1997.
55. Interview with villagers in Jimo, Summer, 1997.
56. Interview with villagers in Jimo, summer, 1997.

CHAPTER 2

Rural Education:
Unfulfilled Promises

Before the Communist Party came to power it had vigorously denounced educational inequality between urban and rural areas and proposed free universal education throughout China. As early as 1926, the CCP Hunan Provincial Committee, in a declaration entitled, *The Minimum Political and Economical Demands of the Peasantry,* demanded free universal education on behalf of the rural poor.[1] That same year, the Hunan Peasant Congress, led by the CCP, resoundingly denounced the social injustices that existed in the Chinese educational system. The rural poor, the Congress declared, bore the cost of education, but they were deprived of educational opportunities. The fruits of poor peasants' labor enabled a small privileged group to enjoy the benefit of education. But this small privileged group then turned around to deceive and bully the rural poor, and to label them as 'ignorant and stupid'.[2] These 1926 Hunan declarations clearly reflect the CCP and Mao's views at the time.

PERPETUATING EDUCATIONAL INEQUALITY

When the Communists came to power they inherited the legacy of pre1949 policies that had financed urban education at the expense of the countryside. While the Communists had denounced the social injustices inherent in this educational system when they were in opposition, once in power, CCP officials began to entrench themselves and their families in urban areas and began to see the existing educational inequality in a different light. Perhaps this was because their children stood to benefit from this educational inequality. In any case, urban education expanded faster than rural education. Educational inequality between urban and rural areas, which was partly responsible for other gaps between urban and rural life, persisted under the Communist rule. Resources were directed to urban "key schools", where officials' children received special treatment, while rural education was largely ignored.

The rationale for China's key school system was to give the nation's most talented more attention in order to produce the urgently needed specialists for national construction. The reality was that in the cities children of old and new elites received better education at the expense of others, particularly of rural people. The consequence of this central government educational policy was that the social inequality created by the elitist pre1949 educational tradition was perpetuated in the so-called new socialist society.

There were key primary and middle schools in Beijing, the national capital, in each provincial capital, and in each major provincial city or county seat to which high officials' children had easy access. These key schools received more government funding and had the service of the best teachers. In essence, this key school system was not much different from the *"zong xue"*,[3] that is, the old school systems set up by the different royal families throughout Chinese history for the privileged children, whose parents had contributed to the military success of the different royal families. Consequently, the key schools in the cities flourished, while rural education suffered for lack of attention and funding from the government.

It would be unreasonable to demand that the CCP-led government provide equal education for rural and urban area in a short time. It was simply beyond the government's ability to do so. In urban areas, the school facilities had been built up over an extended period. The teachers there had received better education and had more experience, which translated into better educational opportunities in the cities.

In many rural areas, schools did not exist when the Communists came to power in 1949. In all rural areas there were not enough schools or teachers to provide all school-age children with an education.[4] In Jimo County in 1950 only 48 percent of children between the ages of seven and twelve years were enrolled in primary school.[5] Only a tiny fraction attended middle school. In 1956, seven years after the Communists came to power, 66 percent of school age children were able to enroll in primary schools.[6] This was certainly progress, but progress could have been much faster.

The odd thing was that the CCP government began to worry that rural education had developed too fast. In 1953, the State Council (*Zheng Wuyuan*) ordered rural education to "overhaul and consolidate, develop key schools and guarantee quality and progress steadily," (*zhengdun gonggu, zhengdian fazhan, baozheng zhiliang, wenbu fazhen*). It wanted rural education to slow down.[7] From 1949 to 1956, government revenues in rural Jimo more than tripled, increasing from 2,642,000 yuan in 1949 to 8,398,000 yuan in 1956.[8] However, educational expenditures in rural Jimo actually declined from 789,000 yuan in 1953 to 721,000 yuan in 1956.[9] If the government had only kept its investment in rural education abreast of the increase of its revenue, rural education would have been in much better shape and the gap between urban and rural education would not have been so great.

THE GREAT LEAP FORWARD AND RETREAT

By the mid-1950s the increasing gap between urban and rural education was obvious. It became one of the factors driving the Great Leap Forward in 1958. During the Leap attempts were made to improve rural education and medical care in order to reduce the gap between urban and rural life. One of the most widely used slogans at this time was to reduce the three big gaps *(san da chabie)*. These gaps referred to the gap between urban and rural areas, the gap between workers and farmers, and the gap between mental and manual labor *(chengxiang chabie, gongnong chabie, naoti chabie)*. Villagers interpreted the introduction of this slogan as an indication that the government had become aware of rural problems.[10] They initially greeted Great Leap Forward policies as a means for rural people to catch up with their urban counterparts.[11]

Great Leap Forward policies led to substantial, if temporary, gains in education in rural Jimo. In 1958, the opening year of the movement, educational expenditure in Jimo increased to 1,662,000 yuan, twice as much as in 1956. The number of primary schools almost doubled from 719 in 1957 to 1434 in 1958. The rate of enrollment of children between the ages of seven and twelve increased from 71 percent in 1957 to 95 percent one year later. This was one of the reasons that rural people initially embraced the Great Leap Forward with great enthusiasm.[12]

However, the number of rural schools was cut back as soon as the government began the economic downsizing following the collapse of the Great Leap Forward.[13] The change in educational policies corresponded with the ascendancy of the different power groups inside the CCP. The pre-Leap rural educational policy was the product of the privileged, urban-based conservative policy makers, while the Great Leap educational policies represented the ascendancy of the radical group inside the CCP. The setback of the Great Leap provided the opportunity and occasion for the conservatives to gain dominance in the educational arena, and they accordingly cut back spending on rural education. It was becoming clear that there were two lines inside the CCP regarding rural educational development. As a result of government neglect of rural schools during most of the period between 1949 and 1966, education in rural areas remained very inadequate. Many village children did not attend primary school and even fewer had the opportunity to attend middle school and high school.

REASONS VILLAGE CHILDREN DID NOT ATTEND SCHOOL

Three factors accounted for non-enrollment of many village children in primary school before the Cultural Revolution. First, children were unable to meet initial entrance requirements or did not pass tests for promotion to higher grades. Primary schools screened prospective students by asking them to count to one hundred, to make simple calculations, and to read and write a few simple Chinese characters. Those who were able to start school then had to pass qualifying exams to get into higher grades. For example, Double

Temple junior primary school, which served three villages, had two classes in grade one, two, and three, but only one class in grade four. The two third grade classes would be reduced to one class in forth grade, which meant that half the students would fail to be promoted. Only half of the fourth grade class could expect to be promoted to the fifth grade in another senior primary school in Fangzi Jie village across the river.[14]

This screening was dictated for the most part by the limited space in the school, not by the educational needs of poor but potentially talented village children. If there had been more teachers and school space, school administrators would not have had to utilize a tough test at the fourth grade level in order to reduce the number of children going up to the fifth grade. Sun Xizheng, a graduate of the government-run Double-Temple junior primary school in South River Village, and Chu Xiuying, a retired school teacher from the same school, said that those who were not promoted from grade four to grade five were good and hard working students. They were not promoted simply because there was not enough space in. Fang Zijie Primary School, which had to accommodate a number of junior primary schools in the area.[15]

Second, some of the parents could not afford to pay tuition and other school related costs. Even though costs were low (1.2 *yuan* for tuition and a few more *yuan* for miscellaneous costs including books, paper and pencils), this amount posed a financial difficulty for some parents.[16]

Third, rural parents needed their children, particularly girls, to do household chores. When children had to walk long distances to go to school in another village, it often meant that they had little time to do household work. Because many village children were not enrolled in school, parents did not find it difficult to rationalize their decision to deny their children an education in order to have helpers in the household and in the fields. They were only doing what their friends and neighbors were doing at the time. An entrenched culture of survival worked against educating children.[17]

Because there were a large number of children outside school and they appeared to be having a "good time," they were an attraction for those children who were not enjoying themselves in school. Zhang Suocheng's case in South River Village illustrates this point. Suocheng was sent to school by his parents, but the other six children in his neighborhood did not go to school. Suocheng hated the idea of parting with his playmates. In the early morning when his parents forced him to go to school, his playmates were not up yet. While in school he thought about the fun his friends were having with their games and self-made toys. After one week in school, he decided to join his friends again without telling his parents. Each morning, he left home with his school bag. But instead of going to school, he went to join his friends. For three months, his family did not know what was going on, and the school did not bother to notify the family of his extended absence. His aunt saw him playing with other children in the neighborhood around 10:00 one morning with his school bag hung over his shoulder and called his parents' attention to it. Only then did the parents realize that their child was playing truant all this time.[18]

Han Xiuying, Liu Meijun, Wang Shuying, Zhou Yuhua, Lu Simu, and Wang Zhenying were six girls from the eighth production team of the South River Production Brigade. None of them finished primary school. Han Xiuying, Lu Simu and Liu Meijun dropped out because their parents needed their services at home. Zhou Yuhua, Wang Shuying and Wang Zhenying were forced out because there was not enough school space. They first helped with the household chores and later worked in the fields. At the time, everybody accepted this as normal.[19]

The situation of children in South River Village was typical of children in rural Jimo. If they were fortunate enough to finish the first four years of junior primary education, which was usually in a school in their own village or in a neighboring village, they had to sit for an entrance examination in order to be able to enroll in a senior primary school. Each child had about a 50% chance in that examination. Those who failed would get a junior primary education diploma and enter the work force. Those who succeeded would enroll in a senior primary school further away from home and study for another two years. If they successfully accomplished the two years of study in a senior primary school, they would be able to sit for another entrance examination in order to enroll in a lower middle school. For rural children who aspired to a middle school education, the hurdles were even more difficult. Before the Cultural Revolution there were only eight middle schools (grades seven through nine) in Jimo County. This was an increase over the two that had existed in 1949, but it was still far too few for a county with a population of 800,000. These schools enrolled a total of 1,300 students in 1966.[20] The competition to get in was fierce, and students had about 50% chance of success. Those who failed the entrance examination for middle school would enter the work force. Those who succeeded in the examination would be placed in a middle school according to their scores.

Children who were not able to get into a lower middle school were between age thirteen and fifteen. Girls would stay at home and help their parents with household chores, and boys would find work in the production teams during busy seasons. They also helped with the household chores, taking care of family animals like goats and pigs, collecting firewood and milling family grain. Occasionally, they became involved in crime.

Even students who passed the test for middle school often found it difficult to continue. In 1960, Zhang Ziyang was the only one among twelve students from South River Village who succeeded in the entrance examination to a lower middle school. He was placed in a lower middle school in Licun, about 25 kilometers away from his home, which made his attending school exceedingly difficult. Financial difficulties forced Zhang to quit after one semester.[21] Ziyang, who was the most talented of his village cohort, became a burglar after he dropped out of middle school. He and his brother Ziling stole from government warehouses and department stores. They ended up in prison twice for a total of 14 years.[22]

Jimo County had only two high schools in 1966, an increase from one in 1949.[23] But with only two schools for a population of over 800,000, most children were denied a high school education, especially those from rural villages. In fact, in the seventeen-year period from 1949 to 1966 there were only 1,616 high school graduates in all of Jimo County, more than half of whom left the county forever to go to college. (see Table 1). The seventeen years of high school education in rural Jimo prior to the Cultural Revolution had not produced even one high school graduate per village. There are 1,011 villages in Jimo County. It would be interesting to figure out how long it would have taken to provide each village with a high school graduate if the pre-Cultural Revolution educational trends had continued.

Table 1: Senior high school graduates and number of people who entered college between 1953 and 1965.

Year	53	55	56	58	59	60	61	62	63	64	65	Total
Number of high school graduates	31	50	117	168	170	198	198	177	166	240	101	1,616
number of college entrants	24	51	102	103	154	160	52	27	36	67	65	841
disparity	7	-1	15	65	16	38	146	150	130	173	36	775

Source: *Jimo Xianzhi,_* 27:21-22.

In addition to there being little opportunity for rural children to attend upper middle school, those who did almost invariably went to the city. Throughout Chinese history, the ultimate goal of education was to have an official career, so as to bring glory to one's family. This part of the traditional culture was never challenged until the Cultural Revolution.[24] Farmers, like the elite, sent their children to school with a hope that they could ultimately leave the village. In Jimo, from 1953 to 1965, except during the three year-period of food shortages caused partly by the Great Leap Forward excesses, most high school graduates left rural villages to work in the city or to enter college. Very few ever returned. Of the 1616 Jimo students who were lucky enough to finish high school, 841 went to college and never returned. Among the 775 high school graduates who failed to enter college, some were absorbed by local governments and industry, and some joined the army. Few returned to the villages.

Of more than 1,200 people in South River Village, only four people managed to obtain a high school education prior to the Cultural Revolution. All four went on to college and left the village forever. Wang Zhexian's only son was the first South River youth to enter college. According to villagers, he did not even come back once after he left for college in 1956.[25] It was said that he graduated from the Academy of Military Sciences and was assigned to work in Beijing. Liu Xiuzhang's son graduated from Shandong Mining College and was assigned to work in a coal mine in Xinwen, Shandong. Two other college graduates were from the Hu family. Mr. Hu was a former capitalist who had a non-agricultural *hukou* (household registration) but he and his family resided in the village.[26] He worked in a factory in Jimo town, and was the only member of his family of eight who worked. Many of Hu's colleagues in the factory wondered why he bore the burden of supporting his big family while his able-bodied sons attended high school. However, they understood the logic when his two sons went to college.[27]

Since few rural high school graduates returned to rural areas upon graduation, it seems reasonable to assume that high school education in rural Jimo made little direct contribution to rural development in the seventeen years from 1949 to 1966. Instead of contributing to rural development, the educational system served as a drain on rural talent. Consequently, the countryside lacked the educated personnel capable of absorbing new knowledge and new techniques in an effective manner, and for that reason rural Jimo progressed very slowly before the Cultural Revolution and remained very poor. The failure to develop the rural education system contributed in no small way to continuing rural underdevelopment.

CURRICULA AND DISCIPLINE

Before the Cultural Revolution, curricula and textbooks were standardized nationally. Since the students from the whole nation sat for the same entrance examination for college, schools had to teach the same textbooks in order to prepare students for these tests. The goal of schooling for parents, students and teachers was the same: to succeed in the entrance examination and to enter college.

As students' success was measured largely by test scores, and teachers' success was measured by students' success, school and teachers worked hard to prepare students for various tests. Apart from long hours of schoolwork from 7:00 in the morning to 5:00 in the afternoon teachers overburdened students with heavy amounts of homework. Added to this crazy workload, there were parental pressures. Chinese parents are notorious for pushing their children to excel in school in order to bring glory to their family and to their ancestors. They placed tremendous extra mental pressure on their children by demanding high scores from them. Some parents or guardians would wake up their children in the wee hours of the morning to study, mostly to recite textbooks.[28] Frequent quizzes and tests plus large amounts of homework left students no time for play and exercise. People said at the time *"fen fen fen, xuesheng de minggen, kao kao kao, laoshi de fabao"* (score, score, score are students' lifelines, and test, test, test are teachers' magic wands).

In the frenzied effort to achieve high scores, teachers would ask primary school pupils to write each new Chinese character twenty, sometimes, one hundred, times a day, and to memorize whole texts and remember all mathematical formulas and patterns. Historical data, such as which emperors did what, and when, were important subject matters to be memorized. Before entrance examinations for lower middle school, upper middle school or college, language teachers would try to guess possible composition titles on the exams and ask each student to write a few compositions accordingly.[29] Teachers would correct them and then ask students to memorize them. Teachers of other subjects would make simulated tests for their students. The examiners, on the other hand, tried to surprise and trap students by giving strange and often insignificant questions.[30] The whole process had become a game to outwit each other.

In this environment, students did have a better grasp of certain knowledge, but only at the cost of many other good things. Some of the knowledge they acquired was very useful for the examinations, but had no use in real life. Time spent on memorizing historical texts was not very well used; this time could have been used to learn many other useful skills, skills that could be important in rural life. Exposed to pressure to succeed and worried about failure from very early on in life, many children were deprived of the opportunity to develop their abilities in accordance with their natural developmental stages. They were forced to behave as adults in early childhood. They endured a lot of mental stress, but experienced very little fun in life. Creativity and imagination suffered. In this struggle for success in the national entrance examination, one sees the legacy of traditional Chinese education, the goal of which was to train loyal and obedient civil servants for emperors rather than creative thinkers for society. The memorizing of huge amount of classics in order to pass the imperial examination and launch an official career was likened to *qiao men zhuan* (the brick used to knock the door open) by critics of traditional Chinese educational practices. Once inside the door, the brick was not of much use.[31] In a similar manner, the frenzied obsession with success in the entrance examination for college proved only *biye song*, (useless after graduation), as one student commented during the Cultural Revolution. He said that students spent all their time in school memorizing these formulas and historical facts. But after they left school they found them to be totally useless in real life.[32] This structure of learning inevitably led to the overbearing dominance of teachers in the classroom. Students' role in the classroom was insignificant, accepting whatever the teachers tried to inject into their minds, and following teachers' instructions carefully in order to achieve high scores on tests and quizzes. Talking, commenting, and discussing in class were forbidden. As *shidao zunyan* (strict teacher's authority) was the order of the day, even good-natured teachers could develop abusive tendencies. It was common for teachers to strike students' heads with sticks and other convenient objects like chalk and blackboard erasers. One female teacher in South River primary school had so much practice hitting students with chalk that she perfected her skill. She seldom missed her targets. She could be writing on the blackboard at the time, but as soon as she heard a student's voice, she could turn around very quickly and shoot out her chalk at the same time. And sure enough, the chalk always landed in the space between the students' eyes. Her students often talked about her skills at chalk throwing among themselves. Strict school discipline and demanding teachers usually resulted in submissive and fearful students, producing young adults who were afraid to take risks or experiment.

Students were not happy with the way schooling was conducted and with the way teachers treated them. Under parental and other social pressures, they had to submit to teachers' authority. A negative report from a teacher or school authorities usually meant trouble for them at home. In school, even small, insignificant disobedient behavior led to severe punishment, sometimes physical. In 1965, I saw three male teachers drag out one student from the classroom and beat him up, punching and kicking him for more than twenty minutes. I did not know what the student had done to warrant violent beating. There was no reasoning or argument and the issue in question was settled by sheer force. Of course this was not the norm for Chinese schools, but such violence was not uncommon in Jimo schools before the Cultural Revolution.

EDUCATION POLICY CHOICES

Before the Cultural Revolution many rural schools were housed in village temples or other makeshift houses. A considerable number of those schoolhouses leaked. When it rained hard outside, it rained inside *(shiwai da xia, shinei xiaoxia),* so that classes had to be canceled and students had to scurry home. Many schoolhouses had broken windows, which had to be sealed with bricks in winter. Still others had no windows and often had no lights. These windowless schools, dubbed "dark houses" by rural people[33] were notorious for placing strains on teachers' and students' eyes. Moreover, in the cold of winter the temperature of the classroom was frequently the same as the outside because schools could not afford fuel to heat the classrooms. Teachers sometimes asked students to take turns bringing firewood to school in order to have a fire in the classroom. When the classroom became too cold to continue the class, teachers stopped the class and asked students to stamp their feet and massage their hands together in order to keep warm.[34] It was difficult to study in a cold room. Somehow rural teachers and students had to manage.

In Jimo County more than 65 percent of rural schools did not have desks and chairs before the Cultural Revolution.[35] Students had to bring their own big stools to use as desks, and their own small stools to use as chairs. Some stools were taller than others. They did not look neat. While proper and similar desks and chairs provide for posture and give order and dignity to the classroom, China's rural classrooms looked as if they were disheveled and disordered. But since the government did not provide the funds to purchase the furniture and equipment, villagers had to manage with what they had.

Rural teachers and students could struggle to make do despite these material obstacles one way or another. However, there were things even the most resourceful rural students and teachers could not overcome, since the state had a monopoly over school administration before the Cultural Revolution. Local people, for instance, could not hire more teachers without the government taking the initiative. Because there were too few teachers and too few schools, many rural children were not able to go to school.

The beneficiaries of the pre-Cultural Revolution educational system that emphasized urban key schools at the expense of rural schools argued that, given the financial constraints of the national government, it was the only sensible way to run the nation's educational system. Not having enough money was not a new problem. This was a problem before the Communists came to power. The Qing Imperial Government and Chiang Kai-shek's Nationalist government could have justified the educational inequality between rural and urban areas using the same excuse.

Given the problem of inadequate resources, there were at least two alternatives for Communist policy makers. They could use the available resources to set up more rural schools where there were none and to help the poor rural schools to catch up with the urban-based schools. The Communists had proposed this policy repeatedly before they came to power. The other option was to direct the resources to urban schools to make the already good urban schools better, thus expanding the existing gap between rural and urban educational inequality. Communist policy makers made the second choice, thus breaking the promise they had made to the rural people when they were courting their support for insurgency in the pre-1949 period.

The pre-Cultural Revolution educational policy makers argued that the key school system was essential for raising the nation's level of science and technology and promoting educational quality. But there were other ways to achieve this goal. They could have raised the educational level in the rural areas where the majority of the Chinese people resided and where the overwhelming majority of illiterate people were concentrated. It is difficult to imagine that a nation's educational level can be high when the majority of its rural people are illiterate and a large number of rural children are denied educational opportunity. Only when the vast majority of China's rural people enjoy adequate educational opportunity can China's overall educational level be raised. But such a conception did not take hold in high CCP and government circles.

Among the vast number of rural people, there were tremendous untapped talents that could have been developed through education to serve the nation and to revive the rural areas. Many CCP officials, including Mao Zedong, Zhu De, and Deng Xiaoping, originally came from rural areas. They were able to distinguish themselves because of the educational opportunities they had enjoyed.[36] They must have known what education could do for rural children and for China as a whole. But they did not do it, just as the Nationalist and Qing Dynasty rulers before them did not. To be sure, the CCP differed from its predecessors in many ways. However, its rural educational policies for most of the period before the Cultural Revolution were not much different from those of their predecessors.

China's recent history of humiliation at the hands of Western and Japanese imperialism created a sense of national urgency among government policy makers, who were convinced that lagging behind in science and technology would lead to foreign subjugation and humiliation. The decision by the United States after World War II to make Japan into its number one military base in the Pacific, U.S. military operations in Korea, U.S. support for Chiang Kai-shek in Taiwan, and U.S. military escalation in Vietnam, only reinforced Communist leaders' sense of urgency. China needed to raise its level of science and technology as quickly as possible in order to fend off the threats from the United States.

Given China's security needs, and the nature of modern warfare, there was no question that China needed to raise its level of science and technology as soon as possible. The only question was how. China could have invested heavily in national education, particularly in the countryside where the majority of Chinese resided and more people would have benefited from such investment. If the educational level of the whole nation were raised, the nation's level of science and technology would also be raised. This approach can be characterized as *"shuizhang chuangao"* (a rising sea will lift the boat). This may appear to be slow, but the end result may be more effective. More importantly, this approach would be steady and safe. But China's Communist decision makers did not choose this approach.

The approach the Communist policy makers adopted was to invest more heavily in urban education and even more heavily in a small number of key schools where the educational level was already high. This approach, which can be characterized *"xiuba tishui"* (to build a dam in order to raise the level of the water), gave a selected small number of urban schools special treatment at the expense of non-key urban schools and rural schools. This approach supposedly would produce results faster than the other approach. Just as the construction of dams involves risk, however, this educational policy had unintended consequence for China's educational development as well as in other areas.

Even if the level of science and technology was raised to a higher level as a result of investing in key urban schools, the question is: how real and how sufficient was the level of science and technology achieved in this way? A few Chinese scientists and technicians were able to make an atomic bomb and send satellites into space. But one reality stands out: a large percentage of China's rural people remained uneducated, or poorly educated. The gap between urban and rural educational inequalities perpetuated inequalities in other aspects of urban and rural life. The lack of education in the countryside represented a major obstacle to rural economic development.

Before the Cultural Revolution, policy makers were so obsessed with raising the educational level that they forgot the ultimate end that raising the educational level was to serve. That end was to improve the quality of human life.

Could the Central government have done more to improve education in rural areas? There was no doubt it could, as the educational reforms during the Cultural Revolution would demonstrate. Lack of money and facilities was a poor excuse. Teachers' salaries were very low in the 1950s and 1960s, as *minban* teachers earned only between 15-30 yuan a month.[37] Rent for a three-room house, big enough for a classroom, was less than three yuan a month in the 1950s and 1960s. The lack of will to improve rural education was the problem, as the education reform during the Cultural Revolution was to demonstrate.

Mao supported the Great Leap Forward initiatives in part, I would argue, because he recognized rural people's demands to reduce the inequalities between rural and urban education, medical care and living standards. Popular demand for reducing the gaps between urban and rural areas was channeled to Mao through the CCP hierarchy.[38] Although Mao was forced to retreat following the Great Leap Forward setback, he did not forget the challenge represented by the growing gap in education and other aspects of urban and rural life. Revival of the Great Leap Forward slogan of reducing the gap between urban and rural areas during the Cultural Revolution showed that concerns about urban/rural inequality continued to influence Mao's thinking as he began that movement in 1966.

Mao was not very happy with China's development strategies before the Cultural Revolution. He had launched the Great Leap Forward, partly to spur rural development. The failure of Great Leap Forward brought him back to square one again. He was never reconciled to the existing gaps between rural and urban life, particularly in the field of education. I would argue that this was one of the reasons he started the Cultural Revolution. I would further argue that to reduce the gaps between urban and rural life, particularly in education, was one of the most important agendas of the Cultural Revolution.

Rural people were not as stupid as people thought they were. They perceived what was going on in the rural school system, and what kept them poor and backward. They were not happy with the Central Government's educational policy in rural areas.[39] This is one reason many of Jimo's rural people answered Mao's call for the Cultural Revolution.

Notes

1. *Jimo xianzhi,* 698-699.
2. *"Hunan Sheng Diyici Nongmin Daibiao Dahui Jueyian"* (Resolution of the First Hunan Peasant Congress, December, 1926, 428. *Diyici Guonei Geming Zhanzheng Shiqi de Nongmin Yundong Ziliao* (Collection of Documents of Peasant Movement During the First Revolutionary Civil War), PP. 402-450.
3. *Ershi Wu Shi, (The Twenty Five Histories),* (Fujian: Fujian Youth

Publishing   House,1991),   vol.   8.   Also   see,   *Cihai*   (Chinese encyclopedia) entry of *"Zongxue"* 2312.

4. School age was from 7 years to 12 years old only at time. *Jimo xianzhi*, 699.
5. *Jimo xianzhi*, 698-699.
6. *Jimo xianzhi*, 701.
7. *Jimo xianzhi*, 699.
8. *Jimo xianzhi*, 451.
9. *Jimo xianzhi*, 456.
10. Interview with villagers in Jimo, summer 1997.
11. Villagers initially regarded the rural public dining halls set up in 1958, which later became notorious symbols of the excesses of the Great Leap Forward, as a way for rural people to catch up with urban workers and government officials, who enjoyed the benefit of public dining halls (interview with farmers, 1994). Du Shixun a former deputy Commune Party Secretary of Liu Jiazhuang People's Commune, Jimo County, reported in a letter to the CCP Central Committee and Mao Zedong that farmers were reluctant to cook their own meals with the establishment of the Commune. They too wanted to be able to eat ready-made meals like the workers and government officials (Jimo *xianzhi*, 34-43).
12. Interview with rural people in Jimo, 1990.
13. Jimo *xianzhi*, 701.
14. Interview with former students and teachers in Jimo, 1995.
15. Interview with Sun Jiaxu, a graduate of rural school in South River Village. Also Chu Xiuying, a retired primary school teacher of the same school.
16. Yuan is the unit of Chinese currency, which amounted to about little more than 50 U.S. cents at the time.
17. Interview with Zhang Deshan, a villager who did not go to school, and whose two elder sisters did not go to school either, 1995. He said that he simply fooled around in the village with other kids who did not go to school. His parents did not seem to care at the time.
18. Interview with villagers in Jimo, summer, 1997.
19. Interview with villagers in Jimo, summer, 1997.
20. *Jimo xianzhi, Education,* 27:20.
21. Interview with villagers in Jimo, 1995.
22. Interview with villagers in Jimo, summer, 1997.
23. *Jimo xianzhi,* 704.
24. Thomas Bernstein, *Up to the Mountains and Down to the Villages,* (New Haven: Yale University Press, 1977), 5.
25. Interview with villagers in Jimo, summer 1997.
26. Every Chinese citizen had a *hukou* (residency registration). There were two kinds of *hukou:* the agricultural and non-agricultural *hukou.* People with non-agricultural *hukou* usually resided in urban areas and the Government provided them with grain and other supplies. Rural people belong to the category of agricultural *hukou,*

meaning people who are involved in agriculture, and the government did not supply them with grain except in times of crop failure and other natural disasters.

27. Interview with villagers in Jimo, summer, 1997.

28. Ms. Xiao Qingfeng, a teacher of English in Jimo Number One Middle School, told me that during her middle school years, her elder brother took upon himself to wake her up at 4:00 in the morning to study for her exams in school. Mr. Hu, a former small capitalist and worker at the Jimo Number One Farming Machine Factory whose two sons went to college before the Cultural Revolution told me in an interview that he had to wake up his two sons at 5:00 in the morning. The two brothers would then go to recite their textbooks along the riverbank close to their home.

29. Interview with Mr. Qiao Jiheng, a Chinese language teacher at Jimo Number One Middle School, 1995. Mr. Qiao told me in the interview that it was very important for his students that he should make good guesses about composition titles in the national entrance examination and that he made quite a few close guesses throughout his career.

30. For example, on the national college entrance examination in the subject of geography in 1963 there was a question asking students to name two countries in the world in which the capital and the country shared the same name. Many students thought Mexico and Panama were the answers.But they were wrong, because the capital of Mexico is Mexico City and the capital of Panama is Panama City.

31. Wu Jingzi's *Yulin Waishi* (The Scholars) (Beijing: People's Publishing House, 1962) is one of the best book describing the *qiao men zhuan* phenomenon.

32. Kang Xiaode, a village primary school teacher in Huluyu Village, Xicun Commune, Xiuwu County, Henan Province, wrote an article "There Should Not Be So Many Courses in Primary and Middle School," in the debate of educational reforms. *Selections of Articles in the Debate of Educational Reforms* (Zhengzhou, Henan: Henan Provincial Revolutionary Committee, May 1970) 5. Mr. Kang admitted in his article that mathematics, chemistry, physics, geography, biology, history, foreign language, art and music are all important, but primary and middle school should not try to cover them all with separate courses. He also said that most of these subjects that he had learnt in middle school were already forgotten after graduation.

33. *Jimo Xianzhi,* 703. Interview with Guan Xuliang and Zhang Aishan from South River Village, Jimo, who went to school in 1960s.

34. Interview with rural school teachers, 1995.

35. *Jimo Xianzhi,* 721.

36. The majority of Communist officials were of rural origins in the early years.

37. There were six kind payments to *minban* teachers. 1. 15 yuan-30 yuan monthly cash payment. 2. Free meals plus 6-20 yuan monthly

salary. 3.15-20 kilo grain plus 5-15 yuan monthly salary. 4. Grain alone, 100-200 kilo grain annually. 5. Work points plus a monthly cash bonus. 6. Work points alone. These different payments represented the equivalent of 15-30 yuan monthly salary in the 1950s and 1960s. See *Jimo xianzhi,* 716.

38. See, Mao Zedong, "Speech at a Meeting of Provincial Party Secretaries," *Selected Works of Mao Zedong* (Beijing: People's Publishing House, 1977) Vol. V. 330-362.

39. *Jimo xianzhi,* 698-699.

CHAPTER 3

Collectivization and Obstacles to Economic Development

The Communist Party sought to rapidly develop the rural economy and provide for the economic security and social welfare for the rural population through the social reorganization of the countryside along collective lines. It was believed that rural collectives would facilitate infrastructure improvements, water control and mechanization, spurring agricultural production. They would also be the foundations on which rural industry would be developed. Collectives would be able to improve social welfare in the countryside and provide members with a modicum of economic security. Ultimately, all of these goals were tied to the fundamental communist promise to reduce the gap between the countryside and the city. This chapter evaluates the first seventeen years of this project of collectivization and rural economic development in Jimo.

COLLECTVIZATION

In the rural areas, the CCP's first move after land reform in the early 1950s was to organize individual farmers into mutual aid groups and later into agricultural cooperatives. These organizations had different names in different places. They were called *"tudi she"* (land association) in some places, and *"hezuo she"* (cooperative) in others. The latter term was commonly used throughout China. In Jimo County people gave their agricultural cooperatives fancy names like *"Liming She"* (Early Dawn Cooperative) *"Guangming She"* (Brilliant Cooperative) and so on.

The rationale of this organizational structure was threefold. One was to prevent the land-poor peasants from losing their newly acquired land from the land reform in order to prevent the economic stratification problem in the rural areas.[1] Individual farmers, particularly poor farmers struggling under primitive conditions, were vulnerable to natural disasters. A crop failure due to flood or drought, or a sickness of a family member, especially an inopportune sickness of the only or major farm hand of the family, could easily cripple a poor household. In some cases, such a disaster could result in the loss of family land.[2] Mutual aid and cooperative organizations provided poor farmers some institutional security that they urgently needed. When one family encountered trouble, other families could come to help it tide over through a short difficulty. In essence, the collective farming was a form of mutual insurance designed to make up for the absence of other forms of social insurance.

Agricultural organization could facilitate the sharing of farm tools and farm animals that poor farmers did not own. Prior to the land reform, the poor farmers who did not own farm tools and farm animals could not plow their land in time; as a result, their crops often missed the season both in planting and harvesting. Consequently, poor farmers' crops were always poorer than others. Some poor farmers exchanged their human labor for the use of farm animals and farming tools. But poor farmers often were shortchanged in this trade, and their crops still were planted later than those who owned proper animals and tools.[3]

Communist-sponsored land reform had confiscated some land, farm animals and farm implements from the landlords, and divided them among the poor farmers. Still, there were not enough farm tools and farm animals to go around. Frequently, several poor families had to share one ox or one plow. It was often difficult to coordinate an efficient use of such shared property without friction. Mutual aid groups provided some institutional coordination for the use of the shared farm tools and farm animals. The agricultural cooperatives, which eventually eliminated private ownership of the big farm tools and farm animals, would further eliminate the friction in the sharing of farm tools and animals and further increase agricultural output, or so the Party assumed.

With better coordination, agricultural collectivization was supposed to make better use of the large pool of labor force in the countryside to improve the agricultural infrastructure, like soil improvement and huge irrigation projects. Individual farmers working on their own often failed to see the benefit of large irrigation projects. Even when they were aware, they lacked the institutional strength to organize and coordinate big irrigation projects. That was one reason why the farming practice in Northern China remained primitive in 1949.[4] Jimo farmers called it *"kao tian chi fan,"* (depend on heaven for a good harvest). When there was right amount rainfall at the right moment the harvest would be good. When there was either too much rain or too little rain, or rain at the wrong moment, crop failure would result. Of 2,093,913 mu of land in Jimo in 1949, only 18,900 mu was irrigated. On the other hand, 600,000 mu of lowland in northwest Jimo County suffered frequent crop failures because of floods in summer and fall.[5]

The organization of collectives in the rural areas went through different stages in a trial and error manner. In the early 1950s, the mutual aid groups composed of five or more closely related households, often from the same clan. During mid 1950s, *chu jishe* (preliminary cooperative) were organized on the basis of mutual aid groups. It embraced about 30 to 50 households working together. In

1956, *gao jishe* (advanced cooperatives) were organized, which usually included an entire village. In 1957, some places set up big advanced cooperatives to include several villages. During the Great Leap Forward, *renmin gongshe* (people's communes) were set up, which often include 30 to 50 villages. Within the communes, village became production brigades, and a brigade was then divided into several production teams. A production team had about 30 to 40 households in it, farming about 150 to 200 mu land. Most of the time, production team was the basic accounting unit, and income was calculated and distributed within the team. Production brigades also pooled resources from the production teams to buy big firm machines or build large irrigation projects for the benefit of the entire village. Communes pooled resources from production brigades to invest in industrial enterprises and engage in gigantic irrigation projects for the benefit of an entire commune. This pooling of resources reached a frenzy level during the Great Leap Forward. County and commune governments often randomly and arbitrarily took resources from production brigades to invest in gigantic irrigation projects. Eventually the government and people realized the detrimental effect of this random and arbitrary extraction from the production teams and brigades, and corrected the mistake by returning to production teams as the basic accounting units, and maintained it until the dissolution of the collective in early 1980s.[6]

The Great Leap Forward was a time of great idealism and enthusiasm in China. National leaders, local government officials, intellectuals, scientists and ordinary farmers were all carried away by the achievements and promise of the potentials of the gigantic collectives. They lost their heads, and became over-ambitious in engaging in too many and too big projects which were beyond their capacity at the time. They learned a big lesson and paid a dear price for it when the Leap failed as a result of several factors combined.

INFRASTRUCTURE IMPROVEMENTS

To some extent, the agricultural organizations, *"huzhuzu"* (mutual aid group) *"hezuoshe"* (agricultural cooperative) and later *"renmin gongshe"* (people's commune) achieved what they were designed to achieve. With the organization of mutual aid groups, Jimo County dug 7,738 irrigation wells in 1952. For the next two years, the agricultural cooperatives in Jimo dug 6,178 more, and bought 2,033 new mechanical water pumps called *shuiche* (water pump) in 1954. By 1955, irrigated areas had increased by 153,300 mu. In a matter of three years, the irrigated areas increased more than eight times.[7] With the establishment of the People's Commune in 1958, construction of irrigation facilities took a great stride. Jimo County built its first 33 big irrigation wells equipped with electric pumps, and the first four medium-size reservoirs. Shipang Reservoir with a capacity of 11,140,000 cubic meters, was started in October 1959, and finished in August 1960. Wangquan Reservoir with a capacity of 43,200,000 cubic meters was started in November 1959 and finished in August 1960. Songhuaquan Reservoir with a capacity of 28,500,000 cubic meters was started in November 1959 and finished August 1960. Nuocheng Reservoir with a capacity of 12,600,000 cubic meters was started in November 1959 and finished in August 1960.[8] Apart from these four medium-sized reservoirs, Jimo County also invested in several other irrigation projects, one of which was Chahe Guanqu Gongcheng (Chahe Irrigation Project). The project began in April 1959 and was completed in early 1960.[9]

These huge irrigation projects took tremendous human sacrifices and financial capital. Shipang Reservoir took 1,715,500 labor days, and a capital investment of 3,029,000 yuan. Wangquan Reservoir took 3,389,500 labor days and a capital investment of 2,147,500 yuan to complete. Songhuaquan Reservoir took 2,254,400 labor days and a capital investment of 793,000 yuan. Nuocheng Reservoir absorbed 2,457,300 labor days and 1,764,400 yuan capital investment. The Chahe irrigation project took another 732,000 labor days and 662,900 yuan capital investment. Altogether, a total of 10,548,700 labor days and 8,396,800 yuan capital investment went to constructing these irrigation facilities.[10] When discussing the Great Leap Forward in China, many people see only the food shortages and other negative consequences. They do not understand that the goal of the Great Leap Forward partly was to improve infrastructure in the countryside. The reservoirs built during the Great Leap Forward benefited the rural areas for decades to come. These infrastructure improvements are why farmers who suffered most during the Great Leap Forward have always viewed it with ambiguity rather than completely condemning it.[11]

LITTLE ADVANCE IN AGRICULTURAL PRODUCTION

The huge investment in the construction of irrigation projects since the start of agricultural cooperation had begun to change the mode of farming and improved the infrastructure for agriculture in Jimo. With the improvement of the agricultural infrastructure, farmers were less dependent on rainfall for a good harvest, and production was expected to increase greatly. There was, however, no dramatic increase in grain yield during the years before the Cultural Revolution (see Table 1). In the years before the Great Leap Forward, grain production in Jimo remained fairly steady, varying with weather conditions. Then in the wake of the Great Leap Forward, grain production plummeted in Jimo, as in the rest of China. An analysis of the reasons for this disastrous decline is beyond the scope of this study. It is clear, however, that efforts to build too much too fast led to neglect of planting and harvesting and poor planning and mismanagement on a massive scale, which, combined with extremely poor weather conditions, resulted in a monumental agricultural crisis. In 1960, 1961, and 1962, Jimo suffered spring droughts, while heavy rain in the summer caused severe floods. Villagers recalled that for three consecutive years, summer floods left the fields covered with water. Sweet potatoes planted in early summer remained the same size at the fall. All the ditches in the fields were filled with water.[12] Unit yields dropped to 30.5 kilo per mu in 1960, 51 kilo per mu in 1961 and 54 kilo per mu in 1962 (see table 1)

Table 1: Grain Yield in Jimo County from 1949 to 1965								
Year	Total			Wheat			Corn		
	Planted area	Unit yield	Total yield	Planted area	Unit yield	Total yield	Planted area	Unit yield	Total Yield
1949	231.2	70.5	1633370	63.40	49.5	31590	1.7	37.5	650
1950	226.2	71	161015	65.70	52.5	34575	6.3	65	4085
1951	243.0	81.5	198650	60.90	57.5	34960	6.7	75	5000
1952	241.7	82	198555	72.40	53	39770	8.8	93.5	8215
1953	239.1	72	172635	70.90	41.5	29560	12	108	12980
1954	227.7	79	180130	65.96	48	31710	15	102	15640
1955	229.7	77.5	178330	68.40	43.5	29760	27	101	20795
1956	231.7	80.5	186925	67.60	48	32315	29	91.5	26890
1957	242.5	67	162775	67.60	40.5	27830	22	101	22850
1958	247.6	70.5	174740	71.80	40	28670	29	71	20215
1959	209.9	67	140160	47.00	37	17385	16	43	6950
1960	191.0	30.5	58025	66.00	36	23820	9.8	20.5	1985
1961	182.8	51	93015	50.00	23	11220	5.7	45.5	2580
1962	202.7	54	109145	46.80	43	13965	7.7	59.5	4580
1963	181.3	67.5	122180	39.40	39.5	15875	12	84.5	10260
1964	187.2	69.5	136630	48.40	57	27575	18	82.5	114475
1965	195.7	83.5	163560	52.30	49	25595	20	101	19655

Unit: unit yield = kilo per mu, total yield = ton, area = 10,000 mu. Source, Jimo *xianzhi*, 242. Here only the total yields and the yields of the two major crops are listed. Figures for minor crops, like sweet potatoes, millet, sorghum, soybean and so on, are not included.

Although agricultural performance recovered in the following years, the results were not that impressive considering all the investment in irrigation projects. The highest pre-Cultural Revolution unit yield, 83.5 kilos per mu in 1965, was not much higher than in the first years after the end of the Civil War, see table 1.

RURAL INDUSTRY

Rural industry was nonexistent in Jimo before 1958. With the establishment of the communes, farmers set up many industrial projects with very little capital. There were two kinds of rural industrial enterprises at the time: ones run by communes and ones run by production brigades. Two thousand eight hundred and fifty four enterprises of both categories had been set up by August 1959, employing a total of 47,932 people.[13] Most brigade run enterprises were small in scale. Their products were shovels, hoes, sickles, papers, water pails, baskets, wines, bean cured and son on, involving mostly traditional craft and skills. In South River, the village printed decorating papers and bean cured.[14] Commune enterprises, on the other hand, were usually bigger and more sophisticated, with some basic machine tools, producing or repairing farm machinaries.

Liu Shaoqi and Deng Xiaoping's readjustment policy following the failure of the Great Leap Forward closed down the new rural industrial enterprises. Only ten rural enterprises in Jimo survived the initial readjustment. These ten enterprises employed only 253 people and their annual output was estimated at only 170,000 yuan.[15] By 1963, all commune-run industrial enterprises came to a stop.[16] The failure of the Great Leap Forward hurt people's confidence in the communes. Because of serious grain shortages, collectives in many places were dissolved. Land was divided for individual households to farm separately. Employees working in commune industries, who had been compensated by the collectives through the collective distribution system, now had to return home to farm their share of land.[17] The rural industrial enterprises, which had been started with encouragement from the center, were also closed on orders from the center.

COLLECTIVES AND RURAL SOCIAL SERVICES

Substantial social security guarantees were embedded in collective distribution system in Jimo. No matter whether a villager could work or not, the collective undertook to provide him and his family with "five guarantees", (wu bao) — food, clothes, fuel, education for his children and a funeral upon death.[18] Yang Liu and Wu Fengqi were bachelors from South River village. Yang Liu was from production team one, and Wu Fengqi was from production team six. Their production teams gave them simple assignments in their old age, like watching crops in the fields, taking care of farming animals or helping bring meals to the fields. In return for their service, the production team provided them with food, clothes and housing. When they were sick, they got free treatment from the village clinic. When they died, the production teams gave them decent funerals.[19]

Seventy percent of the collective harvest was divided on a per capita basis, and only thirty percent of total production was divided according to the input of labor. In the short run, those who contributed more labor to the collective seemed to be shortchanged, and those who contributed less labor to the collective seemed to benefit more from the collective system. But over time, these discrepancies were often evened out. For example, Song Shundao and his wife, members of the eighth Production team in South River, had no children of their own. They worked full time in their middle age. Liu Zengshun from the same production team had six children and only Liu Zengshun himself worked in the collective in the beginning. Song and Liu earned same amount of work points annually. But because seventy percent of the harvest was distributed on a per capita basis, Liu's family got only a little less grain than Song Shundao's on the per capita basis. In a way Song Shundao was helping support Liu's big family by his labor input to the collective. But as Song Shundao grew older and gradually lost his 'ability to work, Liu's six children gradually grew up and entered the working force of the production team, and began to help support Song Shundao and his wife.[20] The collective, thus, provided a de facto institutional retirement plan for villagers. The government had put some thought into this unique social security system in the rural areas.

While economic security and certain social services to families improved due to the collective structure, medical care remained almost non-existent. For small medical problems, villagers had *to ying ai guoqu* (harden it over without seeking medical help). For big problems, some villagers relied on *wuyi* or *shenpo* (witch doctors). These witch doctors claimed that they had the service of some powerful spirits, and could treat people's diseases in their trances. Sometimes they were successful and sometimes they were not. The witch doctor in South River, for example, claimed that she had in her service a range of deities that could diagnose people's diseases. Despite her reputation of being a good witch doctor, her treatments occasionally cost her patients' lives.[21]

Occasionally, villagers sought help from the county people's hospital *(xian yiyuan)*. But doctors in the people's hospitals did not treat villagers very seriously. When Zhang Yingwen's only son had a skin problem in 1958, she took him to the hospital. Yang Weijun, a surgeon just transferred to Jimo from Shandong Provincial Medical

School Hospital, treated Zhang's son. But several months' of costly treatment failed to help the boy's skin problem, leading instead to a serious deterioration of his condition. A coin-sized skin rash developed into infections covering the boy's whole leg. He could not walk any more. When the boy was dying and the Zhang family in despair asked him timidly what was wrong, the doctor simply told the Zhang family that he did not know and that they should not come back to him again, thus kicking the Zhang family out of the hospital.[22]

Tracheitis was a widespread disease among rural residents in Jimo. The problem became worse in winter. Victims of this disease suffered tremendous pain, but many of them refused to seek medical help from the people's hospital. Liu Yinghai, a long time victim of tracheitis from South River, said he would rather die than to go to the County People's Hospitals. The fee was too high for him and he also could not stand the arrogant attitudes and careless handling of the doctors and nurses in the hospital.[23]

Collective organization in the countryside improved some aspects of economic security and social services, which had previously been provided only by the family. Still, the services and economic security provided by rural collectives were far inferior to what was provided to urban workers and cadres in state work units, who received guaranteed wages and pensions and free medical care. Villagers' income not only remained far lower than that of urban residents, it was dependent on the success or failure of the annual harvest of the individual production team and production brigade. And, as we have seen, there was very little access to medical care.

POLITICAL WEAKNESSES OF COLLECTIVE ORGANIZATION

The main weakness of rural collective organizations was political: ordinary members were not politically empowered and were dependent on village and commune officials. The Communists had not fundamentally changed the rural political culture of submission to authority and had not significantly remedied the lack of education in the countryside. Collectivization had made ordinary villagers more dependent on officials by placing economic decisions in the hands of the collective while failing to really empower villagers to take part in the decision-making process. This was not only a political problem: without solving this problem, possibilities for real rural economic development would remain untapped. The modernization of agriculture and development of rural industry required an educated and politically empowered and involved rural population. It also required the investment of resources from the city, particularly in the form of the knowledge required to develop rural education and health care and the technique and machinery required to mechanize agriculture and produce chemical fertilizer. Before the Cultural Revolution these resources were not forthcoming.

Fukua feng (exaggeration of production) became a serious problem during the Great Leap Forward because the commune members were not politically empowered to check the wrong doings of the commune and village leaders. In this sense, the Great Leap Forward failed not just because its overall design and rationale were flawed, but also because China's political culture at the time was out of sync with the new production relationships introduced by the agricultural collectivization. For the advantages of agricultural collectivization to materialize, it was critical to empower ordinary people through education and by changing the rural political culture.

Notes

1. Mao, "*Guanyu Nongye Hezuohua Wenti,*" (Issues Concerning the Agricultural Cooperation), *Mao Zedong Xuanji* (Selected Works of Mao Zedong) Vol. V. 187.
2. Interviews with farmers in Shandong, summer, 1990. Many farmers told me their stories how their families had to sell their land in time of crop failure and to migrate to other places. Local records published in the recent years documented numerous cases that farmers were forced by natural disasters to sell their land and to migrate. See, Zhang Hengxiang, "*1942 Zaihuang Jianwen*" (Stories of the 1942 Natural Disasters), *Xiangchengxian Wenshi Ziliao, (Xiang Chengxian Local History Material,* Vol. 4, June, 1991, 28. See also Li Xiangbin, "Jiu *Shehui Xiangchengxian Tudi Zhanyou Zhuangkuang and Jingying Fangshi,*" (Land Ownership and Management in Xiangcheng County before Liberation) *Xiangcheng Wenshi Ziliao,* Vol. 2, September, 1987, 65.
3. Interviews with villagers in Jimo, 1985. See also *Jimo Xianzhi* 226.
4. *Jimo Xianzhi,* 223.
5. *Jimo Xianzhi,* 287.
6. Interview with farmers in Jimo, 1995.
7. *Jimo Xianzhi,* 301.
8. *Jimo Xianzhi,* 293-295.
9. *Jimo Xianzhi,* 298.
10. *Jimo Xianzhi* 293-298.
11. Interview with farmers, 1995, 1996.
12. Interview with farmers in Jimo, 1995.
13. *Jimo xianzhi,* 9: 2.
14. Interview with farmers in Jimo, 1996.
15. The yuan used in this book is 1970 constant value.
16. *Jimo xianzhi,* 9: 2.
17. Workers in the rural enterprises were paid the same way as farmers working in the fields in the form of working points. In 1963, land was divided into individual household plots in Jimo County. Work

points were not worth anything. Workers of commune industrial enterprises had to return home to farm their share of land to survive the food shortages following the Great Leap Forward.

18. The family remained the basic unit for economic distribution in the collective system and the family head was typically male.
19. Interview with farmers in Jimo, summer 1997.
20. Interview with farmers in Jimo, summer 1997.
21. At the beginning of the Cultural Revolution, families of her victims from Shimudi, Chuantou and Sanlizhuang villages came to settle accounts with her. They paraded her in town, and some angry victim's family members hit her very hard. She almost lost her life during the parade. Interview with villagers in Jimo, Summer 1990.
22. Interview with villagers in Jimo, summer 1990.
23. Interview with villagers in Jimo, summer 1990.

CHAPTER 4

The Cultural Revolution and Political Empowerment

By 1966 a major dilemma had developed in Chinese political life. The Communist Party had been granted the supreme authority by the Chinese Constitution to rule. But without appropriate supervision from the people, the party bosses at all levels possessed the human tendency to become arrogant and corrupt. The corruption of an increasing number of individual party leaders would eventually lead to corruption of the party as an institution—from a quantitative change to qualitative change.[1]

Because a corrupt institution would not be able to exercise leadership in an effective manner, ultimately this development would lead to its death. During the 1950s and early 60s, Mao Zedong had initiated numerous campaigns to prevent that from happening. The Cultural Revolution was Mao's last resort after the previous campaigns failed to do the job effectively. It differed from all the previous political campaigns because for the first time in the CCPs history it circumvented the local party bosses and stressed the principle of *letting the masses empower themselves and educate themselves.*[2]

CHALLENGING THE JIMO LEADERSHIP

At the beginning of the Cultural Revolution, the CCP had total control of Chinese political and economic life. From the Central government down through the intermediate levels of provinces, prefectures, and counties, and all the way down to the communes and the villages, the party committees—and more frequently the party secretaries—held the reins of power at each level. The party committees and party secretaries had the authority to enact, interpret and enforce the laws of the land.[3] As various political campaigns were launched by the party, including those to clean up corruption within the party, party committees often sent out "work teams" to implement them at lower levels.

"Party leadership" had often been presented as a "sacred cow" by CCP leaders at various levels. Challenges to their personal authority and criticism of their mistakes could be labeled "anti-party," and challengers subjected to severe punishment. Party committees and their work teams continued to use this mechanism to suppress challengers at the beginning of the Cultural Revolution. In other words, official work teams, sent out by party authorities in the name of leading the Cultural Revolution, were used to suppress the very activity—independent criticism of Party authorities—that Mao was trying to encourage by launching the movement. This was precisely what happened in Jimo County.

On June 20, 1966, in Jimo Number One Middle School, Wang Sibo, a high school student, and Li Yingliang, a physics teacher, together with many other students and teachers, put out their first batch of big character posters supporting the Cultural Revolution. These posters criticized the school's educational policies and practices. They charged the school, the highest educational institution in the county, with stressing scores too much in recruiting students, which amounted to discrimination against working class children who often lagged behind because they had to work to help out their families. They also accused the school of excluding ordinary teachers and students from the school's decision making process. They demanded an overhaul of the school's educational policies: opening school doors wider to workers' and farmers' children; and allowing students and ordinary teachers a voice in the school's management.[4] This was an unprecedented challenge to the school party authorities. These students and teachers were reacting to signals in the mass media originating from radical supporters of Mao in Beijing that encouraged criticism of school authorities. Why did they want to take the risks associated with their actions?

The Jimo County Party Committee reacted to this challenge very quickly. The next day, on June 21, 1966, it dispatched a work team to Jimo Number One Middle School. It was made up of seventy officials, all of whom held a cadre rank of seventeen or higher. They were mostly heads and deputy heads of various departments in the county government. The team was headed by Zhang Junguang, Chief of the Organizational Department of the County Party Committee.[5] On June 22, one day after the work team entered the school, it labeled the students and teachers who wrote the big character posters as anti-party elements. The accusation was that opposition to the party leaders of the school was opposition to the County Party Committee, which amounted to opposition to the CCP Central Committee and to Mao himself. Imitating the actions of similar work teams in Beijing, the work team labeled Li Yingliang, the physics teacher, Qiu Lijian, the music teacher, and Niu Yingguang, the physical education teacher, as a *san jiacun* (three household village) anti-party clique of the school.[6] To deflect student anger away from the party branch in the school, the work team also directed the attack on other influential teachers of the school. Ding Shiwu, Song Ya and Guo Qiguang, all prominent teachers of the school, were labeled "black gang elements." Teachers with landlord, rich peasant and capitalist family backgrounds were subjected to criticism and harassment by students under the party work team's guidance.[7]

On July 19, with the encouragement of the official work team dispatched by party authorities, teachers and students from Number One Middle School in Jimo, brought twenty senior teachers who were academic authorities of the school to the market place in Jimo town. There, in front of a big crowd, they shaved half of the hair from these people's heads, as a means to humiliate them.[8] Li Yingliang, the first teacher to challenge the party's educational policies, was among those who lost half of their hair that day. In addition, he was accused of being the commander-in-chief of a counter-revolutioniry uprising, a crime punishable by death. Student leaders who led the attack on the party leadership at the beginning of the Cultural Revolution were labeled as anti-party elements. Wang Sibo, Wang Zhanjun, and some thirty other influential students in Jimo Number One Middle School were placed under house arrest for over fifty days.[9]

With their careers, if not their lives, hanging by a thread, the rebel students were desperate. They managed to persuade an elder brother of a classmate who was a Jimo post office employee to send a telegram to the Central Government at midnight to report the oppression they were subjected to and ask the Central authorities to rescue them. However, all the secrecy and planning did not conceal their action. The telegram was discovered, and the post office employee who sent the telegram was also placed under house arrest.

In early August 1966, party committees and work teams supported the organization of official student Red Guard groups.[10] Jimo Number One Middle School's Red Guards, were organized by the school work team. Only students of good family origin were allowed to join.[11] Lu Xiuyun, a female student of capitalist family background was made an exception because she denounced her capitalist father Lu Jingshan at a mass rally.[12] South River Village, like every other village in Jimo County, also had an official Red Guard organization, composed mostly of members of the Communist Youth League and core militia members *(jigan minbing)*. Student leaders who had criticized party authorities were persecuted by the party-led work teams and the official Red Guards under their auspices.[13]

Yu Zhengyang and Zhou Xianjie, two farmers from Datong village of Chenguan Commune, Geng Zengshi from Ba Li Zhuang village of Xiaopo Commune, Zhou Zunxun from Xiatan village of Yingshang Commune, Wang Chengtang from Xiao Yuzhuang of Liangshan Commune, and a few others were arrested for organizing a rebel group called Peasant Revolutionary Rebel Regiment *(nongmin gemin zaofan bingtun)*, and for challenging their village party leaders by writing big character posters. Tian Shidian, head of the County Public Security Bureau *(Gong anju)*, and Zhang Shaofeng, head of the County Military Affairs Department *(Wu Zhuangbu)* labeled these people as anti-party elements on their arrest warrants.[14] At this stage, the Cultural Revolution in Jimo seemed as if it might be a repetition of the 1957 anti-Rightist campaign, in which some of those who had followed Mao's exhortation to "let one hundred flowers bloom" were later punished for airing grievances against party authorities.

DESTROYING THE "FOUR OLDS"

In some other ways, the opening stanza of the Cultural Revolution in Jimo also looked like a second land reform because the traditional enemies of the Chinese Revolution - former landlords, capitalists and rich peasants – were targeted. In order to deflect criticism of their own behavior, officials encouraged renewed attacks against the old class enemies. Luxurious clothes, furniture, ornaments, gold and silver wares owned by Sun Jianan, a prominent landlord from Fangzijie Village, and by Xie Zihui, a former capitalist, were put on exhibit in the market place. Sun Jianan's entire household was open for public visit. In South River Village, official Red Guard groups confiscated luxurious furniture and clothes from landlord Fu Xiangshan's household and distributed them among poor villagers.[15] No wonder at the beginning, many villagers mistook the Cultural Revolution for a second land reform.[16]

Wang Chenxian from the Welfare Association *(Fuli She)* had served briefly as a medical officer in the collaborationist army during the Japanese occupation. Wang was subjected to physical harassment by these official Red Guards, even though he insisted that he had not done anything wrong throughout his life.[17] Liu Zixu, a former capitalist, had in his possession a Nationalist flag, a leftover from the Guomindang past, which was taken by the official Red Guards as evidence of Counter-revolutionary crimes. He was subjected to harassment for that reason.[18]

Chu Pengrui and Chu Leirui, twin brothers from South River village had abused their wives. Their mother was believed to be the instigator of the abuses. They were paraded in the village with big paper hats. Chu's younger sister, who was only twenty years old at the time, protested and was dragged into the parade too. Yuan Youkui from South River Village, a captured bandit affiliated with the Nationalist army turned PLA soldier during the Civil War in the Northeast, had a subordinate in his company whose name was Lin Biao. He used to tell his fellow villagers that Lin Biao had long eyebrows and liked to walk along street edges. Yuan even boasted that he once slapped Lin Biao twice for insubordination. When Lin

Biao rose in prominence during the Cultural Revolution, Yuan was subjected to investigation. Fortunately, the investigation found that the Lin Biao he was talking about was a different person.[19]

Official Red Guards in Jimo County also enthusiastically followed their Red Guard counterparts in Beijing in attacking the *sijiu* (the four olds: old thoughts, old culture, old traditions, and old habits). In Jimo the campaign to destroy the four olds, in its intensive phase, lasted several weeks and led to the burning of old books, old paintings, and destruction of old temples. it was largely the work of the official Red Guards. Official Red Guards from Jimo Number One Middle School led the way and Red Guards from different villages followed suit. In Jimo the main targets were superstitious funeral and wedding ceremonies. Red Guards from Jimo Number One Middle School ordered the three coffin shops in Jimo town to close. Shops that made and sold paper figures and objects for sacrifices at the funerals were denounced and had no customers thereafter. Red Guards burned the decorated sedan carriages used at the weddings and funerals in the market place. They said that only the exploiting classes needed to be carried by others.[20]

The proclaimed goal of the campaign was to change old ways of thinking and old habits. The Red Guards argued that superstitious ceremonies and practices were sheer deception and harmful to social progress.[21] In their overzealous effort to eradicate the superstitious old culture and old habits, they also targeted the instruments of the old ideas and old culture in a very naive way: by destroying them.[22] Liu Xianguta, a famous pagoda at the foot of Ma Mountain in west Jimo, was destroyed by official Red Guards from Jimo Number One Middle School in collaboration with Red Guards from nearby villages. Guan Zhaoyin, a former landlord in South River village, kept a big variety of beautiful hybrid golden fishes inside huge tanks with pretty rocks. He also had some beautiful parrots and three white mice inside a cage playing tricks with various gadgets. The official Red Guards of the village denounced them as the culture of the exploiting classes and destroyed them in public. In the political climate of the Cultural Revolution, many ordinary villagers burnt their own collections of old books and old paintings, some out of revolutionary enthusiasm and others out of fear of trouble.[23]

Of course, from the point of view of local party officials, campaigns to destroy the four olds and attack former landlords, capitalists and political enemies were convenient ways to divert attention from themselves and protect themselves from attack.

CHAOS AND POLITICAL EMPOWERMENT

It was in this situation that Mao presided over the drafting of the

"16 Points" in August 1966, which made the distinction between the Communist Party as an institution and party bosses as individuals in a definitive manner, and which stressed that the *targets* of *the Cultural Revolution were the capitalist roaders inside the party.*[24] Prior to the release of the "16 Points", Mao had already made speeches to that effect. On August 4, 1966 at the Eleventh Plenary Meeting of the CCP Eighth Central Committee Mao said: "Why should opposition to the new Municipal Party Committee in Beijing be labeled opposition to the Party? Why should the new Beijing Municipal Party Committee not be opposed when it suppresses the masses?"[25] After the "16 points" was publicized, it became very difficult for individual party leaders to use "party leadership" as a shield against criticism.[26] The "16 Points" laid out the political platform for the Cultural Revolution, and initiated the sweeping attacks against the "capitalist roaders" inside the CCP at the local level.[27] Mao decided to allow sweeping attacks on local party bosses. The "chaos" that attacks on the local party leaders would cause was the price Mao was willing to pay in order to create opportunities to empower the masses.

Mao's decision to circumvent the authority of local party committees in carrying out the Cultural Revolution was very significant. He did not want his Cultural Revolution initiative to become another anti-Rightist campaign, which would have allowed the local party bosses to protect themselves at the expense of people who dared to challenge them. Cui Jianping, an army regiment commander stationed in Jimo County during the Cultural Revolution, told rebel leaders that both in the military and in civilian agencies those who dared to criticize their superiors, who had independent minds, who were competent at work, and who did not use their time and energy flattering their superiors, always ended up in trouble. In order to have a successful official career, Mr. Cui said, one had to be a "pig" or a "dog". Those who did not want to be pigs or dogs would never succeed in their official careers. Those who had independent minds and who had ability would be eventually filtered out in that political culture. It had always been a pattern in Chinese political culture that those who used their energy and skills to flatter their superiors got promoted, often at the expense of those who were more capable and honest in their work.[28]

The Cultural Revolution threatened this previous pattern in Chinese political life. It empowered ordinary people to challenge the tight control over political resources by party leaders at the different levels. That is why most party leaders condemned it and most rural people supported it. The "16 points" and Mao's support liberated the suppressed rebels throughout China. It also took away the sacred veneer from local "dictators" whom ordinary people called *"tuhuangdi* " (local emperors), and subjected them to mass criticism.

China's pre-Cultural Revolution political culture had provided fertile soil for the growth of *tuhuangdi*. Officials who had not yet become a *tuhuangdi* had the potential to become one when the circumstances were right. Former rebel leaders in Jimo like Lan Chengwu and Wang Sibo say that Mao called his 1966 revolution "cultural" because he wanted to cultivate a more democratic political culture in order to eradicate the *tuhuangdi* phenomenon.[30]

MASS ASSOCIATIONS AND POLITICAL EMPOWERMENT

With the issuing of " 16 points", the official Red Guards organized under the auspices of local party leaders dissolved very quickly. Independent rebel associations began to appear. Many people use the term mass organizations for all the mass groups during the Cultural Revolution. I personally feel there is a need to distinguish between mass organizations and mass associations. The former term would be applied to the organizations like the militia, the Communist youth league, women's association, workers' unions and the official Red Guards which were set up by the CCP and were official in nature. The latter term would refer to the independent Red Guard groups formed largely in the spirit of free association. In Jimo Number One Middle School more than one dozen independent rebel Red Guard associations emerged overnight after the publication of the " 16 points" in August 1966. Before long these independent rebel associations formed a united front under the banner of Jimo Number One Middle School Revolutionary Rebel Liaison General Station. This group, in turn, became a source of leadership for the whole county as farmers and workers came to contact them. The rebel students also went to factories and villages to help organize rebel workers and farmers.[31]

Yang Xizhe from Datong Village resurrected the banned Peasant Revolutionary Rebel Regiment. Jin Weian and Yu Jianzhun started a rebel association among artists. Jiang Xiaoming from the Bureau of Material Supplies formed a rebel association among the different departments of the County government. Huang Xiangcui and Wang Shigui initiated a rebel association among employees of the Public Security Bureau, the Court and Public Prosecution Bureau. Niu Xili headed a rebel association of employees of finance and commercial organizations. Yan Zhide from Jimo Tractor Station, Jin Kexin from Jimo Hardware Factory, and Zhou Peixin from Jimo Lique Factory were the leaders of the workers' rebel association. In a very short time, there were several rebel associations in every village and factory in Jimo County. In order to coordinate their efforts, the rebel associations formed a united front under the banner of Kongda Commune which united different rebel groups in every village and every factory in Jimo County. And the factions that more inclined to defend the party authorities were organized their counrywide organization as Zhu Li Jun.[32] Both the rebels and the defenders of the party Leaders were called Red Guards. The rebels were called *zaofan pai* (rebel faction) while the defenders were known as *bao huang pai* (loyalist, or royalist faction) during the Cultural Revolution which divide people into two major factions. I use the rebel Red Guards and distinguish it from the other faction.

These self-organized rebel groups were fundamentally different from the official Red Guards. Some rebel leaders like Lan Chengwu and Wang Sibo from Number One Middle School had been previously suppressed by the official Red Guards organized by the work team. Other rebel leaders like Yan Zhide from Jimo Tractor Station, Jin Koxin from Jimo Hardware Factory, Zhu Xiangchun from the Transportation Station and Yan Xizhe from Datong Village were all suppressed by the authorities at the beginning of the Cultural Revolution because of their attempts to criticize their party superiors. Therefore they had grievances against the party bosses of their respective units.[33]

Most of these workers and farmers, unlike the young students who had naive and noble notions about the Cultural Revolution, joined the revolution for very practical reasons. They rebelled because they were not happy with the local Jimo party bosses, and with the ways some party leaders conducted their official business. They accused the party leaders of turning their units into small independent kingdoms *(duli wangguo),* of distorting Central Government policies and enacting their own arbitrary rules, of oppressing people who challenged their authority, and of pilfering public funds. At the beginning of the Cultural Revolution, their challenges were labeled as anti-party and anti-revolution by the local party bosses. Now Mao's 16 points" lent them support and they felt empowered. They said: Chairman Mao supports us, and we will not let Chairman Mao down *(Mao Zhuxi ti women changyao, women wei Mao Zhuxi zhengqi)*[34]

The establishment of mass associations in factories and villages gave the rebels unprecedented power. As they linked up with each other in different factories and villages they became an important collective force. Rebel students in Jimo Number One Middle School drove the work team out in late August, 1966, and forced Zhang Junguang, head of the work team, to give up all the "black" materials he and his subordinates collected against rebel students and teachers, and to apologize to the people involved. Rebel students also took Lu Daoping, County Party Committee Secretary, Wang Qingchun, Head of County Government, and a few other county leaders to read big character posters in schools, in villages and in factories, and to listen to rebel broadcasts as a way to educate them.[35] All these things would have been unimaginable without Mao's support and without the institutional support of the mass associations.

The rebel mass associations in Jimo County attacked Tian Shidian, the Police chief, and Zhang Shaofeng, the Chief of the Military Affairs Committee, for their arrest of rebel leaders. Peasant rebel associations in Datong Village held meetings to denounce Tian Shidian five times. Rebel student associations from Jimo Number One Middle School forced Zhang Shaofeng to attend criticism meetings three times. At one struggle meeting some students tore the ensigns off Zhang's military uniform when he refused to admit his guilt in arresting rebel leaders.[36] In the end the rebel mass associations in Jimo County were able to force the police to free Yu Zhengyang and other rebel leaders who were arrested at the beginning of the Cultural Revolution.[37]

Lan Chengwu, a sixteen-year-old student from a South River Village family, was the leader of one of the dozen or so independent rebel associations at Jimo Number One Middle School. He and his comrades called their group the Red Fearless Rebel Team (*Heng Wuwei Zaofan Dui*). He wrote an open letter to support Yu Zhengyang while he was still in prison, and condemned police arrests of the rebel leaders. Farmers copied his letter and pasted it everywhere in Jimo town. Lan Chengwu and his comrades bought a printer with their own money, and worked long hours every day, sometimes without sleep, to publish their *Red Fearless Fighting Newspaper* (*Heng wuwei zhang bao*). Apart from publishing their newspaper, they wrote big character posters to criticize the county and school party bosses. They distributed their newspapers and pamphlets free in the market places.[38]

In the beginning the rebels were not able to engage in these political activities without harassment. Li Hu, a policeman from Chengguan Police Station, tried to stop Lan Chengwu and his comrades Yan Libo from distributing their newspapers in the market places. They resisted. Li Hu took them to police headquarters. Inside the police station, Li Hu confiscated all their newspapers and searched their bodies. After harassing both students for some time, Li Hu dismissed them in the usual off-handed manner. But the two students refused to leave and demanded an apology for the illegal harassment. When they did not get an apology, they immediately started a hunger strike inside the police headquarters. Farmers, workers, students and teachers swarmed the police station to support the two students. Immediately, big character posters protesting police harassment and demanding an apology covered the police headquarters and the neighborhood walls. Sun Changle, the chief of the police station, had to negotiate with the students to end the confrontation. He sent for their parents, hoping they would persuade their children to go home. But the students refused to budge. In the end, Mr. Sun apologized and promised that he would chastise Li Hu for his illegal action.[39]

When rebels such as Lan Chengwu and Yan Libo defended themselves and subjected the arrogant and aggressive party leaders to vehement criticism and physical harassment, defenders of traditional political culture condemned this as "disaster" and "chaos". But this "disaster" and "chaos" also empowered masses to talk back to people in authority.

The emergence of mass associations during the Cultural Revolution played an important role in the process of political empowerment, particularly in the rural areas. The Chinese constitution had granted the Chinese people the freedom of association, but rural people did not enjoy this freedom prior to the Cultural Revolution. The absence of political associations or groups in rural areas except for those like the militia and Communist Youth League which were controlled by the village party branch resulted from the dominating presence of the CCP party branch, which did not allow any challengers. This explains why the emergence of mass associations in the rural areas coincided with the paralysis of the local party organizations.

The villages I studied developed between three and five mass associations each during the Cultural Revolution. South River Village had four mass associations, Yao Zhuang had three, and Guocun had four. These mass associations were formed largely in the spirit of free association, and enjoyed tremendous independence and freedom. They cut across clan and family lines. It was common for people from the same clan and same family to join different associations. People came together because of their political views. With few exceptions, all of the adult population belonged to one mass association or another.

In Jimo, children in primary school had their Red Guard associations. Jin Keqing, Jin Kezhu, Wang Siying, Wang Xiying, Gu Dunmin and Huang Keqiang were primary school children from South River Primary School in their early teens. They set up their own Red Guard groups, designed Red Guards armbands, and printed their own pamphlets. They wrote big character posters accusing their school principal, Song Liaoyi, of eating sweet potatoes the students gleaned from the fields for the school. Chu Jiying, a female primary school teacher who had taken home the toys she confiscated from students for her own children, was asked by the students to make a confession and return the toys to their original owners.[40] These former school children, now in their early forties, recalled this experience in terms that suggest political empowerment.

These mass association had connections with mass associations in other villages, in the county town, and in the provincial capital, which shared similar political views with them. They went to other villages and county towns to support their allies, and got support in return when needed. They all claimed allegiance to Mao Zedong thought and to the agenda of the Cultural Revolution because they empowered them. But their perceptions and understandings of the Cultural Revolution were different. In most cases, the mass associations were divided into two major sides in a village. The major difference between them was whether or not to overthrow the old village party bosses.

Usually, one side was made up of people who had grievances against village party leaders and saw the Cultural Revolution as an opportunity to settle past wrongs. The other side was composed of people who were more favorably disposed toward the former village party leaders and wanted to protect them. Because they did not want to be labeled as *lao bao* (people who protected the power holders) they, too, wrote big character posters criticizing the leaders, but their tone was less harsh and their actions were less bold on the whole. *Heng Wei Zaofan Bingtuan* in South River Village and *Da Wuwei* in Yaozhuang Village, which were both majority associations in their respective villages, aimed at overthrowing the old party leaders in the village. Opposing associations tended to protect the village leaders.[41]

Different mass associations competed with one another for the allegiance of villagers. They held mass meetings to denounce village leaders and forced village leaders to bend their heads and confess their mistakes and wrong doings. In some cases, village party leaders were subjected to violence. In Yaozhuang Village the Party Secretary was beaten. Part of his house was torn down, and the building materials were confiscated. In South River Village, the party secretary and his deputy were taken from their homes at night to attend criticism meetings and their family bicycle was confiscated by the mass associations.[42]

Before the Cultural Revolution, there were no regular channels for ordinary villagers to air their opinions and grievances against the village party authorities. Their anger and frustration could only be stored up, waiting for an opportunity to explode. When the opportunity arrived, the explosion sometimes was violent and excessive. However, placed in the social and historical context of the time, these violent explosions of anger and frustration by villagers had some very positive consequences in the process of empowerment for rural people. Ordinary villagers realized their own power, and former village party bosses witnessed the capacity of the ordinary people. Both were indispensable for the political empowerment of ordinary villagers. Some villagers say that before the Cultural Revolution, villagers felt shorter before village party leaders and always nodded to them first when they met on the street. After the Cultural Revolution ordinary villagers no longer felt diminished before the village leaders and such leaders often greeted ordinary villagers first when they met on the street.[43]

DEBATE, BIG CHARACTER POSTERS AND POLITICAL EMPOWERMENT

Sida, the "four bigs," referred to *daming* (great airing of opinions), *dafang* (great freedom), *dazibao* (big character posters) and *dabianlun* (great debate). These were the political instruments widely used by common people during the Cultural Revolution. After students and teachers in Jimo Number One Middle School put out their first batch of big character posters to criticize the school leadership, *dazibao* (big character posters) became weapons of villagers and workers. Village streets and workshops in factories were plastered with big character posters, airing grievances against village leaders and factory managers. Some of these grievances went back to the Great Leap Forward years. In South River Village, for example, the people put up big character posters asking the village party secretary, deputy party secretary and village accountant to confess how much grain they had divided among themselves without the knowledge of villagers during the grain shortage following the Great Leap Forward. The deputy party secretary's wife died of food poisoning during the Great Leap Forward, and before long, he married the village store keeper. Some villagers suspected foul play in the death of deputy party secretary's wife, but they had no opportunity to air their suspicion before the Cultural Revolution. During the Cultural Revolution, some villagers wrote big character posters, asking the deputy secretary to explain the circumstances of his wife's death and how he got remarried so quickly. Though unable to get to the bottom of the matter because it took place so many years before, the villagers felt empowered, being able to ask him these questions.[44]

The big character poster was a very flexible, effective, and convenient political instrument. All it took was some ink, some paper, a brush, and the ability to write. Even if a person could not write, he or she could always find somebody else to help write a poster. Liu Meiyu, a housewife, did not know how to write herself, so she asked somebody to write a big character poster for her. In her poster she asked the head of her production team Zhang Min, what he had done with the money he exacted from her in the previous few years. Liu's husband was a worker in a factory. For a number of years before the Cultural Revolution, the production team leader asked her to give him money to pay for the grain her family got from the production team. Each time she gave him the amount that was demanded. But she got no receipt, and that money did not make any difference in the distribution of grain. She was suspicious, but she dared not ask any questions, being intimidated by the fierce expression and attitude of the production team head. The big character posters put out by others gave her courage, and finally she put out one of her own.[45]

Powerful village and production team leaders were overwhelmed by the big character posters targeting them. They lost their arrogant air. These subtle changes in everyday politics empowered timid villagers like Liu Meiyu. After putting out her big character poster, she went even further to challenge the production team head face to face, making him admit that he used all the money he got from her over the years for himself.[46]

The big character posters, as a weapon of the weak, served the rural people well.[47] That was the reason why big character posters were a widelyused medium during the Cultural Revolution in rural areas. Street walls were covered with layers and layers of big character posters. After the wall space was used up, wood bulletin boards *(dazibao peng)* were set up to hold more big character posters. Many people say that China does not have a free press, and lament the political consequences of its absence. But few realize that during the Cultural Revolution big character posters more than made up for the absence of a free press. Writers of big character posters did not need to please any editors, and no reputation was required to put one out. This forum was tailored to the needs of ordinary farmers, workers and others for participation in the political life of their units. Villagers say that if they were not happy with what was going on in their villages they could write posters to air their opinions. In a Chinese village a big character poster attracted attention very quickly.[48] Thus an individual could easily put his or her concern into a public forum. Other people could write to engage in the discussion too. Ordinary people were empowered by this convenient political weapon, which was one of the reasons that the Communist Party officials and village party bosses hated it so much.

In addition to big character posters, great debate played a role in the political empowerment of ordinary people. During the initial period of the Cultural Revolution in Jimo, mass associations debated with one another and with party leaders—in public. Like big character posters, these public forums provided ordinary people an opportunity to air their opinions. Lan Chengwu from South River village, Wang Sibo from Lingshan, Wang Zhanjun from a soldier's family, Jiao Chuanfa, an ordinary worker, and many other rebel leaders learned to make effective public speeches during these public debates. They said that the ability to speak publicly was empowering.[49]

Today many people do not recognize the role factional debates, big character posters, and mass meetings criticizing power holders played in empowering ordinary people. Some people regard these events as much ado about nothing, causing trouble, disrupting production and disturbing peace and unity in their units. In the present political climate it is natural for people to dismiss what happened during the Cultural Revolution as politically insignificant. However, former rebel leaders like Lan Chengwu and Wang Sibo believe that the great debates, the big character posters and the mass criticism of village leaders were a process of political awakening for Jimo's rural people. The opinions and criticisms villagers aired through big character posters, at debates and mass meetings may not have had high theoretical content, but both Lan and Wang said that these exercises promoted the democratic habit of free speech among ordinary villagers.[50]

CHUANLIAN AND POLITICAL EMPOWERMENT

Chuanlian refers to the trips made by young people from Beijing during the Cultural Revolution to spread the revolutionary messages, and by people from other places to Beijing and other revolutionary sites like Jinggangshan and Yanan to gain revolutionary experiences. These trips provided young people, particularly those from rural areas, few of whom had ventured beyond their market towns, with an opportunity to see the outside world. In Jimo County, the Cultural Revolution took a dramatic turn after young people returned from trips to Beijing where they gained new perspectives. The independent mass associations emerged, and destruction of the *si jiu* (four olds) stopped after the students returned from their travels.[51]

In 1966, one group of twenty rural youth between fourteen and sixteen years old left their rural middle school in Jimo County on foot for Beijing. They were the first youngsters from their villages who had ever ventured beyond the county town, located fifteen kilometers east of their village. Holding a red flag, they were determined to walk all the way to Beijing. Passing bus drivers stopped and offered to give them a lift. But they refused, determined to walk. They walked during the day and stopped for the night at various reception centers set up at different schools along the way. At these reception centers they met students from other places and discussed the developments of the Cultural Revolution with them. They read and copied big character posters. They collected and read large quantities of the political pamphlets published by different Red Guard associations in cities and towns. As they saw the world, and exchanged ideas with others, they felt politically empowered.[52]

In Beijing and in other cities along the road to Beijing they had some eyeopening experiences. The school classrooms in the cities were much better equipped than those in their own school. They had glass windows, electric lights, and better desks and chairs. The city people ate mostly wheat flour breads, with vegetable and meat dishes. Back home their families grew wheat and raised pigs and poultry. But wheat flour and meat, even most vegetables were too much of a luxury for them. They could afford them only on rare occasions when they had guests and during festivals. They were humbled to some extent, but they also felt indignation over the gap in the living standards between the rural and urban areas.[53] The recognition of this gap in living standards and educational opportunities was an important part of the process of political learning.

In rural Jimo, *chuanlian also* referred to efforts made by people to contact others in other villages, other factories and other schools, to spread information and to make connections. Students who had traveled to Beijing and other big cities spread what they had learned to people in other schools and other places in the county. After they came back from Beijing, Lan Chengwu, Wang Sihe and their comrades, for example, made several trips to remote villages to speak to villagers and students from rural schools. These trips were a learning process for them too. It was during these trips that Lan Chengwu and his comrades learned about the widespread corruption among rural cadres. The outrages of village *tuhuangdi* (local emperors) who stole collective grain, slept with other people's wives and suppressed those who dared to challenge them angered Lan and his comrades and fired their determination to sustain the Cultural Revolution.[54]

Today official historical accounts emphasize the disruptive impact of *chuanlian* on the national transportation system. Large numbers of people traveling free of charge by train jammed the railway system and disrupted the delivery of raw materials to factories. Consequently, industrial production in some sectors declined in 1966. Some scholars have characterized *chuanlian* as free sightseeing tours for bored city youngsters who had nothing else to do as schools were closed.[55] Others have condemned *chuanlian* as a waste of time on the part of school children and a misuse of state resources.[56] But former rural Red Guards emphasize that their *chuanlian* experiences were not only beneficial to themselves but also to rural society. They provided rural children a rare chance to see the outside world and to see the gap between urban and rural education and living standards. Lan Chengwu and Wang Sibo doubted they would have been able to overthrow the county

Communist Party bosses without the contacts with Red Guards of other places and the experience and courage they gained from *chuanlian*.[57]

THE CAMPAIGN TO STUDY MAO'S WORKS AND POLITICAL EMPOWERMENT

In Jimo the study of Mao's works also contributed to the empowerment of rural people. The small red book of Mao's Quotations and the four volumes of his selected works became widely available in rural areas during the Cultural Revolution[58] Directives from Mao and the Central Government were read and explained to villagers at mass meetings. Given the dominant traditional Chinese philosophy, *min ke shi you zhi, bu ke shi zhi zhi*[59](ordinary people should be led but be kept ignorant), this was something very revolutionary. In early 1967, the PLA stationed in Jimo County sent out 3,070 officers and troops to factories and villages to help promote the study of Mao's works. They went to villagers' homes to read and explain the meanings of Mao's works. Zhang Wenying, Jin Aiyu and Lin Xiuying, three housewives from South River Village, still remembered the PLA soldiers who came to their houses to explain Mao's works to them.[60] For a time, virtually everybody was studying Mao's works. Villagers carried Mao's red books in small handbags everywhere they went. When they went to fields, they carried *yulupai* (a wooden board with Mao's quotations written on them). During their field breaks they read Mao's works. In South River, Yaotou and Guocun, young people set up night schools to teach Mao's works. Young people went to the homes of those who could not attend night schools. School children were teaching their illiterate parents and grand parents, and wives and husbands were helping each other read Mao's works. With these massive efforts it was not surprising that everybody could recite some of Mao's quotations and most of them could recite *Lao Sanpian* (the three venerable articles).[61] Young people in many villages organized Mao Zedong thought propaganda teams to stage *yang banxi* (the model Beijing operas) in the village and other self-made programs to propagate basic Maoist principles and ideas to villagers. Mao's quotations were put into songs. Consequently, most rural youth could sing these Beijing operas and quote Mao.[62] Zhang Xiuying in South River Village, an illiterate housewife, learned to sing the quotation songs like "Make a decision, do not be afraid to die, overcome all the difficulties to win victory," and many other quotation songs. Whenever she was faced with a difficult task, she would sing this song to encourage herself to carry on. She said that singing these songs gave her strength.[63]

Fundamentally speaking, *yang banxi* (the model Beijing operas) and Mao's quotations served important social functions. They promoted a democratic modern political culture and established a highly demanding, though loosely worded, code of official conduct. They called on Communist Party members to accept hardship first and enjoyment later. They required government officials to think about the livelihood of the masses. They denounced high-handed oppressive behavior and promoted subtle persuasion in dealing with difficult persons. All these qualities were embodied in the major characters of *yang banxi*. Mao quotations and the main characters of *yang banxi* served two functions. They set up good examples for the officials to emulate, and, more importantly, they provided the ordinary people with a measuring stick of good official conduct.[64]

Yang banxi were not the only literary creation of the Cultural Revolution. Villagers I interviewed described to me many other kind performances with local flavors at the village, commune and county level throughout the Cultural Revolution period. Almost every village and factory had a Mao Zedong Thought propaganda team during these years. These teams produced a large variety of plays with distinct local flavor.[65] We do not see these local level performances any more in China.

To the outside world and to the educated elite, songs based on Mao's quotations and *yang banxi* constitute a personality cult carried to the extreme.[66] There is a measure of truth in such an assessment.[67] But in a way this cult served to empower ordinary Chinese people. Ordinary villagers used Mao's words to promote their own interests.[68] What some outside observers don't realize is that Mao's works had become a *de facto* Constitution for rural people. More importantly, this *de facto* constitution became an effective political weapon for ordinary villagers.

One of the cliches of the Cultural Revolution was that Mao Zedong Thought would become a weapon in the hands of ordinary people in transforming the old world and building a new one. Mao's works did become a powerful weapon in the hands of many ordinary Jimo villagers. They used Mao's words as a weapon in their debates with abusive village leaders, and as a yardstick to measure the behavior of village leaders. Village leaders who used to boss and beat ordinary villagers now had to be subjected to the words of Mao's Cultural Revolution constitution. In this sense, Mao's works promoted the idea of equality between leaders and the led, and ultimately promoted the political empowerment of ordinary villagers.

The Cultural Revolution was a revolution in which ordinary people rose against their superiors, and Mao's words provided ordinary villagers with a strong sense of political power. Guo

Sheng, a seventy-year-old farmer from Jimo's Guojiaxiang village, was illiterate and used to be dismissed as an old fool by others before 1965. During the Cultural Revolution he learned, with the help of others, to recite Mao's three most venerable articles, which was no small feat for an illiterate farmer. During the breaks in the fields, he recited Mao's works and explained to others his understanding of Mao's works. Nobody dared to laugh at him any more. He used the political discourse of the time to gain personal dignity.[69]

Scholarly critics of the Cultural Revolution dismiss the study of Mao's works as blind submission to Mao's words as the final authority.[70] That is very true. It is true that few people in China ever, particularly during the Cultural Revolution, subjected Mao's works to any theoretical scrutiny, which is sad indeed. However, critics sometimes forget the social context of Chinese society in the mid-1960s, and the most urgent needs of ordinary people at that time. For the illiterate and powerless villagers, it was not the business of the day to subject Mao's works to theoretical scrutiny, but to use Mao's words as a weapon to empower themselves against official abuses and to overcome their traditional submissive culture. Submission to Mao's works as the final authority provided ordinary villagers protection against capricious local government leaders who dominated daily life in China, providing the rural people a sense of power they never had before.

To many Western scholars, Mao's Cultural Revolution-era messages were extremely ambiguous. Andrew Walder, for instance, has written: "It takes an extraordinary amount of energy and imagination to figure out precisely what Mao really meant by such ideas as 'the restoration of the capitalism' or 'newly arisen bourgeoisie'"[71] However, to Chinese people, even to the illiterate villagers, these terms were not so hard to grasp. For many farmers I interviewed, "capitalist restoration" referred to the loss of the fruits of the land reform, and a return to the ways of the old society, and the term "newly arisen bourgeoisie" referred to party leaders who did not work but bossed people around like the old landlords and capitalists.[72]

Mao's essay "Serve the People," one of the three essays people were encouraged to memorize during the Cultural Revolution, is less than three pages long, but it contains several straightforward messages. First, it states that the CCP and CCPs army have no other goal than to serve the people. This message undermines the legitimacy of selfish and corrupt behavior on the part of officials. Second, it states that the CCP and CCP officials should not be afraid of criticism, and if the criticism is correct, they should accept it and act on it. On the one hand, this principle provided ordinary villagers with the right to criticize their superiors. If a leader was afraid of criticism and forbade people to criticize him, he was unqualified to lead the masses. Third, it says that everyone in the revolutionary ranks is equal regardless of rank or position. Implicitly, this criterion denounced all practices of beating and cursing by village leaders and other officials. This third message also constitutes part of the code of official conduct promoted during the Cultural Revolution.

The study of Mao's works during the Cultural Revolution served to make this code of official conduct more explicit and more public. Farmers and former rebel leaders said that the leaders of the Cultural Revolution had gone a long way to separate themselves from elitist ideas and style.[73] To what extent was this new development interwoven with the popular study of Mao's works? I would argue that they were connected. It seems that all the three messages from this one small essay by Mao served to restrain officials and promote the political empowerment of ordinary people. Today farmers still say that "Chairman Mao said what ordinary villagers wanted to say" *(shuo chu liao nongmin de xinli hua)*.[74]

China has a political history of several thousand years in which ordinary peasants were victimized by officials. Peasants often followed a tradition of *zhi fan tan guan bu fan huangdi* (rebel against corrupt officials but not the emperor). The Confucian philosophy of loyalty to the emperor and paternal authority probably had a lot to do with it. The Chinese regarded their emperors more or less as parents beyond the family. They tended to classify their emperors in the categories of wise or stupid, just as they would their parents. With few exceptions, they refused to categorize emperors as bad, just as they were reluctant to so label their parents. If anything went wrong, they blamed it on the emperors' officials. This may not have been the case, but this was a common Chinese belief. As with any common belief, there is a justifiable element in it.

This traditional Chinese dualism in the popular attitude toward emperors and their officials had parallels after 1949. Even though people were angry with corrupt Communist officials, they did not blame the CCP and its top leader Mao Zedong as much. During the Hundred Flowers campaign in 1957, most criticism was directed toward the local party bosses, not the CCP or Mao Zedong.[75] During the period of food shortages following the failure of the Great Leap Forward Chinese, farmers suffered most.[76] But very few farmers blamed Mao for their suffering.[77] During the Cultural Revolution ordinary villagers attacked local officials in the name of defending Mao. It would be too simple to explain their actions simply as a continuation of the *zhi fan tan guan bu fan huangdi* tradition, but the parallel is clear. In this case, ordinary villagers gained real power against local officials by following Mao and holding local officials to the code of conduct Mao established. I would argue that one reason why ordinary villagers made such an effort to study Mao's works and why they could recite Mao's quotations and other lengthy works at the time, is because they gained power by doing so.

The study of Mao's works left some permanent marks on China's political culture. The language rural people use to express their indignation against corrupt officials in today's China is still the same language they used during the Cultural Revolution, and the criteria they use to gauge official behavior are derived from Mao's words promoted during the Cultural Revolution.

A NEW POWER STRUCTURE: THE REVOLUTIONARY COMMITTEE

In early 1968, after a year and a half of mass associations, big character posters, great criticism, and great debate, a new power structure began to emerge. In Jimo County, village *Pinxia zhongnong xiehui* (Association of Poor and Lower Middle Peasants), known in some other places as *Pinminhui* (Association of Poor Farmers) were formed and began to exercise leadership in conjunction with mass associations.[78] These associations which included more than ninety percent of the rural population, were more representative than the party branch which had been in power since 1949. In the villages I have studied, the association demanded that production teams and production brigades publish their financial transactions monthly. Production team members also elected a representative to sit on the production team committee. The representatives were present at the production team committee meetings and held one of the two keys that opened one of the two locks of the storeroom. Without the presence of the representatives, production team leaders could not even enter the storeroom, let alone steal public grain, which had been common among production team leaders prior to the Cultural Revolution.[79]

In late 1967, rebel mass associations in Jimo, with the backing of the PLA, began to take over the reins of power formally. Jimo Number One Middle School was the first place where this happened. Wang Sibo, Wang Zhanjun, Wang Silun, three rebel student leaders, Li Yingliang, Jiang Zhenshen, two rebel teachers, and Tong Da, a former administrator, were selected by the masses with the support of the Army to form the revolutionary committee of the school, and began to exercise leadership.[80]

Following the example of student rebels, mass associations in villages and factories set up preparatory committees to organize revolutionary committees. In South River and Guo villages, the preparatory committees were composed of representatives from different mass associations in proportion to the size of their memberships. These preparatory committees and the associations of the poor and lower middle peasants together chose the people who were on the new village revolutionary committees.[81] Those who stood out in the struggle against the old power holders at the beginning of the Cultural Revolution eventually became members of revolutionary committees. Writing big character posters and engagement in public debate helped these new leaders sharpen their pubic speaking skills. Wang Sibo, the former rebel leader from Jimo Number One Middle School, became the deputy head of Jimo Dahua Machine Factory. Workers there were impressed by his ability to make effective public speeches, and his willingness to work very hard on the night shifts with ordinary workers.[82] Wang Sibo later became a member of the Jimo County Revolutionary Committee. According to Wang, he and his comrades on the Jimo Number One Middle School Revolutionary Committee and later on the County Revolutionary Committee, were all baptized in the storms of the mass struggle in which they gained organizational skills and popularity among the masses. Former rebel leaders in Jimo despised Central Government leaders like Premier Li Peng who worked his way up through personal connections, and who could not even make a decent public speech.[83]

The significance of the revolutionary committee was not simply that a new power structure replaced the old. Rather it was an empowering process in which both the leaders and masses learned a lesson. Facing the politically empowered villagers, the old village leaders became more inclined to listen to their opinions. They understood that their power depended on the support of villagers. The new village leaders who gained power largely through criticizing the mistakes and shortcomings of former village leaders tried to avoid their mistakes. They participated in manual labor more conscientiously than their predecessors had. In some localities, it was stipulated that members of the county revolutionary committee had to participate in manual labor for about two hundred days a year, and members of the commune revolutionary committees had to work in the fields for more than two hundred days a year. Village leaders had to work in the fields around three hundred days a year and production team leaders had to work every day with ordinary villagers.[84]

Farmers still remember Ding Qichao, the head of the Jimo County Revolutionary Committee, riding his bike on the dirt road in the fields, carrying a side bag and a water bottle on his back, stopping once in a while to work and talk with farmers. Before the Cultural Revolution, Wang Dechun was Chengguan Commune Party Secretary. Later, he was incorporated into the Revolutionary

Committee by the rebels. He worked and lived with villagers more than two hundred days a year, sleeping under the same roof in the villages and eating the same kind of food with villagers.[85] The political empowerment of the villagers had changed the political culture of the rural areas.

With few exceptions, the major party bosses who were criticized at the beginning of the Cultural Revolution in rural Jimo were rehabilitated between 1968 and 1976. As the head of the Jimo County Government, Wang Qingchun was the primary target of mass anger in Jimo County at the beginning of the Cultural Revolution and was subjected to numerous meetings of mass criticism. Eventually, however, he accepted the rationale of the Cultural Revolution. He was invited to join the County Revolutionary Committee and developed a close relationship with some of the rebel leaders.[86]

THE EMERGENCE OF A NEW POLITICAL CULTURE

The Chinese Communist leadership claimed to have built a new society in China after 1949. However, many Communist leaders and government officials still operated with the assumptions of the Confucian culture of officialdom. Liu Yingji developed the concept of "officialdom culture" *(guan wenhua)* to describe the unique dominance of officialdom in Chinese civilization for thousands of years. This culture had not been seriously challenged until Mao's Cultural Revolution.[87] The political culture of the new ruling elite in the "new" China was in contradiction with the new production relations of the new society. Before the Cultural Revolution the Communist officials, particularly in rural areas, had become increasingly corrupt, arbitrary, and intolerant as their control over resources increased. The tension between officials and the common people was rising.

The culture of submissiveness of ordinary Chinese villagers, and the mentality of survival by avoiding confrontation, had been formed in the context of this long history of official oppression and abuse. For individual farmers, this submissive culture and mentality were useful for survival. Unfortunately, however, they reinforced the tendency on the part of officials to abuse their power. *Jian sun bu lu you zui* (It is a crime not to take advantage of a submissive creature), is an old saying I picked up from villagers during my field work in Jimo. Fundamentally speaking, widespread official abuse in rural China was partly dependent on the collaboration or acquiescence of ordinary villagers. They allowed officials to get away with abusive behavior until it became a quasi-legitimate habit to abuse and beat ordinary villagers. As some village leaders used to say, those who did not beat and curse were not good village leaders. I heard this expression while interviewing farmers in rural Jimo many times.[88]

The Communist Party platform stipulated that Communists had no separate political interests from the people, and no party members should be allowed to act as if they were above the masses.[89] This noble rhetoric was taken seriously by the rebels during the Cultural Revolution and was used as a criterion in the rebels' debates with party officials and in their big character posters criticizing party officials.[90] Many Communist officials had never expected to be challenged this way. It is understandable that they felt frustrated and angry during the Cultural Revolution when the rebels denounced them and subjected them to physical harassment for not living up to their own rhetoric.[91] They viewed this as disorder and chaos.

Chaos is not necessarily bad. When rules and regulations are as rigidly enforced as they were before the Cultural Revolution, they stifle innovation and progress. When vested interests become too bent on protecting rules and regulations they become oppressors of the disadvantaged. Chaos sometimes creates opportunities the oppressed otherwise would not have. Unfortunately for China, the political culture of officialdom has seldom provided opportunities for common people to achieve changes without chaos. In China's traditional culture of officialdom, demands for change were usually perceived as threats and were often crushed ruthlessly. Under these circumstances, chaos was required to break the resistance to change, and it created the conditions for change.

Just as the submissiveness of villagers had contributed to official abuse before the Cultural Revolution, the improvement of official behavior during the Cultural Revolution was achieved through the effort of villagers. They took courage from Mao's works to overcome their submissiveness. The common people used Mao's prestige and his words to empower themselves.

In sum, the empowerment of ordinary villagers during the Cultural Revolution promoted a change of political culture in rural areas. Before the Cultural Revolution, production team leaders were appointed by village leaders and village leaders were in turn chosen by commune leaders. Ordinary villagers had little say in the process. In the villages I have studied this practice changed during the Cultural Revolution. Production team leaders were elected by production team members. If the production team leader did not do a good job, they would lose their position at the end of the year. In some cases, the production team leaders had to be replaced every year.[92] Whether or not this was good for production is hard to say. But this was an indication of the rising democratic consciousness among ordinary villagers.

The new power organ of the Cultural Revolution—the

Revolutionary Committee—was largely chosen through negotiation among different mass associations. By the time local party organizations began to function again in late 1969, after almost three years of dormancy, the political culture had already changed. More people became party members. In Jimo County, the number of CCP members increased from 14,015 in 1965 to 27,165 in 1978. In South River, Yaotou and Guocun, the number of party members increased from three to ten in each villages.[93] The enlarged party membership gave villagers more choice in selecting village leaders. If they were not happy with one village leader, they could appeal to the commune to replace the current party chief with another person. There was competition among the party members as well. Party member who were not in power looked for opportunities to replace the ones in power. In 1972, South River's Party Secretary Wang Yulong slapped one villager. After the incident, villagers appealed to the commune. The commune investigated the incident and called an election for a new party secretary in a short time. The old party secretary was voted out by the party members.[94] Such a change in the political culture is a significant indication of the political empowerment of ordinary villagers. There are some important social, economic and political reasons behind this.

Mao Re

In the last few years there has been an increasing Mao nostalgia in China. Some people may attribute this to the result of Mao's personality cult. However, it is not a sufficient explanation. Since Deng Xiaoping returned to power in 1978, there has been enough implicit and explicit Mao bashing in government documents and in the mass media in China. It would have more than neutralized that personality cult if there had been one at all. But the Mao bashing did not achieve its intended results. Instead, a steady *Mao re* (Mao Craze) has taken hold in rural China in the last few years.[95]

Notes

1.   This process was, in fact, anticipated by Maoist philosophy. See Mao Zedong, "On Contradiction," *Selected Works,* Vol. 306-307.
2.   Wang Nianyi, *Da Dongran de Niandai,* 63.
3.   There is a conflict in Chinese constitution. On the one hand, the Constitution grants the CCP the leadership role in everything. On the other hand, it also designated the National People's Congress as the body representing the highest authority of the nation. But in reality, the People's Congresses at various levels are controlled by the party. As a result the People's Congress in China is habitually called by the people as the rubber stamp institution that only sanctioned the decisions made by the party leaders behind the scene.

4. Interview with teachers and students in Jimo, Summer 1995.
5. Interview with former rebel leaders in Jimo, summer 1997.
6. In the preceding months, Deng Tuo, Party Secretary of CCP Beijing Committee and chief of *People's Daily*, Wu Han, Deputy Mayor of Beijing City and a historian, Liao Mosha, editor of *Qianxian (The Front Line)* were collectively labeled the *san jia cun* (three household village) anti-party clique, and were subjected to criticism in newspaper's and mass meetings throughout China.
7. Interview with former students of Jimo No. One Middle School, 1995.
8. *Jimo xianzhi, 46.*
9. Interview with rebel leaders in Jimo, summer 1997.
10. Red Guard was an umbrella term that covered many different groups. Some were rebels that rose to attack the local party bosses, while others were conservatives organized to fight the rebels and protect the local party bosses even though they claimed allegiance to Mao and his political line of the Cultural Revolution.
11. "Good family origins" referred to students whose parents before 1949 were poor and lower middle peasants, workers or communist cadres or soldiers.
12. Interview with rebel leaders in Jimo, summer, 1995.
13. Interview with rebel leaders in Jimo, summer, 1997.
14. Interview with villagers in Jimo, summer 1995,.
15. Interview with rebel leaders in Jimo, summer, 1997.
16. Correspondence with villagers in Jimo, summer, 1995.
17. Interview with rebel leaders in Jimo, summer, 1997.
18. Correspondence with former rebel leaders in Jimo, 1995.
19. Interview with villagers in Jimo, summer, 1994.
20. Interview with villagers in Jimo, summer, 1995.
21. Interview with former Red Guards in Jimo, summer, 1995.
22. The physical attacks on former landlords and capitalists and the destruction of cultural relics by the official Red Guards were part of the dark side of the Cultural Revolution. The same is true with the armed factional fighting. The Chinese nation needs to learn a lesson from these sad events. But it is not right to use the dark side of the Cultural Revolution to condemn it as a whole. Despite the excesses committed by Red Guards in destroying the four olds, we also need to put their actions in historical perspective. By closing coffin shops and burning wedding and funeral carriages they helped pave the way for new wedding and funeral practices. Superstitious practices like burning paper human figures and other paper objects as sacrifices stopped during the Cultural Revolution years. The dead were no longer buried in the fields. Instead, they were cremated and stored in village memorial halls, a new practice in rural Jimo that began during the Cultural Revolution.
23. Interview with farmers and rebel red Guards in Jimo, summer 1994.
24. Chinese Communist Party Central Committee "Resolutions on the Proletarian Cultural Revolution" *(Guanyu wuchan jieji wen hua da*

geming de jueding) known as 16 points declaration, was issued on August 12, 1966.

25. Mao made this speech on August 4, 1966 at the expanded meeting of the, CCP Political Bureau. See, Wang, *Da Dongran de Niandai,* 53.

26. Interview with former rebel leaders in Jimo, summer, 1997.

27. For example, in *"Zhongguo Gongchandang Zhongyang Weiyuanhui Guanyu Jianguo Mai Yuoguan Lishi Wenti de Juyi,"* (CCP Central Committee Resolutions on Many Historic Issues of the Party since the Founding of the People's Republic of China) regards the Eleventh Meeting of the CCP Eighth Central Committee as the nationwide launching point of the Cultural Revolution.

28. Correspondence with former rebel leaders in Jimo, 1995.

29. This term is derogatory. It refers to local officials who disregarded central government policies and laws and who exercised power in such an arbitrary manner that people under their rule did not have any way to air their grievances.

30. Interview with former rebel leaders in Jimo, summer, 1997.

31. Correspondence with former rebel leaders, 1995.

32. Interview with Rebel leaders in Jimo, summer 1994.

33. Interview with farmers in Jimo, summer 1997.

34. Interview with farmers in Jimo, summer 1997.

35. Interview of students leaders in Jimo, summer 1995.

36. Interview with villagers in Jimo, summer 1995.

37. Interview with rebel leaders in Jimo, summer 1995.

38. Interview with rebel leaders in Jimo, summer 1995.

39. Interview with rebel leaders in Jimo, summer 1995.

40. Interview with former school children in Jimo, 1995.

41. Interview with villagers in Jimo, summer 1997.

42. Interview with villagers in Jimo, summer 1997.

43. Interview with villagers in Jimo, Summer 1995.

44. Interview with villagers in Jimo, summer, 1997.

45. Interview with villagers in Jimo, summer, 1995.

46. Interview with villagers in Jimo, summer, 1997.

47. James Scott, *The Weapon of the Weak* (Yale University Press, 1985).

48. Interview with villagers in Jimo, summer, 1997.

49. Interview with rebel leaders in Jimo, summer, 1997.

50. Interview with farmers, and former rebel leaders, summer, 1997.

51. Interview with former rebel leaders in Jimo, summer, 1997.

52. Interview with former red guards in Jimo, summer, 1997.

53. Interview with villagers in Jimo, summer, 1997.

54. Interview with rebel leaders in Jimo, Summer, 1995.

55. Gordon A. Bennett and Ronald N. Montaperto, *Red Guard—A Political Biography of Dai Hsiao-ai* (New York: Anchor books, 1972).

56. Wang Nianyi, *Da Dongran de Niandai,* 71.

57. Interview with villagers in Jimo, Summer, 1997.

58. Interview with villagers, summer, 1990, 1993, 1994, 1995. See also *Jimo da shi ji, (Chronology of Events in Jimo)* 71. From August 20-29, 1966, Jimo County Government held a conference to promote the

study of Mao's works. 2000 people attended the conference. On Sept. 9, 1966, each of the thirty communes in the County held a mass rally to distribute Mao's works to villagers.

59.   These are Confucius's words.
60.   *Jimo da shi ji, (Chronology of Events in Jimoz),* 72. Interview with farmers in Jimo, summer, 1997.
61.   Interview with villagers in Jimo, summer, 1995.
62.   Interview with villagers in Jimo, summer, 1995.
63.   Interview with villagers in Jimo, summer, 1997.
64.   After 1978, the main characters in the *yang banxi* were denounced by literary theorists as figures that were *gaodaquan* (characters too high, too great and too complete to be true). Consequently, performance of *Yang banxi* was discontinued in China. But what kind of literary theory is this? Do all characters of literary works have to conform to real life? Does the character Bao Qingtian, the upright Song Dynasty magistrate in the traditional Beijing opera who dared to execute the emperor's son-in-laws and other privileged tyrants, correspond to real life? Three South River villagers who could sing most of *Yang Banxi* by heart said they loved the model operas precisely because the figures were larger than life and made them feel more powerful. Today there is a heated debate in China over the fate of *yang banxi*. The common folk like them and want them back. More than eight million copies of *yang banxi* tapes were sold quietly in China in the last few years, and performance of *yang banxi* are very warmly received by common folk wherever they are staged. But many of the educated elite do not want them back because, they say, these *yang banxi* remind them of their Cultural Revolution experiences.
65.   Interview with villagers in Jimo, summer, 1997.
66.   Tang Tsou, *The Cultural Revolution and Post Mao Reforms,* 147.
67.   There was a tendency among radicals during the Cultural Revolution to use Mao's writing as the sole standard in judging China's literary traditions. In the radicals' ambition to change China's political culture, they judged the traditional literary works too harshly and too simple-mindedly. It is not hard to understand the radicals' rationale in banning some old works which, they argued, were vehicles of China's old political culture of officialdom. But banning these literary works created a sense of deprivation among the Chinese people, particularly the educated elite, and had very negative consequence for literary circles. Many writers became overcautious in their writings for fear of being criticized. The creativity of the writers and playwrights was restricted. It should also be pointed out, however, that the radicals' harsh literary standards did not last long. The radicals gradually learned to appreciate more complexity in literature. As Mao encouraged the whole nation to read *Shui Hu (The* Water *Margins), and Heng Lou Meng (The Dream of the Red Mansion)* in the early 1970s, many traditional masterpieces began to emerge again.

68. Interview with farmers in Jimo, summer, 1997. Farmers say that Mao's words are truth for the farmers.
69. Interview with farmers in Jimo, summer, 1990.
70. Walder, "Actually Existing Maoism," 157.
71. Interview with villagers in Jimo, summer, 1997.
72. Interview with villagers in Jimo, summer, 1997.
73. Interview with villagers and former rebel leaders in Jimo, summer, 1995, 1997.
74. Interview with farmers in Jimo, summer 1997.
75. Wang Shaoguang, *Failure of Charisma,* dissertation (Ithaca: Cornell University, 1990) 54.
76. This may seem strange, but it was true that farmers who were the producers of grain should have suffered most in time of grain shortage. Under the Communist rule, government provided workers with grain. When crops failed in one place, the government could get grain from other places to provide workers with grain. On the other hand, farmers were supposed to provide themselves with grain. When crops failed, particularly when it happened in a large scale, farmers often had to suffer the consequence, though there was government relief but it was not always sufficient.
77. During my field trips to Chinese villages, I have talked with over two hundred people, I did not hear even one farmer blamed Mao for their trouble during the 1959-1961 food shortage.
78. Interview with farmers, 1995. *Jimo xianzhi,* 19:40. This organization of poor and middle peasants was different from the one active during the land reform, which had been dissolved later.
79. Interview with farmers in Jimo, summer, 1995.
80. Interview with former rebel leaders in Jimo, summer, 1997.
81. Interview with farmers in Jimo, summer, 1995.
82. Interview with workers in Jimo, summer, 1997.
83. Interview with Wang Sibo in Jimo, Summer, 1997.
84. Interview with farmers in Jimo, July, 1994. Farmers in Jimo say that they saw the head of the county revolutionary committee Ding Qichao frequently in the fields. He rode a bike alone and stopped to work with farmers for some time and continued on his road again. Villagers came to know their commune leaders very well because they had worked with them in the fields. See also *Huanghua County Records, (Huanghua Xianzhi)* (Haichao Press, 1990) 353, see also *Chen Village,* 354.
85. Interview with villagers in Jimo, summer, 1997.
86. Interview with rebel leaders in Jimo, summer, 1997.
87. Liu Yingji, *Confucius and Mao Zedong—The Builder* and the Critic *of Chinese Officialdom Culture* (Kongzi Yu Mao Zedong—Zhongguo Guan Wenhua de Dianji Zhe Yu Pipanjia) (Jinan: Shandong People's Publishing House, 1993).
88. Zheng Yi observed the same thing in Xianglin County, Guangxi Province. See his paper delivered at a conference held at Harvard

    Kennedy School of Government May 11, 1996. It seems this is very
    wide spread in China.

89. *CCP Platform*, 2, (Beijing: People's Publishing House, 1982)

90. Some urban youth told me that Mao's noble words also fired their
    enthusiasm in volunteering to go to the rural areas. Volunteering
    to go to the rural areas seems very unlikely today. But I have
    interviewed quite a few urban youth in Shandong and Henan who
    told me that they genuinely volunteered to go. People of different
    eras have different values and behaved differently. There is no
    reason for people to judge them by today's value.

91. Many old Communist elite wish that Mao had died in his prime
    years before the Cultural Revolution. They believe China would
    have been much better off, and Mao would still be considered a
    great Marxist revolutionary if he died right after 1949.

92. Interview with farmers in Jimo, summer 1997.

93. Interview with farmers in Jimo, summer 1997.

94. Interview with farmers in Jimo, summer 1997.

95. Zheng Zhilin, *"Yu Bi Tong Pi Yu Yi,"* (Mao's Secretary lashed out at
    Mao's Doctor," *Mingbao Journal,* June, 1996. See also, Jacob
    Heilbrunn, "Mao More Than Ever," *The New Republic, April* 1997.
    20-24.

Typical rural school classroom. Children have to bring their own chair.

A child who does not have a chair has to sit on the floor.

A rural school classroom.

Village youth out of school but too young to work.

Typical rural schoolhouse.

Schoolhouse in need of repair

Village primary school students. The girls on the left and right ends
have repeated the first grade three times

Village youth between the ages of 13 and 15. All are no longer in school. This situation is typical in many villages

Many rural enterprises see little changes in building or equipments 25 years after their beginnings.

The author in his old village factory. This shaping machine he used in
1974

CHAPTER 5

Rural Education Reforms During the Cultural Revolution

Education was the most contested terrain of the Cultural Revolution.[1] The central guidelines established by Mao Zedong at the beginning of the movement, contained in the Central Committee's May 16, 1966 "Decision on the Cultural Revolution," stated that "the task of the Cultural Revolution is to reform the old educational system and educational philosophy and methodology."[2] Before the Cultural Revolution, the educational policies of the Communist party, like other policies and decisions, were regarded as sacred and were never subject to any critical discussion among the people. The CCP simply *presumed* that it represented people's best interests in China, when in fact it had become a vested interest itself. There was little public debate in the policy formulation process. Central Government policies were simply passed down from top to bottom and carried out according to the interpretation of the party bosses at each level. During the Cultural Revolution, rebels questioned the party's authority and its educational policies and demanded fundamental changes in education.[3] The impact of their actions on farmers and workers was profound. In fact, their actions established a new more democratic code of political conduct in Jimo, a code that placed a temporary break on party dictatorship. Farmers and workers, influenced by the actions of the students in Jimo, began to perceive and contemplate the unfairness of the educational policies as well.

CHALLENGING THE JIMO EDUCATION SYSTEM

As discussed in the previous chapter, the first shot of the Cultural Revolution in Jimo County was fired in Jimo Number One Middle School. Rebel students there put out the first big character posters questioning the school party committee's educational policies and practice.[4] Their challenge was met with a fierce counter-attack by the school and county party authorities and the work team dispatched by County Party Committee.[5] What was at issue was the school's educational philosophy. The rebels raised specific questions about how the school should be run. What should be the admissions policy? What kind of teaching materials should be used? And what kind of students should be produced? It is important to note here that the challengers to the existing system had excelled in the system. Wang Sibo, a high school senior, and Lan Chengwu, a middle school freshman, were leaders of the first two rebel associations in Jimo Number One Middle School. They were both from poor peasant families and were on their class Communist Youth League committees. They were academically competent and politically trusted by school authorities before the Cultural Revolution. A high school senior, Wang Sibo was preparing for the national college entrance examination at the time. His plan was to enter Beijing University or Shandong University.[6] Like the students in Beijing Number One Girls High School who wrote to the CCP Central Committee demanding fundamental changes in the nation's college entrance examination system, Wang Sibo and his comrades were not motivated by personal interests. They were virtually guaranteed a college education in the existing system. With a college education, they would go on to become a member of the social elite.[7] They challenged the system because they felt it contradicted the ideological belief in social equality with which they had been indoctrinated by the Communist Party.[8] Partly for that reason, Wang Sibo and his senior classmates felt excited when the Central Government decided to halt the college entrance examination in June 1966 pending educational reforms.[9]

The challengers demanded an overhaul of the existing educational system to make it open to disadvantaged segments of Chinese society, children of the so-called poor and middle peasants and the workers. Since the beginning of the Great Leap Forward, the Chinese Government had been talking about eliminating the three gaps: between urban and rural areas, between mental and manual labor, and between workers and farmers.[10] For the eighty percent of the Chinese population living in rural areas, the slogan of eliminating these gaps was very powerful and appealing. But a slogan was only a slogan. It was only during the Cultural Revolution that some students took it so seriously that they adopted it as a concrete goal of their struggle. They believed that the government's educational policy, instead of helping eliminate these gaps, was actually perpetuating them. They saw with their own eyes that a very small number of educated youngsters from elite middle schools entered college and never returned. Those high school graduates who did not enter college became government employees and urban workers; few ever came back to the rural areas.[11] Because the challengers believed strongly in the need to eliminate the three gaps, they did not give up their fight when the work team suppressed them.[12]

Lan Chengwu and his friends went to other schools in rural Jimo to mobilize their counterparts.[13] They spoke to farmers in the villages and workers in the factories. They also went to PLA barracks in Jimo County to propagate their ideas.[14] The turning point in their struggle was the support Mao and his followers in the

Central Cultural Revolution Small Group extended to rebels in Beijing. Mao's support was the deciding factor in the rebels' ascendancy in Jimo. The army unit stationed in Jimo decided to support them, partly because of Mao's attitude, but also because the rebels' point of view appealed to them.[15] As a result the rebels became dominant in Jimo, and won the right to set up the revolutionary committees.[16] Wang Sibo, Li Yingliang, Jiang Zhensheng, Wang Zhanjun, Wang Silun, Lan Chengwu and other rebel leaders all become prominent members of the revolutionary committee in Jimo Number One Middle School, the most important educational institution in Jimo County, thus paving the way for the bold educational reforms in the county.[17]

Mao's sketchy "May Seventh directive", which was actually part of a letter to Lin Biao written on May 7, 1966, was the philosophical foundation for the educational reforms of the Cultural Revolution. In his letter, Mao had proposed that the length of schooling should be shortened and revolutionary changes should be made in education. The dominance of bourgeois intellectuals in the school system should not be allowed to continue.[18] The letter was a source of inspiration for the workers, farmers, soldiers, and rebel students and teachers in schools who formulated the "Preliminary Educational Reform Program" in Jimo County in April 1968.[19] The Jimo educational reform program called for the elimination of exams as a means of selecting students for middle schools and high schools. It proposed that each village set up its own primary school and that neighboring villagers set up joint middle schools. The length of schooling was to be reduced from six years to five years for primary school, and from three years to two years each for middle and high school. The Preliminary Education Reform Program also called for the compiling of new textbooks that took into consideration local needs and new teaching methods that would promote empowerment of students in the classroom.[20]

NEW VILLAGE PRIMARY SCHOOLS

By the time Jimo Preliminary Education Reform Program was issued in April 1968, the pro-reform Red Guard rebels were already in charge of Jimo County.[21] Immediately, many villages began to set up their own primary schools. Before the Cultural Revolution, South River, Guo Jiaxiang, Yaotou, three villages with a combined population of about 4,000, shared a junior primary school housed in an old temple, which had only offered classes up to the fourth grade. There were two classes in grades one, two and three, but only one class in grade four. Now each of these three villages decided to set up its own primary school and to create a joint middle school with four other villages.[22]

At the time, these villages were very poor, South River and Guo, Jiaxiang particularly so. Farmers in these two villages barely had enough to feed themselves. In fact, during the previous few years, some households in South River had needed government relief grain in order to tide them over during the difficult spring months.[23] They did not have money, but they were not daunted. What these villages did have was an abundant labor force. In South River Village, the Revolutionary Committee, together with ordinary villagers, chose a piece of land inside the village, and made a building plan for the school. After the fall harvest of 1968, villagers began to cut stones in the village quarry and trees from the village forestry. They worked the whole winter, and by early spring 1969, they had gathered all the necessary building materials to begin to build their own primary school. Before spring planting time, South River village had finished the construction of its primary school with five big classrooms and one three-room office.[24] By the winter of 1969, all the three villages had their own primary school. With glass windows and electric lights, these new village primary schools were better equipped than the previous government-run primary schools housed in the old temple.[25]

Teachers in these village schools were themselves villagers with a junior middle school education, and in some cases only a primary school education. Li Meihua, Zhou Chongqi, and Zhao Limei, who had only primary school education, were hired to teach at the South River Village Primary School. Guan Xufen and Zhou Lifen, graduates from middle school in 1968, were the two best-educated teachers in South River Village Primary School. None of the teachers in South River village primary school had any teachers' training except one who had taught in a government school and was hired to head the village school. By any standard, these teachers were very poorly trained. They provided students with basic literacy instruction and training in mathematics. There was also some singing and drawing, and not much else, in the first few years of the existence of the village school. Physical education was no more than relay running in the village street or tug of war. This was true in most other newly created village primary schools.[26] Critics of Cultural Revolution educational reforms note the low standards of the village schools. But what else could village people do? Should they have waited for better teachers to become available? A child has only one chance for education in a lifetime. Once that opportunity has been missed, it can never be regained!

Village schools operated on a flexible schedule. During the busy season, teachers would take students to the fields to help with the harvesting in whatever ways they could, like gleaning wheat fields, or sometimes singing songs for villagers at breaks. As extracurricular activities, students of the fourth and fifth grades engaged in some projects to earn money for the school, making paper boxes and envelopes. Money from these projects was used to pay for trips to see movies and cover some of the costs of the school.[27]

Sun Shiyu from Guo Jiaxiang Village told of his experience as a child who had wanted very much to go to school but was unable to do so before the Cultural Revolution. His family needed him to take care of the family goats. Every morning he watched other children going to school with envious eyes. He also made a point of taking his goats to the pasture outside the school window, so he could peer through the windows while they grazed. Other children who could not go to school gathered there as well. One day the third grade class he was watching was studying an excerpt from Gao Yubao' famous autobiography, "*I want to go to school*," describing his childhood aspiration to go to school and his family's inability to send him there before the CCP came to power.[28] Mr. Gao's autobiography was very popular at the time, and that was why it was adapted in a primary school textbook. Ironically, the unequal educational opportunities under Nationalist rule denounced in Gao's autobiography still existed and were dramatized by the children right outside the classroom window. The teacher and the students all became aware of this. The teacher, touched by the irony, asked Sun Shiyu and his playmates outside the classroom window whether they would come to school if she got them tuition waivers. But, of course, tuition waivers alone could not help these children. Their families could not spare their services.

Sun Shiyu and some of his fellow shepherds joined a third grade class in 1967 during the educational reforms. Even though Sun Shiyu was four years older than most of his classmates when he entered school, the rural educational reforms proved timely for him. He was able to finish primary school and continued to middle school. After middle school, he worked in Guo Jiaxiang's village factory and became an important technician there.[29] Jimo's experimental village primary schools during the Cultural Revolution offered solutions to the various problems that had caused many children not to attend school. First of all, it provided enough school space for every child in the village. There was no need to reject any child for lack of space. Second, the school was free. Parents did not need to pay tuition for their children's education.[30] Third, children went to school in their own village and school hours were flexible, which meant children could have more time to help their parents with household chores. During busy seasons when parents needed their children's help most, the school was closed. Last but not least, it was no longer easy for parents to deny their children the opportunity to go to school. The fact that all children were now expected to attend school brought pressure on parents to send their children to school. According to Jiang Zhihe, the head of South River Village Revolutionary Committee, village leaders questioned parents if they did not send their children to school at this time.[31]

Since village schools removed most of the obstacles that prevented rural children from enrolling in school, the enrollment rate went up as soon as the village primary schools were built.[32] The enrollment of school aged children in Jimo County reached 90.5 percent in 1968, 98.3 percent in 1973, and 99.1 percent in 1976.[33] According to Zhou Chengqi, a retired village school teacher who taught in the South River Village Primary School for over 20 years, with the establishment of the village school, non-attendance was no longer a problem.[34]

NEW JOINT VILLAGE MIDDLE SCHOOLS

Even more important than the establishment of village primary schools was the founding of joint village middle schools. This made middle school education possible for every village child in Jimo County. By 1969, 130 joint middle schools were set up in the county, averaging one for every seven villages.[35] South River and six neighboring villages, Guo Jiaxiang, Hu Jiacun, Yaotou, Huayuan, Moshi, and Fu Jiazhuang, pooled their resources to set up a joint middle school. With a combined population of 8000, the seven villages set up a committee composed of representatives from each village to coordinate the building efforts. Each village contributed building materials in proportion to its respective size. South River and Guo Jiaxiang were bigger than the rest, and contributed more. Most basic building materials were available locally. South River and Guo Jiaxiang had stone quarries, and they contributed most of the stone materials. Yaotou Village produced bricks and contributed more bricks and tiles to the construction of the school buildings.[36]

Once the building materials were assembled, a construction team composed of masons from the seven villages began to build seven new classrooms. The school was built on the site of the government-run junior primary school which had previously served Yaotou, South River and Guo Jiaxiang. This school had been housed in an old temple located between South River and Guo Jiaxiang. In order to build the joint village middle school, more land was needed. But the land next to the former temple school had been used by people from the two villages as vegetable gardens for many years and was very valuable to them. It would be very difficult to persuade these people to relocate their gardens. For the sake of their school, the rebel-dominated governments of the two villages persuaded these villages to give up their old gardens for new ones further away from home.[37]

Construction of the joint middle school solved the problem of school buildings. Finding teachers to teach in the school was a more difficult task. It was relatively easy to find people who could teach primary school. Teaching middle school was much more demanding. In order to teach junior middle school, teachers at least had to have a high school education, which only a few people in the rural areas had at the time. South River Joint Middle School decided to ask two former government teachers, who had formal teachers' training, and four rural teachers, who had finished high school and had teaching experience, to teach middle school classes. Fortunately, Hou Zhenmin and Wang Qingyu's proposal that government teachers return to their hometowns to teach was strongly promoted in newspapers. Consequently many government teachers from urban areas returned to their rural hometowns.[38] South River joint Village Middle School had six such returning teachers.[39] This policy, unpopular among many government schoolteachers, turned out to be a windfall for Jimo's joint village middle schools.

With the joint village middle school arrangement, rural children who finished primary school could all enroll in middle school. There was enough space for everybody. An entrance examination was not needed to keep anybody out. All primary school graduates from the seven villages would automatically enter the middle school without any examination.[40] With the construction of the joint village middle school, every rural child in Jimo could have a free middle school education in a school not far from home.

NEW COMMUNE HIGH SCHOOLS

Before the Cultural Revolution there were only two high schools in Jimo, which had a combined enrollment of 88 students in 1962, 132 students in 1963, 99 students in 1964, and 212 students in 1965.[41] Because of limited space, only about one fifth of the graduates from middle schools were able to enroll in high schools before the Cultural Revolution.[42]

Jimo's Preliminary Educational Reform Program called on people's communes to build their own high schools. By 1969, the number of high schools in Jimo County had increased to seventeen, and 3,020 students were enrolled in high schools. By 1976, the number of high schools increased to 84. The commune high schools were all constructed and financed by communes. There were thirty communes in Jimo County and by 1976 there were about three high schools in each commune (see table 2). In 1976, the freshman class of high school students in Jimo reached 8,264 and the graduating class had 4,095 students. There were 13,172 students enrolled in all

Table 1. Junior Middle Schools in Jimo County					
	Number of Schools	Number of Classes	Number of Enrollments	Number of Graduates	Number of Students in School
1949	2				950
1950	1				1,177
1951	1				1,350
1952	1				1,328
1953	2				2,029
1954	2				2,675
1955	1				1,600
1956	4				3,073
1957	4				2,667
1958	8	79	1,994	408	4,072
1959	8		1,928		4,761
1960	13		2,601	880	4,762,
1961	13	72	1,407	2,957	
1962	8	52	850	509	1,953
1963	7	46	1233	554	2,107
1964	9		1169	319	2,979
1965	8	69	1303	642	3,573
1966	7	90			4,892
1967	7	90	1385	960	4,852
1968					
1969	130	760			28,782
1970	143		14,729	8,065	22,795
1971	210	796	19,737	9,287	33,101
1972	144		16,093	13,185	34,235
1973	144	756	14,171	16,902	30,269
1974	138	618	11,382	12,710	24,693
1975	138	775	22,196	12,637	33,605
1976	269	1,164	29,666	10,937	52,031
1977	255	1,246	27,630	20,788	56,814
1978	173	1,086	23,466	23,466	51,390
1979	141	932	17,855	18,453	43,351
1980	134	942	16,487	9,635	43,272
1981	149	970	17,917	9,546	45,646
1982	141	902	16,437	10,751	43,126
1983	135	791	9,939	10,595	38,358
1984	131	706	10,550	10,513	35,108
1985	106	669	14,444	11,351	34,995
1986	109	810	16,338	10,836	42,554
1987	106	828	15,734	10,665	43,007

Source, *Jimo xianzhi*, 704-705. Missing figures are missing from the original.

Table 2. High Schools in Jimo County					
	Number of Schools	**Number of Classes**	**Number of Freshmen**	**Number of Graduates**	**Number of Students in School**
1950	1	1	3 1		3 1
1951	1	1			3 1
1952	1	2	5 0		8 1
1953	1	4	117	3 1	151
1954	1	4			151
1955	1	7	171	5 0	272
1956	1	8	202	117	357
1957	1.	1 0	96		453
1958	2	1 6	410	168	685
1959	2		465		900
1960	2		451	198	877
1961	2	2 2		198	770
1962	2	1 6	88	177	582
1963	2	1 3	132	166	493
1964	2		95	240	334
1965	2	9	212	101	433
1966	2	9			433
1967	2	9		123	423
1968					
1969	17	6 0			3,028
1970	17		1,758	941	2,860
1971	2 3	105	3,894	1,251	5,695
1972	2 3		4,430	1,444	8,195
1973	2 3	133	3,500	3,737	7,797
1974	2 3	146	4,247	4,119	7,783
1975	2 3	177	5,054	3,420	9,238
1976	8 4	250	8,264	4,095	13,172
1977	8 9	371	12,186	4,762	19,825
1978	9 4	366	7,552	7.753	19,087
1979	3 0	221	5,996	8,708	11,349
1980	2 7	188	31935	4.900	9,502
1981	1 0	7 3	2,029	5,245	4,055
1982	1 0	7 2	1,710	1,745	3,585
1983	1 0	6 8	1,663	1,676	3,463
1984	9	7 3	1,687	999	4,109
1985	9	8 9	1,670	703	5,150
1986	9	8 8	1,685	1,546	5,554
1987	9	9 9	1 1,936	1 1 819	5.669
Source, *Jimo Xianzhi, 704*. Missing figures are missing from the original					

Table 3. Middle and High School Teachers and Staff			
Year	Government Teachers	Village Teachers	Total
1949			52
1950			95
1951			113
1952			121
1953			204
1954			151
1955			152
1956			156
1957			191
1958			260
1959			292
1960			474
1961			142
1962	289	6	295
1963	273		273
1964	292	9	292
1965	307	8	307
1966			297
1967			302
1968			
1969	698	664	1,362
1970	1,348	500	1,848
1971	1 737	731	2,468
1972	1,676	813	2,489
1973	1,605	767	2,372
1974	1,583	748	2,331
1975	1,664	1,179	2,843
1976	1,804	2,426	4,230
1977	1,893	3,243	5,136
1978	1-944	2,785	4,629
1979	2,117	2,054	4,171
1980	2,072	1774	3,846
1981	2,187	1,485	3,672
1982	2,271	1,251	3,522
1983	2,162	1,122	3,284
1984	2,140	1,044	3,184
1985	2,229	912	3,141
1986	2,658	1,291	3,949
987	2.762	1,263	4,015

Source, *Jimo Xianzhi, 75.* The missing figures are missing from original.

the high schools in Jimo in 1976.[43] During the seven years after the Preliminary Education Reform Program was implemented in Jimo, that is from 1969 to 1976, there were 19,130 high school graduates, thirteen times more than there had been during the seventeen years before the Cultural Revolution. In the same period there were 84,727 junior middle school graduates, seventeen times more than there had been during the years before the Cultural Revolution (see Tables 1 and 2).

Of the 4,230 teachers and staff in Jimo high schools in 1976, 2,426, more than half, were paid in work points, which meant that the burden of supporting these teachers and staff was shared by villagers collectively (see table 3). The rural teachers got the same amount of work points as farmers worked in the fields or in the village factory. They also got two *yuan* cash subsidy from the commune government each month. Of course, it would be better if the government could foot all the bills for education, but government itself does not produce money. It can only get money by taxing the people. Very few people like to be taxed, yet without taxes there would be no public services. In the commune structure the tax was invisible, and the cost of government was greatly reduced by this system because the government did not need to finance a tax-collection bureaucracy.[44]

WORKERS' AND FARMERS' PARTICIPATION IN SCHOOL MANAGEMENT

During the early period of the Cultural Revolution, Beijing and Qinghua University experimented with the idea of getting workers, soldiers and farmers involved in the school management. In the summer of 1968 Mao Zedong proposed that the whole country adopt that idea. In Jimo, the response to Mao's initiative was immediate. Workers' teams entered Jimo Number One Middle School, Jimo Number Two Middle School, Chenguan Middle School immediately. And farmers' representatives became part of school management in all the rural schools. The Workers' Team that entered Jimo Number One Middle School was composed of seven workers from the largest and most important state enterprise in Jimo County, the Jimo Farming Machine Factory. Six workers from Jimo Chemical Fertilizer Factory, led by He Zongyin, entered Jimo Chenguan Commune Middle School to preside over the education reform. In the rural areas, farmers sent their representatives into village primary schools and joint village middle schools. The team that supervised South River joint Middle School was composed of Zhang Dechi and Zhang Zuojiao from South River Village, Lan Yingyu from Yao Tou; Chu Jilan and Zhang Ziyong from Moshi, and Huang Kerong from Guocun, and Yu Lixing from Hu Jia Village.[45]

Since 1978, elite educators as well as some ordinary people have ridiculed the practice of allowing workers and farmers participating in school management because these workers and farmers had deplorable educational credentials. Zhou Songbo, the head of the workers' team in Jimo Number One Middle School had no formal education. He started to work in a factory when he was twelve years old. He learned to read and write simple words at night schools sponsored by his factory.[46] Other workers in his team were not much better educated. Zhang Meien, the only female member of the team, became literate through attending night schools as well. None of the other five members had finished primary school. He Zongyin, an army veteran who headed the workers' team in Chenguang Middle School, had a middle school education. He was the best educated of his team.[47]

The credentials of the peasant representatives were no better. Zhang Dechi, the head of the Peasant Association in South River Village, had no formal education. He began looking after a landlord's animals when he was only 9 years old. Huang Kerong, the deputy head of the Peasant Association in Guocun, did not finish primary school. Zhang Ziying, the deputy village head, and Chu Jilan, the head of the Women's Association in Moshi, who had both finished primary school, were among the better educated farmers' representatives in rural schools in Jimo County.[48]

From the standpoint of traditional Chinese beliefs, allowing these less educated farmers and workers to lead the educational reforms was outrageous. How could the less educated lead the better educated? Fundamentally, this was a philosophical question. The criticism reflected the arrogance of the Chinese educated elite[49] and their narrow mind-set toward knowledge. While these workers and peasants had no formal education, what they did have were practical knowledge and a different perspective on education. They braved the traditional bias and prejudice in Chinese schools and society because they felt they had a mission in the educational reforms.[50] Their experiences in schools varied. Those who were more capable won respect and cooperation from teachers and students quickly; those who were less capable had a harder time winning respect and cooperation.

At first, teachers and students from Double Temple School laughed behind Huang Kerong's back because at his first school meeting he said the unusual words *"xiang Mao Zhuxi Xuexi"* an unusual grammatical way of saying learn from Chairman Mao.[51] Zhang Dechi became a joke among teachers and students of South River Village School because he talked about his experience of having to work while suffering from food poisoning, the result of his landlords having fed his hired farm hands with diseased pork.[52]

In face of jesting and ridicule, they did not back down. They continued to work with students and teachers. Teachers and students' attitudes began to change when Huang Kerong ran to the train station at midnight to recover equipment stolen by a former administrator who had been transferred to another school. Gradually, those who had no formal education won the cooperation and respect of teachers and students when their practical knowledge and judgment began to reveal their ability. Students learned that Zhang Dechi was the most respected farm hand in his production team. The wheat seeds he planted were always more evenly distributed, and had higher yields. They also noticed that Zhang Dechi and Huang Kerong were helpful to students. The South River joint Middle School did not have hot water for lack of a boiler. Zhang Dechi managed to get one for the school. In winter, Huang Kerong persuaded his village to spare some coal for the school to heat the classroom.[53] At the same time, Zhang Ziying and Chu Jilan, who were experienced public speakers, won cooperation and respect from teachers and students from the very start. Teachers discussed problems with them and for the most part their opinions were respected.[54]

On the whole, workers seemed to fare better than farmers in schools because of their higher social status.[55] Students and teachers gave the workers very warm receptions when they arrived at schools. Former students and worker team members still remember the warm reception today.[56] In general, workers were also better organized and disciplined than farmers were. All of the seven workers who entered Jimo Number One Middle School lived on campus, eating in student dining halls. They also made frequent visits to student dorms. In the first year, they seldom went home during weekends, since many students from distant rural areas did not go home either.[57]

When workers first entered the school they organized students to open a number of vegetable gardens to produce fresh vegetables for the student dining hall. Zhou Songbo, head of the workers' team, and his fellow workers worked in the garden with the students after school. They turned human excrement into organic fertilizer and used it in the garden. One teacher informant asked rhetorically: What kind school leaders were these workers who dirtied their hands with manure and bothered themselves with vegetables?[58] But according to former members of the worker team, they came to know the students well and won students' respect by working with them.[59] Some former students said that working in the garden was a good thing because students from the rural areas had an opportunity to show their classmates gardening skills, while students from the non-rural families learned how to garden. Positive interaction took place as a result of these activities.[60]

According to several of my interviewees, the workers and farmers in Jimo schools made an effort to learn about students' lives. Zhang Meien and Wang Kezhuang said that they went to student dorms frequently because they wanted to know more about students' lives.[61] Zhang Zuojiao and Zhang Dechi from South River Village knew every villager and their children. When a child did not do well in school, they would accompany teachers to visit the parents to find out what was going on with the child at home.[62] Chu Jiying, a teacher in South River Middle School, said that she spent a great deal of time in the village getting to know the parents of children in her class.[63] Gong Zhaolin and Zhang Suocheng, two students in Ms. Chu's class, got into a fight after school, and Zhang's head was broken. Ms. Chu learned about the fight the same day as she visited parents after school. The next day, she was able to discuss with the class the lesson that could be learned from the fight.

One student in Jimo Number One Middle School routinely wet his quilt at night. Fearing his classmates' ridicule, he did not dry it during the day. When the workers found out about the student's predicament, they helped him. Zhou Songbo took him to the school doctor. Zhang Meien, the female member of the workers' team, washed his quilt and stuffed it with new cotton. They also talked to other students, and asked them to understand their classmate's difficulty, and not to exacerbate his situation by laughing at him.[64]

Zhang Dechi and Huang Kerong said that when a student was tardy or absent from school a few times, they and the teachers would talk with the child's parents and find out what the problem was.[65] The workers also helped the teachers solve some of the difficulties in their lives. Li Junping, a physics teacher, was pregnant, and needed help at home. The workers transferred her younger sister from Taian to study in the school so that she could help her elder sister do household chores. Xiao Qinfeng, an English language teacher, was under mental stress as a result of a domestic problem. The workers talked with her husband and reduced her teaching load for a semester so she could get more rest. In winter, there was a coal shortage in Jimo, and the workers made sure that teachers got enough coal to heat their houses.[66]

Zhou Minsheng, a Chinese language teacher, was frustrated by his wife's quarrels with his mother. Whenever he came home he faced some dilemma. His aged mother wanted him to bring her a chair. His wife did not want him to do it. If he brought the chair for his mother, his wife would pick a fight with him. If he listened to his wife, he failed his responsibility as a son. In desperation, he talked with the members of the workers' team. Zhou Songbo talked with his wife and his mother, first separately and then together, about the difficulties their quarrels caused Zhou Minsheng. He also explained Zhou's responsibility both as son and husband, and discussed with them ways the family could live harmoniously. They also asked Zhou Minsheng to play his role as husband and son creatively and to take more initiative to solve their domestic problems.[67] The workers' team involvement helped Zhou solve his family problems.

Tang Kezheng, a chemistry teacher, and Zheng Yiming, a physical education teacher, got into a fistfight over a joke in the teacher's dining hall. Tang was beaten, and felt humiliated. He visited the workers several times, insisting that the workers criticize Zheng in a joint meeting of teachers and students. The workers convinced him that humiliation of Zheng in public would not help him in the end. Instead, it would only deepen the hatred between them, and that an apology from Mr. Zheng at the teachers' meeting would be a better solution.[68]

Zhou Minsheng was a devoted Chinese language teacher. He prepared his courses very carefully, and his language lectures were filled with vivid stories, aimed at getting students interested. Largely because of his teaching methods, students in his two classes out-performed those in other classes. In the two classrooms where he taught, he put up slogans like *"xue bu hao gongke, dui buqi jiu xing"* (if we do not study hard, we are letting Chairman Mao down). He was a popular teacher among students. However, he failed to impress his colleagues. At the end of each year, the workers' team and school revolutionary committee always recognized a few teachers who did an excellent job during the year as model teachers. Since these teachers had to be elected by teachers, Zhou Minsheng was usually not recognized. He felt he had been treated unfairly. He expressed his resentment to the workers and asked why he could not be selected as a model teacher. The workers saw his point. They encouraged him to talk with other teachers, and suggested that he invite his colleagues to sit in on his classes. He followed the advice and improved his relationship with his colleagues. In the end, he was chosen by his colleagues as a model teacher.[69]

All the above cases suggest that the workers were providing counseling service as much as educational leadership in the school. One former worker team member said in an interview that he tried his best to help the teachers and students.[70] This was in accord with prevailing Chinese conceptions of leadership. Chinese society was organized in such a way that employees often required people in leadership positions to provide many services unrelated to their professional capacity. The demarcation between public and private domains in Chinese society was not always clear-cut. People expected a good leader to be a friend who could give advice in time of need. When there was a quarrel, leaders were expected to be magistrates who could arbitrate disputes among family members, neighbors and colleagues. Leaders were expected to provide loans and credit for unexpected financial difficulties and to help solve housing problems. A good Chinese leader could not say no to a subordinate who came to seek help.

On the whole, the majority of teachers and students showed the workers and farmers who worked in their schools a lot of respect. Zhou Songbo, the uneducated old worker, had become so popular among the teachers that when he left the school after four years, teachers wanted him back. In the end he came back, and he stayed in Jimo Number One Middle School for seven years altogether.[71]

Some teachers, on the other hand, found it offensive when workers and farmers were allowed to participate in the discussion of educational reforms. They enjoyed exposing workers' ignorance and showing off their profound knowledge of Marxism and Leninism. Mr. Wang Yukwei from Jimo Number One Middle School, who specialized in Marxist political economy, liked to challenge workers on theoretical issues and made fun of their ignorance whenever it was convenient for him to do so.[72] Many Chinese educated elite believed that they had superior education. Everybody else should learn from them, but they did not need to learn from others. This attitude and behavior is a legacy of traditional Chinese Culture, where book learning was raised above every other activities, and other practical engagements—farming, craftsmanship, and commerce (*wan ban fie xia ping, wei you du shu gao*) were looked down upon. This traditional elitist bias is, no doubt, partly responsible for China's lagging behind the West in science and technology.[73] It is also the reason Mao Zedong stressed the need to reform the educated elite in the process of China's modernization.[74] China's educated elite needed reforming, which meant learning new things, just as Communist Cadres needed reforming.

COMBINING EDUCATION WITH PRODUCTIVE LABOR

The construction of village primary schools, joint village middle schools and commune high schools was only part of the educational reform that the 1968 Jimo Preliminary Education Reform Program envisioned. It also called upon teachers and students to reform old curriculum and teaching methods. The old curriculum was denounced for its divorce from real life. The old teacher-centered teaching approaches were also criticized.[75]

Textbooks in China had been compiled by a few experts in Beijing and other big cities. These experts did not understand, and did not bother to focus on, what rural children needed, or on the prerequisites of rural development. Rural teachers and students denounced the old educational practices during the Cultural Revolution partly because the old curricula and textbooks were divorced from the real lives of rural children and put rural children at a great disadvantage. Much of the abstract materials covered by mathematics, physics and chemistry textbook had little relevance for daily life, while concepts and formulae that were useful in rural life were not taught.[76] To change this, students and teachers in Jimo Number One Middle School decided to develop new curricula and a new set of textbooks themselves with the encouragement of the workers' team stationed in the school. Textbook compilation teams were composed of teachers, students, workers, and farmers. Chemistry, physics, and biology were incorporated into two major courses called "Basic Industrial Knowledge" and "Basic Agricultural Knowledge." Mathematics began to cover practical knowledge like bookkeeping, accounting, and budgeting.[77]

What constitutes a good education? The reformers of the Cultural Revolution wanted students to have a more rounded education. Students were intended to take academic study as their main task, but they were also to learn some industrial and farming skills, and, most importantly they were to learn to develop a critical mind.[78] There was a tendency during the Cultural Revolution to elevate physical labor above academic learning, and as a result many students were assigned too much physical labor. The mix of academic work and physical labor, however, varied greatly from place to place and from time to time.

In Jimo Teacher's Training School, students rotated working in the school's plastic workshop and vegetable garden one shift of three hours a week. Students and teachers from Jimo Number One Middle School spent three months in 1968 in different factories. With the help of workers and engineers, they compiled textbooks on the operating principles of internal combustion engines and electrical motors, on how to draw and read blueprints, and on other industrial skills and knowledge. In the process of compiling the textbooks, students learned how to draw blueprints and how to operate different machines.[79] The middle school students and teachers also spent two months working in villages in Northern Jimo that year. They compiled textbooks on crops, fertilizers, and farming machines and also spent time working with farmers.[80] But this practice of spending extended periods of time in factories and on farms did not continue. Later students spent one afternoon a week working in the school's vegetable gardens or workshops. Occasionally, they would spend an extra afternoon to help villagers in the fields when they were called upon to do so.

In South River joint Middle School, students engaged in two kinds of manual labor. They cut hay in spring, gleaned wheat in summer, and gleaned sweet potatoes in the fall for the school. And in winter, they smashed stones into gravel. The goals of these activities were to increase the school's annual income and to develop a love for physical labor in the students. In these productive activities, students were also able to apply academic learning to solve problems encountered while working and to learn new ways of interacting with each other and with teachers.

In 1973 and 1974, *kaimen banxue* (running an open door school) was encouraged. In addition to one afternoon a week of routine physical labor, students could also go to a hospital or factory for four weeks to learn a skill largely of their own choice. Some learned how to administer first aid and to give injections. Others learned how to repair machines or radios. The average time spent on non-academic engagement was about four hours a week for the high school classes of 1971 and 1972. For high school classes in 1973, 1974 and 1975, it was about 7 hours a week, one-sixth of the total school time.[81]

Over time, schools established ongoing relationships with particular factories and villages. Jimo Number One Middle School had a relationship with Jimo Number One Farm Machine Factory, the largest factory in Jimo County, and also with the Wine Factory.[82] South River joint Middle School built connections with a small collectively-owned transport machinery factory and with an army unit. Students went to the factory to learn about blueprints and how to operate machine tools. They also invited workers and farmers to give lectures in the classroom. When they were studying bookkeeping and accounting as part of math training, they invited village accountants to give lectures.[83] According to Zhang Suocheng, the skills he learned during the educational reforms were readily applicable when he started working in his village industrial enterprise in 1974 after he returned after graduation.[84]

Apart from going out to factories and farms and inviting workers and farmers to give lectures, schools also founded their own workshops and farms both for conducting experiments and to generate income. By the end of 1970, most schools in Jimo County had built one or more workshops and farms.[85] Jimo Number One Middle School had one factory, two workshops, and two small farms. South River joint Middle School set up a workshop casting iron parts, a workshop that produced organic fertilizer, and a small farm composed of two small pieces of land opened up by students and teachers. Here they experimented with different seeds and farming methods.[86] Students would take turns to work in the school workshops and on the school farm, about one afternoon a week.[87]

These industrial and agricultural projects were made possible with help from factory workers and villagers. Factories and villages provided schools with logistical support. The Number One Farm Machine Factory in Jimo County, for example, provided the equipment needed by Jimo Number One Middle School for its first workshop, and also lent the technical support for the operation of the workshop in the beginning.[88] The army provided students with military training.[89] South River Joint Middle School got financial and material support from production brigades in all seven villages. Guojia Xiang Village helped the school set up the first workshop casting iron parts, and helped train students to use the equipment. South River village purchased and transported coal for the school every year.[90]

ASSESSING CULTURAL REVOLUTION CURRICULUM REFORMS

Critics of the Cultural Revolution educational reforms have said that physics courses from the period, for example, were reduced to the study of "three machines and one pump"—generators, diesel engines, electric motors and water pumps.[91] The educational reforms is seen as static. In fact, the curriculum during the Cultural Revolution education was dynamic, and went through a process of evolution. During the initial stage of the educational reforms from 1968 to 1970, practical knowledge about machines and pumps was stressed at the expense of more abstract theories. These textbooks were called *shiying kebei* (trial textbooks), indicating their experimental nature. But by 1971, these textbooks reached a more mature stage, and their contents were more balanced than the previous ones. The physics textbooks used in Jimo and other counties of Shandong Province, for example, embraced many theoretical elements such as magnetic fields, static electricity, and thermodynamics, as well as the application of these theories to the real world. These later textbooks were no longer called *shiying kebei.*[92]

Influenced by current Chinese Government's assessment, and the criticism of Cultural Revolution by the educated elite, some farmers in Jimo feel today that their children were shortchanged by the rural educational reforms of the Cultural Revolution. They say their children did not learn as much as graduates of the old school system; their children's handwriting was not as good; or they did not memorize as many Chinese characters and as much historical data. Song Yongfa, former Deputy Party Secretary in South River Village commented that though he had only four years of primary education before Liberation, his handwriting was better than most of the graduates of South River joint Village Middle School.[93] Liu Shizheng, former accountant of the Eighth Production Team of South River Village, remarked that of the ten graduates from the commune high school in his team, none had very good handwriting.[94] Hu

Dawei, who was one of the fifty students among 50,000 former and current high graduates who passed the standard college entrance examination in 1977, was ridiculed at the railway station for his poor handwriting. A train station clerk, looking at his handwriting, commented with contempt: how did you manage to succeed in the college entrance examination with such lousy handwriting?[95] To use handwriting as a measure of talent and schooling was natural and proper in the old China because that was how children were trained. That was what counted then, and many people used their handwriting talent to decorate themselves. But handwriting as a measure of quality for modern schooling is ridiculous.

There are many people who see the Cultural Revolution rural educational reforms differently. Yu Bo is such a person. He pointed out the tangible achievements of rural educational reforms in rural Sanhe County. In rural Sanhe, during the period of educational reforms, 1,500 high school graduates learned how to repair diesel engines, electric motors, water pumps, radios and amplifiers. Over 1,800 graduates mastered the skills of cultivating new crop seeds and other agricultural techniques. Another 4,000 were trained to treat common animal diseases while completing the required curriculum of the time. These high school graduates became the mainstay of rural Sanhe's technicians and continue to play crucial roles in contemporary rural development.[96]

Apart from these achievements, Yu Bo also points out that from 1970 to 1981 school-operated factories and farms in rural Sanhe generated a total of 13 million yuan. The money not only contributed to the improvement of school facilities, it also paid tuition for all students in all 405 middle and primary schools in the county. Approximately 196 schools paid for textbooks, and 96 schools provided students with paper and pens. Children who had been kept out of school because of financial difficulties were all able to enroll, and the enrollment rate in rural Sanhe remained at above 97 percent, with more than eighty percent children finishing middle school.[97] In Jimo, as well, schools used the money generated from the school factories to improve their facilities. Among other things, Jimo Number One Middle School bought its first tractor with the money the school factory had earned.[98]

Huang Bingde, a former teacher of South River joint Village Middle School, said that the Cultural Revolution educational reform opened school doors wide to rural children who had always been disadvantaged in education. He cited three major achievements of the educational reforms in Jimo. First, rural schools built during the educational reforms trained large numbers of local youth in practical industrial and agricultural skills and knowledge, which has long-term impacts on the development of rural areas. Economic development in Jimo relied on this practical knowledge. Second, the educational reform began to alter the views of teachers who had previously looked down upon farmers. When they were obliged to participate in some forms of manual labor, they learned to respect villagers and other working people. Third, it empowered villagers. Farmers no longer viewed the educated elite with mystic feelings because they knew the educated teachers better after working with them. According to Huang, despite their limitations, the educational reforms during the Cultural Revolution served the historical needs of the rural areas extremely well.[99]

Many people expressed concerns that too much participation in manual labor and obsession with practical knowledge led to a general decline in China's level of science and research during the Cultural Revolution decade. This is a very legitimate concern, and there is always the danger of overreacting to, or overcorrecting, a previous problem. Chinese call this *jiao wang guo zheng* (go too far in correcting past wrongs). It is hard to definitely establish a line between what is the right amount and what is too much as far as practical knowledge and participation in production is concerned. Needless to say, too much or too little is always a relative issue, depending on one's perspective.

Is the fact that a much larger percentage of the population acquired a middle and high school education, and more importantly acquired important technical know-how, an indication of the advancement of a nation's science and technology? Does the fact that more villagers began to apply scientific knowledge in farming and more rural people used machines in farming and produced machines in their village factories advance the level of a nation's science and technology? Or should we only acknowledge important breakthroughs in sophisticated research as indicators of advances in education, science and technology?

It is not that China did not have its own share of scientific breakthroughs during the Cultural Revolution years, like the explosion of thermo-nuclear bombs and the launching of satellites. These are important indicators of a nation's technical level, but their relationship to the people's livelihood often is not as close as small technical innovations in farming tools and better crop seeds. The educational reform during the Cultural Revolution, and its impact on the empowerment of the rural people, promoted exactly these kinds of small technical innovations.

CHANGING THE RELATIONSHIP BETWEEN TEACHERS AND STUDENTS

One of the important changes the Cultural Revolution brought about in schools was in the different relationship between teachers and students. The Cultural Revolution destroyed the supreme authority teachers had over students, and this helped empower students. Students, even pupils in primary school, began to adopt a critical attitude towards their teachers and scrutinized teachers' behavior. Students, children in primary school, wrote big character posters to air their grievances against their teachers at the beginning of the Cultural Revolution. In Double Temple Primary School, students from the third and fourth grades classes wrote big character posters denouncing their teachers. One student in a big character poster accused his teacher of confiscating his playing cards and an antique knife and gave them to her own son.[100] Another student denounced the teacher for striking him with a stick simply because he talked with his classmate.[101] The school walls were covered with big character posters criticizing teachers. If anything, these big character posters set a new tone in the classroom, and many teachers took criticism from the students very seriously. Some teachers indicated to me during interviews that they learned to respect their students' opinions more during the Cultural Revolution and never struck them afterwards.[102] Ms. Sun Zhixian, the skillful chalk thrower, said that after reading the big character posters, she gave up the habit of hurling chalk at students' faces. Once in a while she would invite some students to her house to cook together, and get to know students more.[103]

In fact, not all teachers were happy with the way schools conducted business before the Cultural Revolution. For one thing, frequent testing and sharp competition between schools and classes created tremendous pressure on teachers. But the political climate of the pre-Cultural Revolution years did not allow them any control over the situation and they had no choice but to follow the tide of the time, even though some of them were aware of the absurdity of the level of academic pressure in schools.[104] During the Cultural Revolution many teachers, particularly young teachers, revolted against the school authorities as well and demanded the reform of school administration. Among the rebel Red Guards who first rose to criticize the school authorities in Jimo were many teachers.[105] In the several dozen volumes of debates about education reforms published by different provinces during the Cultural Revolution, the most vocal condemnation of the old teaching methods came from teachers, and the most vehement proposals for changes were also made by teachers.[106]

Many teachers began to encourage students to ask questions in the classroom, and to engage in discussions among themselves and with teachers. Some teachers made extra efforts to involve students in preparing new lessons. Students and teachers also chose a class representative for each major subject who was entrusted with the task of getting feedback from the students to the teachers.[107]

According to Chu Jiying, a retired village middle school teacher, some teachers and students prepared lessons together, and she actually experimented with her class by allowing students to take turns teaching some classes.[108]

The relaxation of teachers' authority in the classroom gave rise to a bigger student role in class. Students discussed, debated, and sometime challenged teachers. There were cases when students abused their newly gained freedom in the classroom. Wang Xinfa, who had been a naughty boy, now became a big distraction in the classroom. He would intentionally get into an argument with his teacher. Knowing there was not much his teachers could do to him, he would insist that the teacher was wrong and he was right in any argument.[109] Song Yanchang, another naughty boy, played finger guessing games with his classmates when he was bored in the class.[110]

The deterioration of order and discipline in the classroom appalled some teachers and parents. Relaxation of the strict regimentation of the pre-Cultural Revolution classroom meant that students no longer had to sit with their hands behind their backs. But the majority of students wanted to study and did not want to promote disorderly conduct. Faced with disruptive students, teachers were not completely helpless. They could inform the parents of the students' behavior in school. Song Yanchang's teachers did this. Yangchan's parents took the problem very seriously, and disciplined him in their own way. Afterwards, he behaved himself in class. The teachers could also mobilize the students to bring peer pressure on the disruptive students. Wang Xinfa's teachers did this. After Wang Xinfa disrupted class twice, Sun Zhenxian and Chu Jiying, the two teachers in charge of the class, discussed the matter with his fellow students, and the whole class decided to have an open debate with Wang Xinfa. During debate, the majority of students expressed their disapproval of Wang Xinfa's disruptive behavior. In the end, they passed a resolution that Wang Xinfa had to write a report of repentance before he was allowed to continue his schooling. Wang Xinfa was isolated, and he angrily left the classroom. The teachers and student representatives informed Wang's parents of what was going on in school. Wang Xinfa stayed out for a week. But in the end, he turned in his report of repentance and was allowed to resume class. He learned his lesson.[111] Some teachers were more experienced and more resourceful in dealing with problematic students than others. Some teachers actively dealt with the deterioration of classroom order, while others became very cynical about it and turned a blind eye.[112]

It was not easy for Confucian-minded, teachers and parents to accept some equality in the classroom. Understandably, they were critical of the lack of discipline during the Cultural Revolution, and they changed back to supporting a more regimented classroom when the Cultural Revolution was denounced in China. This shows that it is not easy for a new democratic culture to take root. Some people say that it takes three generations to bring up a noble man. The cultivation of democratic culture and values will definitely take time.

The issue here is how to balance the gains and losses by a more enlivened classroom environment. First of all, the freedom students enjoyed in the classroom certainly made the teachers' job in the classroom more difficult and more challenging. They could not suppress student questions and demands by simply relying on teachers' authority. They had to make their lessons more interesting. Otherwise, students would not listen to them, and would begin to cause them trouble. Jiang Nihu, a high school math teacher, was considered to be a boring teacher. Zhang Xiuyi, a student, was bored and began to cause trouble. The teacher tried to control Zhang Xiuyi by telling him he was *zhen bo yao lianpi* (you are shameless). Zhang Xiuyi, mimicking his teacher's voice, said the same thing, causing the whole class to laugh. In the end, Jiang was forced to talk with Zhang Xiuyi privately and also worked to improve his teaching method in the classroom.[113]

Liu Yuande was a high school physics teacher, who also served as a homeroom teacher. He wanted his class to outperform other classes, partly because of his own ambition. But the students in his class did not cooperate with him. They were doing moderately well but not great. In his disappointment, he denounced the class as *kuxiao yi ge muyang* (cries and laughs with the same expression). He labeled the whole class as mediocre. His unreasonable criticism of the class in this blanket manner angered the whole class. They decided to boycott his effort to collect the 1.2 yuan school fee at the beginning of the next semester. He was not able to collect it after several attempts. When he realized the class's intention was to embarrass him, he was forced to ask the school to transfer him to another class. When a different teacher was appointed to the class, everybody paid the school fee promptly. According to students in the class, not only did Liu not respect his students' feelings, but he was not very good at teaching his subject matter, and he needed to be taught a lesson.[114]

Did deterioration of discipline hinder students' learning and growth? Four notorious trouble makers in South River joint Middle School during the Cultural Revolution decade all are in their late thirties and early forties now. Wang Xinfa is a very successful businessman, the owner of a trucking company. Zhang Xiuyi runs a very successful clothing business. Zhou Jiashan is an engineer of his village construction company. Song Yanchang owns a very successful restaurant, and manages it with creativity.[115] During my trip to Jimo in the summer of 1997, I met Wang Xinfa when he was engaged in an interesting conversation with a group of neighbors. He was loudly denouncing the corruption and stupidity of the local government in public. From the way he was talking, I could clearly see the imprint the Cultural Revolution left on him.

EDUCATED YOUTH IN THE COUNTRYSIDE

Instead of educating the rural population, the pre-Cultural Revolution educational system was depleting the countryside of talent. The few rural students who were able to attend high school went on to college or got a job in the city. Few ever returned to the villages. Villagers' lack of education, as I have pointed out, contributed to wide-spread corruption and abuse among rural officials and led to slow economic development in rural areas for lack of educated personnel to absorb new skills and knowledge. A fundamental aim of the Cultural Revolution was to bring knowledge and skills to the countryside. This was accomplished by rapidly expanding the rural school system, orienting it towards rural needs and breaking the direct progression between high school and college. Rural high school graduates were expected to return to their villages and millions of urban high school graduates came to the countryside.

In June 1966, institutions of higher education suspended the scheduled national entrance examinations.[116] From the perspectives of the individuals whose dreams of going to college were shattered, this reform of the college entrance examination system was deeply disappointing. But from the perspective of rural development, this reform measure, not unlike a blood transfusion for a sick patient, brought knowledge and skills that revived rural areas. Going to college immediately after graduation was no longer an option for high school students. Every student had to work in rural areas or in a factory for at least two years before becoming eligible for college. Academic performance was not a sole criterion in the selection of candidates for college. Students had also to prove themselves as good farmers or workers before going to college. Starting in 1976, college students from rural areas were required to go back to their original villages after graduation to serve the villagers who sent them to college.[117]

The *shangshan xiaxiang* (going up the mountains and down to villages) movement was intensified following the suspension of college entrance examinations. Students of the graduating class of Jimo Number One Middle School returned to their home villages. In

Jimo, high school graduates with urban *hukou* (household registration) went to settle down in Wagezhuang and Duan Polan communes, in North and Northwestern Jimo. Most stayed there for two years, and a few only one year, before they got jobs in town. The government built some collective residences for them, and provided food supplies for them for the first year. Parents of these urban youth were eager to secure preferential treatment for their children. They used their influence to help the local people in the villages where their children lived. Some helped local people get more fertilizer and farming machines. Others helped the villages set up rural industrial enterprises and provided them with contracts. The local people in return treated the urban youth very well. They inducted them into the Communist Party, provided them with good recommendations when opportunities came for them to join the army, or helped them gain admission to college.[118] A two-way transaction took place between urban and rural areas. The educated urban youth served as a bridge between the two. My interviews with both former urban youth and local people gave me the impression that the local people welcomed the educated urban youth. They regarded them as Chairman Mao's guests. And the young people generally appreciated what the local people had done for them.

In addition to native youth, from January to July 1968 alone, 883 educated youth from Qingdao City came to live and work in rural Jimo.[119] The influx of educated youth, of both rural and urban origin, into rural areas changed the educational structure and talent base of the rural population. In Jimo County between 1966 and 1976, 65,597 junior high school graduates and 19,130 senior high school graduates, an average of 85 per village returned to their villages in Jimo County.[120] These students, became the new teachers, medical personnel, and skilled workers and technicians on which rural development depended. The reform of the college entrance system and the movement of encouraging educated urban youth to go to the rural areas broke the vicious circle in Chinese education.[121]

The rapid expansion of schools in rural Jimo during the Cultural Revolution was typical of rural China as whole. For the first time in history all children in rural China had the opportunity to go to primary school and the great majority of children had the opportunity to go to middle school and high school. For the perspective of the village, the Cultural Revolution decade, far from being a disaster for education, as it is routinely presented by Chinese education officials today, was a period of unprecedented development. Formally, Chinese Communist Party was beginning to seriously fulfill the promise it had made to the rural people to bring universal education to the village. This would have a profound effect on rural economic development.

Notes

1. Wang Nianyi, *Da Dongran de Niandai, (The Years of Great Chaos)*, 354. See also Suzanne Pepper, "Education and Revolution: The 'Chinese Model' Revisited," *Asian Survey*, Number 9, 1978, 847.
2. CCP Central Committee, *"Zhongguo Gongchandang Zhengyang Weiyuanbui Guanyu Wuchan jieji Wenhua Da Geming de Jueding,"* (CCP Central Committee' Decision on the Cultural Revolution), May 16, 1966.
3. The first thing the red guards did in their school was to question the educational line of the party authorities. Interview with Lan Chengwu, summer, 1997.
4. Interview with former Jimo rebel leaders, 1995
5. Interview with former Jimo rebel leaders, 1995.
6. Interview with former Jimo rebel leaders, 1997.
7. Julie Kwong, *Cultural Revolution in Chinese Schools May 1966-April 1969*, 17
8. Interview with Jing Aiai, the monitor of the Graduating Class of Beijing Number One Girls High School, who, together with her classmates, wrote to the CCP Central Committee demanding an overhaul of the Nation's college entrance examination system, 1993.
9. Interview with former rebel leaders, summer, 1997.
10. The press, and other public media were talking about the eliminating the three gaps for a number of years prior to the Cultural Revolution. There were popular songs about eliminating the three gaps, see also Kwong, *The Cultural Revolution in Chinese Schools*, 17.
11. Interview with former rebel leaders, summer, 1997. The Students from Beijing Number One Girl Middle School who wrote to the *People's Daily* on June 6, 1966, expressed the same ideas. See also Kwong, *The Cultural Revolution in Chinese Schools*, 17.
12. Correspondence with former rebel leaders, 1996, 1997.
13. Jimo Number One Middle School was located outside the town where the county seat was located too. Compared with other cities, the town is a rural town, because the overwhelming majority of its residents were rural, but compared with other rural areas in the county, it was urban, because it was the commercial center of the whole county.
14. Correspondences with Rebel Leaders, 1994, 1996.
15. The Army was called upon to support the revolutionary leftists by the center. But since there was no concrete criterion for the revolutionary leftist, it was really up to the soldiers in the fields to decide who they wanted to support.
16. Correspondences with rebel leaders, 1995.
17. Interview with former rebel leaders in Jimo, summer, 1997.
18. Mao Zedong's May Seventh letter to Lin Biao, which was called May Seventh Directive, was published on May 15, 1966. See Wang

Nianyi, *Da Dongran de Niandai*, 4.

19. *Jimo xianzhi, Chronolgy of Events in Jimo County*,74
20. Interview with former rebel leaders,1997
21. *Jimo xianzhi* 47, Interview with former rebel leaders,1997
22. Interview with villagers, 1997.
23. Interview with villagers, 1995.
24 Interview with villagers, 1997.
25. Interview with villagers, 1995.
26. Interview with former members of farmer representatives, 1995.
27. Interview with Ms Xue Xiulan, the head of village primary school in South River Village, 1995.
28. Gao Yubao's book, *Wo you shang xue (I want to go to school)* was very famous in China and his writing was used as text book for primary school children throughout China.
29. Interview with former village school students, summer, 1997.
30. Interview with villagers, summer, 1997.
31. Interview with villagers, 1995.
32. Interview with villagers, 1995.
33. *Jimo Xianzhi, Education,* 27:16.
34. Interview with villagers, summer, 1997.
35. *Jimo xianzhi, Education,* 20.23.
36. Interview with villagers, 1997.
37. Interview with villagers, 1997.
38. In October 1968, Jiaxiang County Teacher Hou Zhenmin and Wang Qingyu proposed that government teachers return to their hometown to teach and be paid in work points like village school teachers. Their proposal was debated in the press and finally was adopted in some places. This proposal was very controversial among government teachers because it meant that they would lose the salary and benefit as government employees. See *People's Daily,* Nov. 14, 1968.
39. Interview with villagers, 1995.
40. Interview with villagers, 1995.
41. *Jimo Xianzhi, Education,* 20:24.
42. *Jimo Xianzhi, Education,* 20:22.
43. *Jimo Xianzhi, Education,* 20:22.
44. There were no personal income tax and property tax in the Chinese system at the time. But because the public servants, like teachers were paid by the work points, the value of the work points actually reduced as a result of that. But unlike taxing, people did not feel that way.
45. Interview with villagers, 1995.
46. Interview with former members of the worker team, summer, 1997.
47 Interview with former worker team members, 1995.
48. Interview with former schoolteachers, 1995.
49. Unlike the western tradition, the Chinese refers to everyone who has a relatively good formal education as an intellectual. I think it makes more sense to distinguish intellectuals from other trained

professions. An intellectual who is someone working to seek answers to fundamental social issues is different from those who are trained to do some special tasks. I want to stress this difference by using the "educated class" here.

50. Interview with farmers and workers who participated in the educational reform, 1995.

51. There was nothing grammatically or politically wrong to say "learn from Chairman Mao," but the teachers and students never heard anybody say it, and as a result sounded strange and funny to them.

52. The teachers and students thought it was vulgar to talk about dysentery in school.

53. Interview with former village school students, 1997.

54. Correspondences with former schoolteachers, 1997.

55. In the rural primary schools, there were no revolutionary committees.

56. Interview with former students and worker team members in Jimo, summer,1997.

57. Interview with former members of workers' team, summer, 1997.

58. Conversation with a college professor about educational reform during the Cultural Revolution, summer, 1995.

59. Interview with former members of the workers' team in Jimo Number One Middle School, summer, 1995.

60. Interview with former students, summer, 1997.

61. Interview with former members of workers team, summer, 1997.

62. Interview with farmer representatives in school, summer, 1997.

63. Interview with former school teachers in Jimo, summer, 1997.

64. Interview with members of former worker's team and former students, 1995.

65. Interview with villagers, summer, 1993.

66. Interview with members of former workers' team, 1996.

67. Interview with former members of the workers' team, 1995.

68. Interview with former members of workers' team, 1995.

69. Interview with former worker team members, 1997.

70. Interview with former members of workers' team, summer, 1997.

71. Interview with members of former workers' team, summer, 1997.

72. Interview with former middle school teachers, Summer, 1997.

73. Numerous theories have been raised by both Chinese and Foreign scholars to explain why Chinese science and technology fell behind since the 15th century. One of the theories suggests that a significant segment of Chinese intellectuals had strong bias against practical knowledge, an attitude which had been developed partly as a result of the imperial examination system. People do what they get the most reward. If reciting the classics would get what they wanted in life, that is what they would perfect and respect. This hurt Chinese development of science and technology.

74. Wang Nianyi described Mao's call for reforming intellectuals as an indication of his bias against intellectuals and as an example of his leftist mistakes of the Cultural Revolution.

75. Red Guard Jimo County Headquarters, "Preliminary Educational Reform Program," 6.
76. Zheng Gong, Xiang Nong and Zhou Bing, "The Curriculum Should Be Concise and Related to Real Life," *Selected Articles in the Debate of Educational Revolution,* Ed. by Henan Provincial Revolutionary Committee, Educational Bureau, Vol. 10, May, 1970. 2.
77. Interview with former students, summer, 1997.
78. Interview with former students, summer, 1997.
79. Interview with former students from Number One Middle School, who together with two teachers and one member of Workers' Mao Zedong Thought Propaganda Team stationed in the school participated in compiling the textbook for combustion engines. They stayed in the Number One Farming Machines Factory, the Electric Company, and Farming Implements Factory for a total of three months during the process of writing the textbook for Basic Industrial Knowledge.
80. Interview with former students of Jimo Agricultural Middle School in Jimo, summer, 1995.
81. Interview with former high school students in Jimo, summer, 1997.
82. Interview with former students, 1995.
83. Interview with former teachers, summer, 1995.
83*. Interview with villagers, summer, 1997.
84. *Jimo Xianzhi, The Chronology of Events,* 78.
85. Interview with former school teachers at South River joint Middle School, who was in Charge of building the school's workshop casting iron parts at the time, 1995.
86. Interview with former school teachers and students, 1997.
87. Correspondence with members of former workers' Mao Zedong Thought Propaganda Team in Jimo Number One Middle School.
88. Interview with Liu Changzheng, a retired soldier who led a group of soldiers to help the educational reform in the school, 1995.
89. Interview with former farmer representatives, 1995.
90. Canton dispatch, *Wen Huipao,* Hong Kong, November 23, 1977; staff correspondent, *Ta Kung Pao,* Hong Kong, November 24, 1997, cited by Suzanne Pepper, "Education and Revolution: The Chinese Model Revisited," *Asian Survey,* Number 9,1978,875.
91. Interview with former teachers, 1996.
92. Song Yingfa served as deputy party secretary from 1969 to 1974. He is in his mid-sixties and is semi-retired.
93. Liu Shizheng was best educated in his team. He graduated from high school before the Cultural Revolution, and went to a teachers' training college. He taught a few years. But in 1960 during the period of severe food shortage in Jimo County following the Great Leap Forward he left his teaching post outside Jimo and came back to his home village to take care of his parents and wife.
94. Hu Dawei, a music teacher in a high school now, is one of the most talented among his peers. He was among the first 54 college students in 1977 chosen from over 50,000 candidates who took the

national entrance examinations on six subjects in Jimo County. Because it was the first such examination held since the beginning of the Cultural Revolution in 1966, every middle and high school graduates from the previous 12 years were qualified to sit in the examination after paying a fee of ten yuan. The candidates aged from 35 years old who graduated from high school in 1966, to 17 years who were still in high school in 1977. As the space in college was limited, it was the most spectacular competition of its kind in Chinese history.

95. Yu Bo, "Brief Discussion about Participation in Labor," jiao Yu Yanjiu, (Educational *Research), Number 9. 1982. 26.

96. Ibid., 28.

97. Interview with former teachers, 1995.

98. Interview with Huang Bingde. Huang graduated from a teacher's training school in Leiyang County in 1968 during the Cultural Revolution. He would have been assigned to teach in a key school in urban areas without educational reforms of the Cultural Revolution. The educational reform brought him home to his home village. He taught in South River joint Village Middle School until 1979 when he got a government position. Now he heads the municipal department that manages the affairs of retired officials in Jimo County.

99. Interview with former students of Double Temple Primary School, 1995.

100. Interview with former students of Double Temple Primary School, 1996.

101. Interview with former teachers of South River Primary School, summer, 1997.

102. Interview with former teachers and students, summer, 1997.

103. Interview with former school teachers in Double Temple Primary School, 1995.

104. Interview with Lan Chengwu, 1995. He said when he and his classmates organized the red guard group in the school to criticize the school's education authorities, teachers participated in their discussion and help them prepare some of the big character posters.

105. Each Province published several dozens of volumes of selected articles in the Debate of Educational reforms. The articles were very short and informal, contributed mostly by primary school and middle school teachers, students, workers, farmers and soldiers, covering every aspect of education at every level.

106. Interview with former students, Summer, 1997.

107. Interview with former teachers, summer, 1997.

108. Interview with former teachers, summer, 1997.

109. Interview with former teachers, summer, 1997.

110. Interview with former teachers and students, summer, 1997.

111. Interview with former teachers and students, summer, 1997.

112. Interview with former teachers and students, summer, 1997.

113. Interview with former students, summer, 1997. The Chinese

character *xian* (fresh and delicious) is made up with two characters for fish and lamb. Song Yanchang got inspiration from analyzing these characters, and created a unique and delicious menu by cooking fish with lamb in an unusual combination, which attracted a large number of customers and made his restaurant a big success.

114. Interview with Song Yanchang, summer, 1997.
115. Editorial, *Renmin Ribao (People Daily)*, June 18, 1966.
116. Interview with villagers in Jimo, summer 1997.
117. Interview with former urban youth in Jimo, summer, 1997. This reform was reversed in 1978.
118. *Jimo xianzhi, chronology of Events in* Jimo, 79.
119. *Jimo Xianzhi*, 27:25.
120. Of course it was not the same everywhere. Many urban youth had bad experiences.

CHAPTER 6

Rural Economic Development During the Cultural Revolution

During the Cultural Revolution decade agricultural production more than doubled in Jimo County. At the same time, rural industry, which had been negligible before 1966, grew to become nearly 36% of the Jimo economy. This chapter will describe these remarkable advances in detail and analyze the changes that made them possible. I will argue that two key factors were products of the Cultural Revolution—a change in political culture, which empowered ordinary villagers and enhanced collective organization and rapid improvement in education, which provided literacy, numeracy and technical knowledge that made the adoption of modern technique possible.

INVOLVING VILLAGERS IN PRODUCTION DECISIONS

In Chapter four I wrote about the empowerment of rural people during the Cultural Revolution. The word empowerment sounds abstract. In practical terms, empowerment meant changes in the way things were done. Production team leaders, as I have noted, were now elected instead of being appointed from above. Another indication of empowerment can be seen from the way production was planned and the way plans were implemented. On March 11, 1967, the Jimo County Production Office called a mass meeting of leaders of various mass political associations that had emerged in the previous months. The meeting discussed production plans for the next year. After that it became a normal practice during the Cultural Revolution decade to hold a mass meeting in early spring to discuss the production goals and plans of the year.[1] The meeting was colloquially called *wan ren dahui* (ten-thousand person-meeting) or *siji ganbu dahui* (four-level-cadre meeting), because there were about ten thousand people involved, from county leaders to the most basic level of leadership—production team leaders. These meetings reflected the democratic orientation of the Cultural Revolution. The rebel leadership of the Cultural Revolution did not want to conduct its business in the old manner. Instead, they wanted the production team leaders to be part of the planning and to communicate with ordinary villagers about production goals and plans for the year.[2] This simple act turned villagers from passive followers into active participants. This annual event also provided a forum for villagers to share information and aspirations with each other. Lessons about better farming practices and methods were exchanged through these meetings.[3]

During the Cultural Revolution decade, rural collectives in Jimo once again took up the kind of large-scale economic projects that were attempted during the Great Leap Forward. This time, however, the decision-making; process was different. During the Great Leap Forward production decisions were typically handed down by higher level authorities.[4] Provincial leaders decided the production quotas and development projects for counties, and county leaders told the commune leaders what they were expected to do. The commune leaders then ordered village leaders to implement the plans. Village leaders for their part hustled ordinary villagers to do what they were told. At harvest time, government leaders decided how much they wanted to take from the village without consulting with ordinary villagers. During the Great Leap Forward, Jimo built three big reservoirs. But in the planning process, little input came from ordinary villagers.[5] Villagers were press-ganged to construct these projects, often without direct benefits in sight.

During the Cultural Revolution, local popular initiatives began to play a more important role than before. The production team and production brigades had much more control over their resources. For example, when South River village built a big irrigation project during the Cultural Revolution decade, it was built with input from ordinary villagers regarding the site and methods. It was a decision collectively made, and villagers could expect direct benefit from the project. In this regard, the Cultural Revolution was very different from the Great Leap Forward. The enthusiasm Jimo farmers demonstrated in their work had a lot do with this fundamental change of political culture.

In the new political culture of the Cultural Revolution decade political campaigns remained an important component. Because these campaigns were the products of a special political climate and tradition, they have to be understood in this context. In this context, these political campaigns could be very practical and produce enthusiasm for collective endeavors.

The campaign to criticize Lin Biao and Confucius carried out in 1973 and 1974 was a good illustration of this. What had Lin Biao or Confucius, to do with the common villagers? Why should common farmers be concerned with the power struggles among the top leaders or with what an ancient philosopher said more than two thousand years ago? For thousands of years, Chinese villagers lived very apolitical lives, seldom getting involving in politics. The fact that Mao and other Cultural Revolution leaders saw the need to involve common villagers, most of whom were illiterate and were considered ignorant by the educated elite, was in itself revolutionary and democratic. According to some villagers, rural people were thought by urban people to be *lao niai* (numb and senseless). They supposedly refused to be provoked even if they were kicked. But a central point of the campaign to criticize Lin Biao and Confucius was that rural people were not stupid. This was a completely different kind of politics that empowered farmers.

To many of the educated elite, the anti-Lin Biao and anti-Confucius campaign seemed vague and abstract. But it had specific meaning for ordinary people. The major theme of the campaign was to criticize the elitist mentality in Chinese culture. It denounced the Confucian philosophy of *shang zun xia yu er bu* yi (it is a general rule that the elite is respectable and that ordinary people are stupid). It promoted Mao's idea that the masses are the motive force of history and that the elite are sometimes stupid while the working people are intelligent.[6] These were not empty words. Villagers toiled all year round, supplying the elite with grain, meat and vegetables. But they were made to feel stupid in front of the elite. They did not know how to talk with the elite, and accepted the stigma of stupidity the elite gave to them.[7] In the eyes of the Chinese elite, farming was a lowly occupation. The campaign encouraged the rural people to straighten up their backs and helped them recognize their own worth.[8] In this sense the campaign served to help common Chinese villagers discover their dignity. Some Jimo villagers said that they began to look at their work in a different perspective. Farming was hard, but important. Other people had no right to look down on them, because they could not survive without their toil.[9]

COLLECTIVE WORK ETHIC

The Cultural Revolution consolidated the collective economy. The "socialist" line of development was promoted and contrasted with Liu Shaoqi and Deng Xiaoping's so-called "bourgeois" line of development. To be fair, the difference between the "socialist" line of development and the "bourgeois" line was never entirely clearly defined. But this ambiguity left room for local people to figure out for themselves what the difference meant. In rural Jimo, the "socialist" line of development was understood to mean cultivating and encouraging loyalty to the collective. This encouragement played a significant role for the development of the collective economy. Without this kind of encouragement, initiatives to develop agriculture infrastructure and mechanization as well as rural industry, all of which relied on collective organization, would have had a hard time getting off the ground.

Collective endeavors, such as soil improvement and irrigation projects, were taken up with new enthusiasm by Jimo villagers during the Cultural Revolution decade. It could be argued that the Cultural Revolution broadened the horizon of ordinary people. They seemed to live and work for something bigger than their day-to-day concerns. In 1972, Jimo County initiated a major irrigation project in the northern part of the county. Many rural adults went to work on it. Children at the village schools got up earlier than usual in the morning to fetch drinking water from the river for families whose members participated in the irrigation project.[10] They did not have to do it. But they did it because they wanted to contribute to "the cause of revolution."[11]

In 1968, the South River Production Brigade began a major irrigation project. During the day, a special group of people worked on the project. At night, villagers who worked on other projects during the day all came out to put in a couple hours of work. During the crucial stage of the project, schoolteachers, students, and local government employees all came to help. They worked from 7:00 p.m. to 10:00 p.m. each day for several days until the crucial stage was completed. While the villagers got paid in work points and would benefit directly from the irrigation project, government employees' and school teachers' neither got work points nor direct benefit. Nevertheless, they volunteered to work on the project at the night.[12] I interviewed a government worker, Chu Jiying, who participated in the project. She said that she, like others, volunteered to work at these projects at the time because it was an honorable thing to do.

There was a widespread pattern of doing volunteer work in China during the Cultural Revolution. Liu Guixing, Lan Shenli, and Zhang Suocheng, three village school students got up one hour earlier in winter to start a fire in their classroom for several years. Fu Zhenjian, Gong Zhaolin, Sun Shijun and their classmates spent one afternoon each week fetching drinking water and cleaning houses for soldiers' families in their neighborhood.[13] Liu Chengshui, Liu Jiamin, Wang Sijiang, young people of the Eighth Production Team of South River village, would transport organic fertilizers to the collective field at night.[14]

After the failure of the Great Leap Forward, many farmers in Jimo were so bitter about the food shortages that they declared they would not do any more work for the commune.[15] Why, then, were Jimo farmers willing to work hard for the collective during the Cultural Revolution? What was behind this change of attitude? Some workers and farmers testified that the practice of cadres' participation in production during the Cultural Revolution made an important difference. They said that when leaders worked hard, common villagers would work hard with them.[16]

In rural Jimo before the Cultural Revolution, village party leaders often had become a "race apart" since they did not work in the same harsh, skindarkening, outdoors environment as ordinary peasants.[17] This situation began to change in rural Jimo during the Cultural Revolution. The new leaders, who had emerged after discrediting the former village party leaders for corruption and failure to participate in farm work, learned a lesson from their predecessors. More importantly, village youth, politically emboldened through Cultural Revolution conflicts and educated in the new schools, were ready to challenge party leaders if they did not work with the ordinary people.

In South River Village, no one among the village leaders was exempted from manual work except Li Dezhi and Xue Zhifu, who were both over seventy years old and were assigned to take care of the village office, store room and financial accounts.[18] Villagers said that members of the Village Revolutionary Committee were all required to work in the fields with villagers to earn work points, except when they attended occasional meetings at the commune. Members of the Production Team Committee (*dui wei hui*) had to work harder than common villagers. Production team leaders got up earlier than everyone else in the team. They used the village loud speakers to wake up team members, tell them what tools to bring, and describe the task of the day. At the end of the day members of the production team committee were usually the last to go home, as they had to discuss what had to be done the next day.[19]

The reason why the leaders worked harder during the Cultural Revolution was simple. Common villagers would not tolerate lazy leaders. If leaders did not work, villagers refused to work as well, which would lead to a decline in production and living standards. If leaders did not work hard, villagers would elect someone else to replace them in the year-end election, someone who was ready to work hard.[20]

Village leaders were easily discredited during the Cultural Revolution if they could not or would not work hard. Zhang Xiuzheng from South River Village returned to the village in 1971 after serving in the army for four years. Like other PLA veterans, he was highly respected by the young people in the village at the time. When the village Communist Youth League was resurrected in 1971, he was elected its secretary. In the winter of that year, he was asked to lead a group of young people to work on an irrigation project in the northern part of the county. The work was very hard. People worked from early morning until midnight in a spirit of competition with other villages. They ate six instead of three meals a day because of the long working hours. The work involved pushing wheelbarrows filled with mud weighing one thousand pounds from a riverbed up over the riverbank. It took four people to work one wheelbarrow, one pushing from the back and three men pulling in the front with short ropes. As the road was very wet and soft, the wheel often sank deep in the mud. In order to move the barrow, the four men actually had to lift it. In such circumstances, the person who was pushing in the back bore half the total load while the three men in the front shared the other half. People took turns pushing the wheelbarrow at the back. PLA veteran Zhang, the leader of the group, had to do the same. But his army life had never put him to the test of such hard work. The moment the three people lifted the wheelbarrow in the front, he was weighed down by the load. He simply could not do it. He thus became the *naozheng* (the incompetent person) of the group, and soon his incompetence was talked about in the whole village. In the next election, Zhang lost. This was the way villages in Jimo operated during the Cultural Revolution. It was important that leaders could talk high sounding-words, but they had to live up to what they said at the same time. Otherwise nobody would listen to them.[21]

This politically-inspired work ethic also transcended the class labels that had defined villagers since the land reform in the early 1950s. Class labels, reflected the divisions of the land reform, and continued to reinforce those divisions. In Jimo, villagers of poor peasant background did not want their children to marry into families of former landlords and rich peasants if they could help it. Such a marriage could affect the chances of their children joining the PLA or the CCP. But apart from that, Jimo farmers cared very little about class labels. Wang Fangjun of the Eighth Production Team of South River Village was held in high respect despite the fact that he was the son of a rich peasant whose father fled to Taiwan with the Nationalist army in 1949. Far from being an untouchable, he actually married Zhao Limei, one of the most attractive women in the village. Zhao's younger brother and mother, who were very unhappy about the marriage, tried to stop it and expressed their anger and frustration at the wedding ceremony, but were not able to stop it. Wang served as one of the two village militiamen for a number of years. Because Wang was a good worker, his opinions were often respected in his team.[22]

Zhou Youliang, the son of another rich peasant from South River Village, served in the village militia during the Great Leap Forward years, and worked as a technician in the village factory during the Cultural Revolution, a highly desirable position. Guan Dunxiao, the son of the most prominent landlord in the village, returned to South River at the beginning of the Cultural Revolution upon graduation from high school. He was one of the first technicians in the village factory, and became deputy manager of the Village factory during the Cultural Revolution decade.[23]

On the other hand, if one could not work hard and became known as a *naozheng* of the team one would not be respected by other people, whatever class label one bore. Zhang Youshan was from a poor peasant family, but he was the laughingstock of his peers. He was not a good worker and he often made improper remarks. Guan Dunyou and Guan Dunchuan, sons of a landlord who worked on the same team as Zhang, often jeered at him like everybody else.[24] The CCPs policy then was: *you chenfen, dan bu wei chenfen* (class labels are important, but they are not the exclusive factor in judging a person). Of course, it was a big disadvantage to have negative class labels in China before and during the Cultural Revolution years. It was impossible for young people with negative class labels to join the army, and very difficult to join any political organizations at the time.

EDUCATION AND PRODUCTION

The educational reforms of the Cultural Revolution were also very important in making rapid economic development possible in rural Jimo. The educational reform contributed to economic advances in at least two ways. First, tens of thousands of local village youth received middle and high school education. Without the education reform, a much smaller number of rural youth would have been able to go to middle and high school, and those who managed to go to high school would most probably have left the rural areas. The reform of the college entrance examination brought home many local educated youth and other educated youth arrived from the cities. Without the large number of educated youth, large-scale scientific agricultural experiments and mechanization in rural areas would have been unimaginable.

Second, the education reforms led to the adoption of more practical curricula tailored to the local needs. School children learned agricultural, mechanical and industrial skills in school, which they could make good use of upon their return to their villages.[25] Village middle schools and commune high schools quickly trained thousands of rural youth with technical knowhow. Thousands of graduates learned how to repair diesel engines, electric motors, water pumps, radios and amplifiers. Thousands of others learned how to cultivate new seed crops and conduct agricultural experiments. Thousands more were trained to care for animals and treat animal diseases. The curriculum of the rural schools served the needs of rural Jimo at the time. There was a direct link between educational expansion and rural economic development during the Cultural Revolution. The large number of rural youth with the special training from joint village middle schools and commune high schools helped farmers improve the economic situation in the village. Unlike their illiterate predecessors, the newly educated young farmers had the conceptual tools to modernize production.

AGRICULTURAL EXPERIMENTATION

The changing political culture together with rural educational reforms broadened villagers' minds and horizons. They began testing new farming methods and new crop seeds. In 1966, 244 of 1,016 production brigades in Jimo set up experimental teams to cultivate new seeds, and test new farming methods. By 1972, the number of experimental teams had increased to 695, employing 4,043 people, and by 1974, the figure had increased to 851. At the same time, about 1,015 production teams had set up experimental groups.[26]

These teams and groups experimented with a variety of means to increase production. Traditionally, farmers in Jimo had used about 2-2.5 kilos of wheat seeds per mu. The experimental teams increased the quantity of seeds per mu until they found that the best amount was 4-5 kilos per mu for rich and irrigated land, 5-6 kilos per mu for average irrigated land and 7.5-8 kilos per mu for hilly and non-irrigated land.[27] Various methods in cultivating corn were also tried during these years. The teams experimented with the intervals between rows of corn, using alternating narrow and wide rows instead of equally spaced rows. They developed a method of cultivating corn plants in small paper containers on a small piece of land until the large fields were ready. Later they transplanted the corn plants with their paper containers, which held the plants and soil together, to large fields. The productivity of the land increased because this method of transplanting seedlings increased growing time for the corn by three weeks.[28] The experimental teams also increased the number of corn plants per mu from 2000 to 4000.[29] During the Cultural Revolution decade, these experimental teams in Jimo tested more than 1,000 different seeds, and carried out more than 10,000 controlled experiments. Through these experiments they selected about forty three varieties of wheat seeds, thirty nine varieties of corn seeds, fourteen kinds of sweet potato seeds, twenty varieties of peanut seeds, eleven kinds of sorghum seeds, eighteen varieties of bean seeds, seventeen kinds of millet seeds and eighteen kinds of rice seeds. These new seeds helped increase crop yields. Previously hemp did not bear seeds under natural conditions in northern China. In 1976, the experimental team of Qing Zhengbu Production Brigade in Jimo shortened the daylight hemp received by covering them up before sunset. Under this condition, hemp began to bear seeds for the first time in northern China.[30]

IRRIGATION AND LAND IMPROVEMENT PROJECTS

Since the 1950s, the CCP Jimo County government had intensified efforts to address the problems of flood and drought. It organized numerous massive irrigation projects, but farmers in rural Jimo remained at the mercy of natural forces. The three reservoirs built in 1959 during the Great Leap Forward did not solve the problem, because they were not equipped with the necessary facilities for irrigation and because they were far from adequate. A small number of traditional wells dug during the Great Leap Forward also were not much help in times of serious drought. These wells were shallow, and when the underground water level went down during a serious drought, these wells often became dry.

Thus, whenever there was a serious drought or flood, villagers were helpless, and food shortages loomed. However, this situation began to change during the Cultural Revolution. Jimo villagers led by the new leadership of village, commune and county revolutionary committees began to grapple with their shared environmental dilemmas. They began to challenge nature. From 1966 to 1976, farmers using shovels, baskets, carts, and later tractors, built more reservoirs and other irrigation systems than those built during the years prior to and after the Cultural Revolution decade combined. All the eight medium-sized reservoirs in Jimo County in service in 1987 were built during the Cultural Revolution.[31] Of the 37 small reservoirs in service in 1987, 19 were built during the Cultural Revolution.[32] From April to the end of June 1970, alone, 1,636 large wells, ponds and dams had been completed, which increased the irrigated acreage by 400,000 mu, about one quarter of the total arable land in Jimo County.[33]

Large wells with electric pumps was critical to irrigation. The number of these wells was greatly expanded during the Cultural Revolution decade. Traditionally, wells for irrigation were small. A *lulu*, a manual device consisting of a pail, a rope and a round wooden device that rotated around a wooden axis, was the only means available to draw water up to the ground. Its capacity was very small. One day's hard work could only irrigate a third of a mu.[34] *Shui che,* a simple mechanical device introduced in the 1950s, was still slow and labor intensive. Four people pushed a horizontal pole in a clockwise direction to get water up to the ground through iron pumps. Its capacity was about one mu a day.[35] During the Great Leap Forward, farmers in rural Jimo began to use gas and diesel engines for the first time for irrigation. But very few wells were equipped with engines. There were only 33 by 1959.[36] The number of big wells with electrical motors and diesel engines began to expand rapidly during the Cultural Revolution decade.

South River dug its big well in 1969. Equipped with an electrical pump donated by a local factory, it irrigated about 450 mu of land, about one half of the total land in the village. The new village leadership, the Revolutionary Committee, led by Jiang Zhihe, organized an irrigation team, which worked exclusively on digging the well. Other villagers, who worked on other projects during the day, came to help at night. Government employees, store keepers, and teachers from the joint Village Middle School all came to help at night.[37] Chu Jiying, a woman teacher in her mid 40s, took her sixth grade class to work two hours a night for a number of days.

These teenagers and their teachers were not effective workers, but their presence helped with morale. When outsiders, especially government functionaries and teachers who were part of the educated strata elite and who had no direct material interest in the production of the village, came to help, an atmosphere conducive to achieving a common goal was created. People felt good about their work.[38] Many other villages, including Yaotou, Guojiaxiang, Hujiacun, Huayuan, dug wells during these first two years of the Cultural Revolution. In 1970 atone, 751 such huge wells were dug in Jimo County.[39]

The construction of wells and reservoirs made large-scale irrigation possible. But the fields had to be leveled before irrigation could be realized. The land-leveling projects required more strenuous efforts than the construction of wells and reservoirs. From 1966 to 1976, during winter and early spring, which traditionally are slow seasons in rural areas, thousands upon thousands of farmers were engaged in building irrigation channels and leveling fields so that water could flow smoothly through the fields. The slogan at the time was "There is no winter slack season in Shandong Province. We work just the same even when the earth is frozen to a depth of three feet." Another slogan said: "Jimo people will not take a holiday at the Spring Festival. After eating *jiaozi*, we will continue to work the next day."[40]

In the winter of 1971, in the northwest low land of Jimo County alone, 100,000 farmers were engaged in a basic land improvement project. In the course of the winter, they built 63 drainage channels, 645 irrigation channels, the total length of which amounted to 300 kilometers. They moved 1,310,000 cubic meters of earth and built 1,378 irrigation projects in the process. By removing the salty soil on the surface of the land and covering it with 300 wheel barrow loads per mu of good soil collected from else where, 57,000 mu of salty land was transformed into high quality land. The productivity of these lands improved by thirty per cent the following year.[41] Three hundred ninety thousand mu of land was transformed into terraced land. Farmers divided the salty land into large pieces and built a 30cm ridge around each piece. They filled each piece of land with water for some time. When they let the water go through the ditches dug in the fields, water carried the salt and alkali away. This process alone, which farmers called "land washing," increased the unit grain yield of salty land from fifty kilos to one hundred kilos per mu.[42] In 1975 alone, Jimo farmers spent about 190,000 working days on land improvement projects. They increased the depth of soil of the 75,000 mu of hilly land from 20cm to more than 40cm using soil collected from elsewhere, and covered it with 10,000 jin of organic fertilizer per mu, greatly improving the productivity of the land.[43]

MECHANIZATION

Farm machinery became available on a wide scale for the first time during the Cultural Revolution decade. The Central Government stressed the importance of agriculture, prompting factories to show their support for agriculture by producing farm machines. At the same time, as will be discussed below, many rural industrial enterprises were built during the Cultural Revolution decade. These small factories began to produce a large number of farm machines, which were adapted to local needs at relatively affordable prices. In 1975 alone, commune industrial enterprises in rural Jimo produced 1,108 farm machines. In 1976, 35 commune farm machine factories in rural Jimo produced 5,112 farm machines, including tractors, mills, grinders and planters.[44]

The machines introduced during the Cultural Revolution decade included tractors, planters, sprayers, harvesters and mills and tracks which greatly aided in planting, harvesting and other field work. Collectively owned tractors would transport organic fertilizers to the fields and crops to threshing grounds. Harvesting and plowing was done mostly by machines. Motorized and engine driven pumps, as we have seen, made large-scale irrigation possible by the end of the Cultural Revolution.

From Table 1 we can see that the use of machines only started during the Cultural Revolution. In 1965, the total mechanical power capacity in Jimo County was only 8,271. That translated into 8.1 horsepower per village. By 1970, the total power capacity in Jimo increased to 25,676 horsepower, which translated into 25.3 horsepower per village, more than three times of that in 1965. By 1975, the total power capacity reached 116,586 horsepower, which averaged among 1,016 villages in Jimo County was 114.75 horsepower per village, 14.2 times that in 1965. The rapid growth in the number of appliances like grinders and mills also played a significant role in improving rural living. Today, people take machine-processed food for granted. But in 1965, most people in rural Jimo still used stone mills and grinders to process their grain. Women and children spent a large proportion of their time doing this slow and tiring work. By 1976, electric mills and grinders completely replaced the stone mills and grinders. Women and children were liberated from this dreaded household chore.

Table 1: Use of farm machines in Jimo County						
Year	**unit**	**1958**	**1960**	**1965**	**1970**	**1975**
total power	HP	1120	6116	8272	25676	116586
big tractors	No.	1	54	76	76	1137
	HP	35	1848	3841	3841	25206
small tractors	No.				19	231
	HP				168	2503
trucks	No.			2	2	3
	HP			125	125	191
diesel engines	No.			131	1029	4571
	HP			1842	15294	68858
electric motors	No.			129	309	2116
	HP			1071	3831	18607
gas engines	No.			258	620	887
	HP			1072	2280	2913
sprayers	No.			7	50	924
grinders	No.			36	1051	1839
mills	No			175	761	1283

Source: *Jimo Local Records*, 5:27.

Villagers' lives became easier.[45]

At the beginning of the Cultural Revolution, South River Village had only a small gas engine connected to a small water pump. By 1975, it had two tractors of 20 horsepower each, two 100-horse-power trucks, ten electric motors which were used to drive lathes and planes in the village factory and grinders and mills to process food and animal feed. Several diesel and gas engines were used to drive water pumps. The village also owned a number of grinders, mills and other farm machines. Most farm work was mechanized by 1976.

The use of chemical fertilizers was greatly increased during the Cultural Revolution decade. In 1965, Jimo built its first Chemical Fertilizer Factory. It produced 117 ton synthetic ammonia in the first year. In 1966, its yield increased to 3,685 ton, and to 7000 ton, by 1973. By 1976, its yields increased to 15,000 ton.[46] In 1971, Jimo built its Phosphate Fertilizer Factory. By 1974, it produced and sold to farmers 2,576 ton phosphate fertilizer. In 1978, it produced and sold 15,543 ton.[47] The use of organic fertilizers was also greatly increased in Jimo during the Cultural Revolution decade. In 1971, the Experimental Team in Zhang Jia Yanxia Village produced and used an organic stimulator called "920" on its crops, and increased the crops yield by 12 percent.[48] In 1973, farmers in Ducun, Nancuan, Liu jiazhuang, Gaoyu and Huashan Communes made and tried a bacteria manure called "5406" in the wheat fields, and increased the yield by 20 percent on average. In the same year, farmers in Chengguan, Duncun, Liu jiazhuang, Nancuan and Fengcheng Communes tried a phosphate bacteria manure on their wheat fields, and increased their yields by 13 percent on average.[49]

DRAMATIC INCREASE IN AGRICULTURAL PRODUCTION

As result of hard work, scientific experimentation, land improvement, irrigation, mechanization, and increased use of both chemical and organic fertilizers, total grain output in rural Jimo more than doubled during the Cultural Revolution decade (see Table 2). The average total unit yield in Jimo County was 69.1 kilos in the period between 1949 to 1965. Even if we do not count 1960, 1961 and 1962, the "three bad years" when natural disasters and the failure of Great Leap Forward gravely hurt agricultural production, the average total unit yield was still only 74.2 kilos.

Grain production per mu of land in 1976 reached 180 kilos, 2.16 times that of 1965. Even though the area of cultivation decreased in those years because of the change of administrative boundaries and loss of land to construction, total grain yield in 1976 was 2.12 times that of 1965. The quality of grain also improved significantly. Production of wheat, which is the favorite food for villagers in northern China, increased to almost four times that in 1965. Production of corn, the second favorite food, increased proportionately. Unit yield for wheat increased from 49 kilos per mu in 1965 to 126 kilos per mu in 1976, and 209 kilos per mu in 1985. Unit yield for corn increased from 100 kilos per mu in 1966 to 226 kilos per mu in 1976 and to 353 kilos per mu in 1987.

During 1967, 1968 and 1969, annual precipitation amounted to only 460 mm, half the usual annual precipitation, the worst and longest drought in Jimo in several decades.[50] Despite these drought conditions, unit yield reached 96.5 kilos—43 percent higher than 1957 when natural conditions were comparable. The unit yield in good years like 1974 and 1975 more than doubled that of the best year before the Cultural Revolution. These were the immediate results of Jimo's scientific experiments and collective efforts to improve production. In these ten years, Jimo suffered no less serious

Table 2. Grain-Output in Jimo County from 1949-1979								
year	total			wheat			corn		
	area	unit yield	total yield	area	unit yield	total yield	area	unit yield	total yield
1949	231.20	70.5	163,370	63.40	49.5	31590	1.70	37.5	650
1950	226.20	71	161,015	65.70	52.5	34575	6.30	65	4085
1951	243.00	81.5	198,650	60.90	57.5	34960	6.70	75	5000
1952	241.70	82	198,555	72.40	53	39770	8.80	93.5	8215
1953	239.10	72	172,635	70.90	41.5	29565	12.00	108	12980
1954	227.70	79	180,130	65.90	48	31710	15.40	102	15640
1955	229.70	77.5	178,330	68.40	43.5	29760	26.70	100.5	20795
1956	231.70	80.5	186,925	67.60	48	32315	29.40	91.5	26890
1957	242.50	67	162,775	69.20	40.5	27830	22.20	100.5	22850
1958	247.60	70.5	174,740	71.80	40	28670	28.50	70	20215
1959	209.90	67	140,160	47.00	37	17385	16.10	43	6950
1960	191.00	30.5	58,025	66.00	36	23820	9.80	20.5	1985
1961	182.80	51	939015	50.00	22.5	11220	5.70	45.5	2580
1962	202.70	54	109,145	46.80	43	13965	7.70	59.5	4580
1963	181.30	67.5	122,180	39.40	39.5	15875	12.10	84.5	10260
1964	187.20	69.5	136,630	48.40	57	27575	17.70	82.5	14475
1965	195.70	83.5	1639560	52.30	49	25595	19.50	100.5	19655
1966	191.90	128	245.030	53.00	70	37025	28.20	145.5	41085
1967	195.44	109.5	214,375	64.90	65	42155	29.22	142.5	41695
1968	185.24	99	183,505	59.69	56.5	33670	27.08	134	36400
1969	190.60	96.5	183,990	59.20	59	34935	28.40	128	36430
1970	193.04	98.5	190,645	58.70	62	36490	32.89	122.5	40275
1971	203.66	120.5	240,455	69.41	69	47820	32.13	160.5	51505
1972	208.63	130	270,280	72.18	80.5	58045	25.37	171	43415
1973	207.69	142	2949875	68.94	69	47780	13.02	164	50960
1974	197.04	157.5	310,025	69.32	99.5	69085	33.61	188.5	63400
1975	193.03	191	369,000	75.66	113	85510	35.64	220.5	78525
1976	191.4	180	344,000	79.26	126	99730	40.17	226	90780
1977	189.83	167	319,129	79.01	116.5	92195	40.42	204.5	82615
1978	186.93	185	3469135	76.08	102.5	77795	43.81	198	84140
1979	182.36	209	381,130	74.47	181	134920	43.18	258.5	111635

Source: *Jimo Local Records,* 5:35. Area unit=10,000 mu, Unit yield=kilo, Total yield=ton. Much of the variation in area of cultivation resulted from changes in the boundaries of Jimo County. Chengyang Commune and Jihengtan Commune, for instance, were switched from Jimo to Laoshan County in 1961. Areas from other administrative units were also added to Jimo County, as in the case of Da Guandao, which became part of Jimo County in 1962.

and no fewer natural disasters than in previous decades. There were altogether four serious droughts, four serious floods, four wind disasters, nine hailstorms and three serious insect disasters.[51] Nevertheless, agricultural production steadily and rapidly increased.

Some critics assert that implementation of the Central Government's directive to "take grain as the key link" (yi *liang wei gang*) led to an overemphasis on grain production at the expense of other agricultural products during the Cultural Revolution decade.[52] This was not Jimo's experience, as we shall see below. During the Cultural Revolution decade local initiative flourished. Central policies, such as "taking grain as the key link" were only advisory, because production decisions were made locally. If local farmers did not want to carry out a particular central policy, as one Jimo farmer commented, there was no way that anybody could force them to.[53] If farmers cut down orchards and filled in fish ponds during the Cultural Revolution years, one villager in South River village said, they most probably did it for good economic reasons. The orchards might have been too old to be productive. The fish pond might not have been profitable enough to maintain, or it might have hindered the use of farm machines on a large piece of land.[54]

After the baptism of the Cultural Revolution, farmers refused to follow policies from above blindly, unless they were convinced that these policies would advance their living standards. Throughout the Cultural Revolution decade, the county and commune governments in Jimo sent functionaries to villages to participate in agricultural production and to give villagers advice. But villagers did not have to listen to them. In fact, there were cases of farmers driving away outside cadres.[55] Many Jimo farmers had paid a high price during the Great Leap Forward when they listened to the bad advice of outsiders. They were not going to let that happen to them again. In a sense, the Cultural Revolution was an effort to make sure that the Great Leap excesses would not happen again in rural areas.

The famous "May Seventh Directive," which Mao issued in the early days of the Cultural Revolution, encouraged farmers to develop in many directions simultaneously, including agriculture, forestry, fishery, animal husbandry and rural industries. Jimo farmers did exactly this.[56] The new revolutionary committees in Jimo were concerned with improving farmers' living standards. They enthusiastically implemented the central policy that encouraged farmers to make the best use of local conditions and engage in multiple enterprises (*yin di zhi yi, duo zheng jing ying*).[57]

South River, Guo Jiaxiang, and Yao Tou villages started their first attempt at *linye* (forestry and fruits) with the encouragement of Mao's May Seventh Directive at the beginning of the Cultural

Revolution in 1966. Fu Zengshan, Wang Shufang and other educated youth who returned to their own villages at the beginning of the Cultural Revolution set up the *linye dui* (Forest team) in South River, Guo Jiaxiang and Yao Tao villages. They planted peach, apple, and pear trees on the sandy land. Fu Zongshan, Fu Zengjie, Wang Shufang and many other educated youth went to study how to cultivate and graft these fruit trees. In the space between fruit trees, they planted watermelons in the spring and peanuts in the fall. It was the first time people in these villages planted watermelons and peanuts. Along the riverbanks, they planted poplars, elms, Chinese parasols, and Chinese scholar trees to break the winds in spring and protect the riverbank against flood in summer. Along the roadside, they planted pepper trees. For the first time, villagers received apples, peaches, pears, watermelons and peppers from the collectives. Later on, they also added pigs and goats to their operation. In the spring, they were able to provide villagers who wanted to raise pigs with small piglets. On Chinese New Year and other festivals they would supply villagers with pork. They used twigs from the fruit trees and shrubs on the riverbanks to make baskets in winter and sold them to villagers. Fu Zengshan and Wang Shufang, the founders of South Rivers' *linyedui,* commented with pride that the operation turned out to be a big success.[58]

It was also during the Cultural Revolution that South River set up a vegetable team. Before the Cultural Revolution, villagers planted vegetables on their private plots if they were close to the village and could be irrigated. Otherwise, farmers would plant grain in their private plots: wheat in winter and corn in the summer. Apart from selling vegetables on the market, those who had a vegetable garden could enjoy fresh vegetables frequently. Those who did not have vegetable gardens had to buy vegetables on the market. As cash was scarce, villagers who did not have vegetable gardens did not have a big variety of vegetables. They only had two kinds of Chinese cabbages, three kinds of turnips, and mustard which villagers pickled for use during the whole year. It changed as a result of the work of the vegetable team. Zhang Tongxu and Sun Kexian, the two best vegetable gardeners in the village, were chosen as the head and deputy head of the vegetable team. Together with a group of house wives from the village, they managed a big vegetable garden of twenty Chinese mu. They were able to provide villagers regularly with a variety of vegetables throughout the Cultural Revolution years and they were able to make money by selling vegetables on the market, too.[59]

The cash crops in rural Jimo include peanuts, hemp, tobacco and vegetables. Peanuts grow best in sandy land. They do not like too

Table 3. Area and output of cash crops in Jimo County 1936-1979

year	peanuts			hemp			vegetable	tobacco		
	area	u.o.	t.o.	area	u.o	t.o.	area	area	u.o	t.o.
1936	14.80	84	12465	0.06	25	15	8.51			
1949	16.00	66	10470	0.10	15	15	9.50			
1950	16.00	71	11445	0.10	40	40	4.60			
1951	13.20	109	14370	0.20	92.5	185	2.30			
1952	20.50	104	22330	0.50	85	425	4.10			
1953	16.70	95	15900	0.30	80	245	4.30			
1954	20.00	100.5	20135	0.20	67.5	135	6.20			
1955	18.60	104.5	19405	0.30	43.5	130	4.50			
1956	11.80	123.5	20740	0.30	61.5	185	6.90			
1957	15.90	103	16375	0.10	24	240	6.60			
1958	13.60	143	19480	2.00	53.5	106	12.10			
1959	2.40	111	2660	0.80	90	720	14.80			
1960	6.60	23	1525	0.30	3.5	10	5.56			
1961	4.52	55	2485				5.75	0.04	37.5	15
1962	5.90	51	3000	0.20	10	20	3.82	0.05	40	20
1963	6.88	69	4745	0.60	8.5	50	4.05	0.12	41.5	50
1964	11.43	72.5	8290	0.70	22	155	6.21	0.08	44	35
1965	11.00	82	9000	3.63	99.5	610	4.98	0.09	55.5	50
1966	14.95	150.5	22485	5.24	128	6710	3.80	0.07	78.5	55
1967	20.80	114	23760	6.73	125.5	8430	3.57	0.08	81.5	65
1968	16.69	107.5	17955	8.46	110	9310	5.80			
1969	15.10	62	9365	3.70	81	3000	5.33	0.20	72.5	145
1970	15.09	87	13180	3.79	107.5	4050	5.54	0.20	75	150
1971	14.43	127.5	18410	5.02	119.5	6000	4.98	0.10	83.5	135
1972	15.45	101.5	15655	5.00	96	3460	5.93	0.21	140	175
1973	14.47	128	18540	5.20	110	5715	6.11	0.15	100	210
1974	17.58	112	18685	7.39	123.5	9115	6.12	0.17	144	170
1975	18.96	86	16340	9.56	174	16635	7.37	0.26	127.5	375
1976	18.18	S9	10755	9.64	103.5	10020	7.31	0.31	115	395
1977	14.83	82.5	1226S	8.34	106	8825	8.68	0.27	141.5	310
1978	17.26	124	21380	8.36	164	13715	9.20	0.23	143	325

Source: *Jimo Local Records.* 5:39-40, u.o. = unit output = kilo per mu, t.o. = total output = ton, unit of area = ten thousand mu

much rain. Hemp, on the other hand, grows best in tight black soils, and is flood resistant. Farmers in Jimo typically grew vegetables on land that was close to villages. Farmers grew small quantities of tobacco mainly for their own consumption. From Table 3, we can see that the amount of land used for these crops varied from year to year. But the variation was not caused by pressures from the government. It was dictated by weather conditions and the local market. The amount of land used for peanuts was between 110,000 and 200,000 mu before the Cultural Revolution, except the four years from 1959 to 1963 when there were many floods. Variations in the amount of land used for peanuts during the Cultural Revolution was between 144,300 mu and 208,000 mu. The average unit yield in the ten years from 1966 to 1976 was 117 kilos. This represents an increase of seventeen kilos, or fifteen percent, over the comparable period from 1949 to 1959, which was 101 kilos per mu.

Hemp acreage ranged from 600 to 36,300 mu, with an average of 6,112 mu per year, before the Cultural Revolution. During the Cultural Revolution decade, hemp acreage ranged from 37,000 mu to 96,400 mu, with an average of 63,436 mu per year, a huge increase over previous years. The unit yield of hemp during the Cultural Revolution decade was 116 kilos, a 79 percent increase over the comparable period between 1949 and 1959, when the average unit yield was 64.9 kilos.

Vegetable acreage variation was a little more complex because of changes in Jimo County's administrative boundaries. There were three years before the Cultural Revolution when vegetable acreage appeared to be big: 95,000 mu in 1949, 120,000 mu in 1958 and 140,000 mu in 1959. There was a simple explanation for this. In 1949, the three rural districts close to Qingdao City were still under the jurisdiction of rural Jimo. In 1950, these three districts, Chengyang, Jihengtan and Taocun were ceded to Qingdao City. In 1958, the three districts were returned to Jimo County again, because at this same time Jimo County was ceded altogether to the jurisdiction of Qingdao City from Laizhou Prefecture. As traditional vegetable suppliers for Qingdao City, the addition of these three districts accounted for the increase of vegetable acreage in 1958 and 1959. In 1960, Jimo County was ceded to Yantai Prefecture, and the three districts which provided Qingdao City with vegetables were taken away from Jimo County as a compromise.[60] That was why the amount of vegetable acreage declined in 1960. But starting in 1968, the amount of vegetable land rose again. Land for tobacco rose as well during Cultural Revolution decade.

Animal husbandry in rural Jimo did not suffer as a result of the drive for more grain production during the Cultural Revolution either. Pig raising is one of the major animal husbandry activity in rural Jimo. Pigs are the major source of meat and organic fertilizer. In 1949, when the county's territory was at its largest in modern times, there were 22,400 pigs in Jimo. This number increased to 148,000 in 1963. During the Cultural Revolution, there was a drive to raise more pigs in order to produce more organic fertilizers for agriculture. The number of pigs increased to 306,000 in 1967, 345,400 in 1973 and 422,000 in 1975.[61] This was 18.8 times the number of pigs in 1949 and 2.8 times the number in 1963.

Traditionally hares were raised as pets in rural Jimo. But hares became a source of income in 1957, when there was a demand for hare meat and fur on the international market. The total number of hares in Jimo soared to 18,700 in 1957, and 37,500 by 1960. During the Cultural Revolution the number of hares reached its peak level of 300,000 in 1967. Afterwards, the number declined as demand for its meat and fur on the international market dipped.[62]

Chicken is another favorite source of protein for farmers in rural Jimo. Most farmers in Jimo raised a few hens for eggs and one rooster for meat during the Chinese spring festival. According to 1932 statistics, the total number of chickens in Jimo was 289,700, an average of 2.17 per household. By 1957, the number of chickens reached the pre-Cultural Revolution peak level of 416,700, an average of 2.64 per household. Following the failure of the Great Leap and the natural disasters, the number of chickens dropped to 119,00 in 1960, an average of 0.75 per household. When people did not have enough food, they could not afford to raise chickens, for chickens competed with humans for grain. During the Cultural Revolution, the number of chickens began to increase, as grain production increased. In 1970, the number of chickens reached 371,100, and by 1980 the number of chickens had soared to 769,000, about three times that in 1932 and 1.8 times that in 1957. Chicken raising-was also on the rise during the Cultural Revolution decade.[63]

RURAL INDUSTRY

Rural industry flourished in Jimo during the Cultural Revolution. As was discussed in Chapter Three, the fledgling rural industrial enterprises established briefly in Jimo County during the Great Leap Forward depended on collective organization and did not survive the post-Leap retrenchment, when the collective organization was weakened and land was divided and farmed separately by individual families. In the early 1960s, in the entire county there were only ten rural industrial enterprises which combined employed only 253 people.[64] During the Cultural Revolution, the collective agricultural economy was consolidated in rural Jimo, providing the economic and organizational basis for resuming rural industrial enterprises with local initiatives. With the educational reforms of the Cultural Revolution, more and more educated young people with technical knowhow were available to work in rural industries.

In 1966, fifteen commune-run industrial enterprises were set up.[65] Many villages began to set up small industrial enterprises. From humble beginnings in 1966, rural industrial enterprises developed into full-fledged industrial systems in just ten years. By 1976, there were 2,557 rural industrial enterprises in Jimo with an average of 2.5 enterprises per village. These rural industrial enterprises employed a total of 54,771 people and annual output amounted to 91,360,000 yuan (1970 constant value).[66] By then, rural industry accounted for 35.8 percent of the total income of the thirty communes in rural Jimo.[67]

Agriculture nourished the rural industrial enterprises by providing them with raw materials. Rural industrial enterprises in turn helped agriculture develop. They produced machines that made farming easier. The irrigation facilities built during the Cultural Revolution decade would not have worked without electrical pumps, electric motors and gas engines. To equip the wells and reservoirs, the Jimo County Revolutionary Committee mobilized all the technical resources in Jimo and started *nongji da huizhan* (a big campaign to produce farm machines). In eighty days, from April 12 to the end of June in 1970, three hundred diesel engines of twenty horsepower each were produced in Jimo County. In the following eight weeks, Jimo County produced sixty tractors.[68] The National Ministry of Machine Industry called up engineers from 39 research institutes to evaluate the quality of these products. All of them passed inspection.[69] Considering the limited technical resources in rural Jimo before the Cultural Revolution, when workers only produced shovels, sickles, caldrons and wheelbarrows, the achievements of these campaigns were impressive indeed. It took the initiative and expertise of both ordinary workers and technicians to produce these novel machines. More importantly, the educational reforms had provided the local industries with educated youth who had acquired technical know-how while in school. Many ordinary workers organized small groups to tackle technical problems during the Cultural Revolution years.[70]

In 1966 South River Village started its first industrial enterprise, later known as the Henan Welding Factory *(Mao Han Chang)*. The village owned the factory collectively. In the beginning, it was run by the Eighth Production Team and employed only three people, making decoration pieces for furniture. The whole enterprise started with a twenty yuan investment for two big scissors and two big hammers. The raw materials were waste materials from factories, which did not cost much. It used the Eighth Production Team's office as a temporary workshop. The project was a success. During the winter of 1966, it generated two thousand yuan. In the spring of 1967, the village took over the business, more people were employed, and a bigger factory building was built. In the summer of 1967, the village selected ten young people who were returned primary and middle school graduates and sent them to Jimo Farm Machine factory to learn 71 different industrial skills.[71]

When these people returned to the village after six months' training, the village workshop's expertise improved. With their combined technical ability, these ten rural youth began to make machine tool parts for the Jimo Farm Machine Factory.[72] The Farm Machine Factory agreed to compensate their work by giving the village factory some machine tools. At the end of the year, the Farm Machine Factory gave the village factory a thirty-ton press and a small drill as part of compensation for the work done by the village young people. With the new equipment, the village factory began to make ventilation fans for textile factories. The profit from these products enabled the village factory to acquire three lathes, two planers, a sixty-ton press and a big drill, which further increased the factory's technical capacity. By 1976, the village factory owned thirty electric welders, two gas welders and cutters, three lathes, two planers, two drills and two presses. More importantly, it had 179 skilled workers. The managers and the majority of the workers were graduates from the commune high school. Its annual profit reached 300,000 yuan and its products ranged from gearboxes for motor boats to mobile overhead cranes by 1976.

With few exceptions, the farm machines owned by South River Village were purchased with profits from the village factory. The first electrical motor of the village was a gift from a factory in 1968, and the two pickup trucks were assembled by the village factory in 1974. Villagers salvaged two engines and gearboxes from two World War II U.S. jeeps in a pile of waste in another factory. They used these old engines and gearboxes, and made other parts to assemble the two small trucks.[73] The factory also maintained all the farm machines of the village.[74]

Many factors contributed to this development of rural industry, but the human factor was critical. The Cultural Revolution educational reforms provided the rural areas with a large number of educated youth. While in school they learned what was useful for the rural areas, and when they returned to their home village upon graduation they could make good use of what they had learned.

RURAL INCOME INCREASES

Increasing agricultural production and the development of rural industrial enterprises increased the per capita income for the rural population of Jimo. Grain possession per capita among the rural population in Jimo increased from 239 kilos in 1965 to 421 kilos in 1976, (see Table 3).[75] In South River, grain consumption per capita increased from around 130 kilos in 1965 to 220 kilos in 1976.[76] Before the Cultural Revolution, South River villagers had to buy grain from state grain shops and on the free market, because they could not produce enough grain for themselves. Starting in 1968, however, they had enough grain every year.[77] In the old days, Jimo farmers could only afford to eat wheat flour food on special occasions, like festivals or when entertaining a guest. With the increase of wheat production, they could afford to eat more and more wheat flour.

Income from rural industrial enterprises increased the value of work points and consequently improved the living standards of the rural population. The South River Village factory paid the workers in work points in the same way as people who worked in the fields. The income from the village factory was distributed village-wide. The factory, thus, played an important role in improving all villagers' living standard. South River and Guo Jiaxiang were average villages in Jimo. The value of a single work point in these villages ranged from eight cents to fourteen cents, amounting to a daily work point income of eighty cents to 1.4 yuan in the mid 1970s. In above-average villages, such as Moshi, Yaotou, Geli and Nanguang, work point value ranged from 15 cents to 20 cents, amounting to an income of 1.5 yuan to two yuan a day, which was on par with ordinary urban workers' income at the time. The goal of the South River village factory in the 1970s was to maintain villagers' income level at 1.5 yuan a day while maintaining an aggressive level of capital investment.[78]

Table 4. Annual Per Capita Grain possession and income in rural Jimo 1958-1985							
year	1958	1960	1965	1970	1975	1980	1985
grain possession	288	88	230	232	421	423	386
income per capita	27	24	37	50	79.6	117.3	558
Source: *Jimo xianzhi*, 3:27. Grain unit = kilo Income unit = yuan							

Per capita annual income of rural Jimo residents more than doubled during the Cultural Revolution decade, increasing from 37 yuan in 1965 to 79.6 yuan in 1975 (see Table 4). Even the 1975 figure is, of course, not a high income. But we must take into account the fact that farmers calculated income in their own particular ways, and likely under-reported their incomes.

While incomes of rural Jimo residents rose substantially during the Cultural Revolution decade, the incomes of urban residents in the town of Jimo stagnated or actually fell. The average annual income of a worker in a state-run factory in Jimo decreased from 480.7 yuan in 1956 to 427.8 yuan in 1976.[79] If a state worker had four dependents to support, then his family per capita income in 1976 would have been 85.4 yuan, only a little higher than a typical peasant family's per capita incomes.

Table 5. Monthly grain possession for the non-agricultural population in Jimo 1955-1987				
Category	grade	1955-1960	1960-1978	1979-1987
Special labor	1	37.5	26	28
	2	30	24.5	26
	3	27.5	22.5	24.5
heavy labor	1	23	26.5	23
	2	21.5	19.5	21.5
	3	20	17.5	19.5
mental labor	1	18	16	18
	2	17	15	17
	3	14.5	14	16
students college		17.5	16	17.5
senior high		16	15	16
junior high		15	14	15
ordinary citizen		13.5	11.5	13.5
Source: *Jimo Local Records*, 3:28. Unit = Kilo				

While grain consumption of peasant families rose sharply during the Cultural Revolution decade, urban residents' grain consumption actually fell (see Table 5). Rural Jimo County residents' per capita grain consumption increased by 55 percent between 1965 and 1975, (see Table 3) while urban Jimo residents' per capita grain supply was reduced. The per capita grain supplied to an employee categorized as Grade 1 special labor decreased from 37.5 kilos per month between 1955 and 1960 to 26 kilos per month between 1960 and 1978. Grade 2 special labor suffered a monthly loss of 5.5 kilos. Other categories of urban residents sustained monthly losses of 1-3 kilos, or 12-36 kilos annually. It is beyond the scope of this book to analyze the reasons for the stagnation or decline of urban incomes during this period. This fact coupled with the significant increase in rural incomes, however, led to a closing of the gap between urban and rural living standards, a communist goal that Mao particularly emphasized during the Cultural Revolution.

MEDICAL CARE COMES TO RURAL JIMO

During the Cultural Revolution the urban-oriented medical policies of the initial post-revolutionary years were denounced and a system of rural medical care emerged for the first time. At the beginning of the Cultural Revolution, Mao denounced the people's hospitals as *chengshi laoye yiyuan* (hospitals for urban lords only). The film *Chun Miao (Spring Shoot)*, produced during the Cultural Revolution, vividly described the lack of medical care in the rural areas and the mistreatment of villagers by the staff of urban hospitals. It was acclaimed by villagers in Jimo.[81]

In 1967, 105 villages in rural Jimo set up village clinics. By 1969, 525 villages had their own clinics. Some 238 villages adopted the village medical insurance system *(hezuo yiliao)*. Each villager paid fifty cents annually to the village clinic, which would then provide villagers with rudimentary free medical care for a whole year. By 1970, 910 villages—93 percent of all villages—had set up their own village clinics and all had rudimentary medical insurance policies for villagers.[82]

The rural "barefoot doctors" who staffed village clinics were mostly returned educated rural youth, who had received rudimentary medical training while in high school. Because of the educational reforms of the Cultural Revolution, many high schools sent students to work in hospitals as interns for a few months. They learned basic medical theory and acquired some basic skills. When they returned home upon graduation they began to work in the village clinics under the supervision of doctors from commune hospitals. They also received regular in-service training from hospitals and medical schools. Zhou Yulan, Han Xiuyun, Guan Dunguo, barefoot doctors in South River village, and Zhang Xiaozheng, Sun Jilin from Yaotou, Wang Shicai and Sung Yonghua of Huayuan village, all received their first medical training in high school. They became village barefoot doctors upon graduation.[83]

Each village sent two or three young people to receive regular medical training to become barefoot doctors in the village clinic. The village paid these barefoot doctors in work points, the same way it paid village teachers. The barefoot doctors then provided villagers free medical care. If a villager fell ill and needed to be hospitalized, the village would try to pay for his or her medical bills. If the village could not pay, the commune would help. If the medical bills became too big for both village and commune, the hospital would waive the charges.[84] Zhang Guilan' of Yao Village went to Beijing to have an operation in 1969. When the hospital found out that neither he nor his village could pay the bill, it waived the charge.[85] In 1973, Zhang Kechang from Guo village told the hospital staff that he was not able to pay his medical bills, but when his sons grew up they would make the payment. The hospital waived his bills in the end.[86]

To be sure, the rural cooperative medical system was of low quality. The barefoot doctors did not have much professional training, and the village clinic did not have much medical equipment, supplies or medicine. But it was the best system of medical care villages in Jimo had ever had and it provided villagers with important services and peace of mind. The value of the barefoot doctors to Jimo villagers cannot simply be measured by the formal training they received. They were from the same villages as their patients. They were available 24 hours a day in all weather conditions, even during the Chinese New Year or during a big snowstorm. Their medical training was adequate to treat common problems, and for big problems they would get help from regular doctors from the commune or county hospitals. For common problems like colds and tracheitis, the barefoot doctors had a standard treatment. At the early stage of the problem, they provided standard pills. For the more serious cases, they used intravenous drip to relieve patients' suffering.[87]

Of course, it would have been better if villages had doctors with more professional training, but they were not available at the time. Doctors with rudimentary training were better than no doctors.

Life expectancy in Jimo County increased from 35 years in 1949 to 70.54 years in 1986.[88] Behind this impressive increase there were many factors. The barefoot doctors of the Cultural Revolution undoubtedly played a crucial role, particularly in spreading modern medical knowledge and in providing basic medical care to rural people.

ASSESSING ECONOMIC DEVELOPMENT DURING THE CULTURAL REVOLUTION DECADE

The rapid economic development in rural Jimo County during the Cultural Revolution decade was not unique. Across rural China, mechanization, irrigation, land improvement projects and experimentation transformed agricultural production. Crop yields increased dramatically. Rural industry developed from a negligible base and expanded rapidly.

Many of the rural development goals pursued during the Cultural Revolution decade were similar to the goals pursued during the Great Leap Forward. During both periods there were efforts to rapidly build rural infrastructure, expand agricultural production and develop rural industry. During both periods these efforts were based on an intensification of collective organization. While the Great Leap Forward efforts collapsed causing tremendous hardship in the countryside, however, the Cultural Revolution efforts succeeded in transforming the rural economy and permanently improving the conditions of villagers. A comprehensive analysis of the reasons for the distinct results of the two periods is beyond the scope of this study. Such an analysis would have to consider management and planning, resources at hand, and resource allocation on a countrywide level. On the basis of this study of a single county, however, it is possible to confidently point to the key contributions of two factors that were a direct product of the Cultural Revolution: a change in rural political culture and the rapid expansion of rural education.

The Cultural Revolution gave ordinary villagers a voice in production decisions, encouraged local initiative and compelled cadres to work together with ordinary farmers, creating political conditions in which villagers were empowered within the collective structure. The old village party power structure was overthrown and in its place a new power structure, more responsive to the farmers' aspirations, was set up. The schools created as a result of Cultural Revolution reforms also provided rural areas, for the first time, with young people who had the technical knowledge required to modernize agriculture[89] and develop rural industry.

Philip Huang has argued that the growth in agricultural production during the Cultural Revolution decade was *growth without development.* In his investigation of the Yangzi Delta region, Huang challenged the standard Chinese government portrayal of the Cultural Revolution as an economic disaster, documenting the substantial growth of crop yields per land unit during the Cultural Revolution decade. He, however, concluded that this was accomplished by intensifying labor input to an extent that the marginal returns per workday declined. This continued a long-term tendency of *agricultural involution,* he argued, in which population pressure forced Chinese farmers to intensify labor at the expense of labor productivity. The cycle of agricultural involution was broken and real development began, he wrote, only after surplus rural labor was diverted from agriculture to rural industry. This did not take place, he concluded, until the post-Cultural Revolution reform period.[90]

Huang's distinction between involutionary growth and real development is valid and useful. Yet, if we use his definitions, during the Cultural Revolution, rural Jimo experienced real development, not simply involutionary growth. Practices designed to increase productivity per mu through intensification of labor, such as multi-cropping and transplantation of seedlings, which Huang identified as involutionary, were, indeed, an important aspect of the advances in grain yields in Jimo. At the same time, however, mechanization greatly reduced field labor. This allowed a massive diversion of labor to rural industry, which, as we have seen, grew rapidly, making up nearly 36% of Jimo's economy by the end of the Cultural Revolution decade. Moreover, while Jimo's labor force grew rapidly, Cultural Revolution education reforms diverted tens of thousands of young people from productive activity by placing them in school.

Huang correctly identified the building of rural industry as the key factor that broke the cycle of involution in rural China. The building of rural industry in Jimo County, however, began as a result of the Cultural Revolution and was already well under way before the onset of Deng's rural reforms. Moreover, this was also the case in the area that Huang investigated, as his careful study showed,[91] as in much of rural China. It was, in fact, the Cultural Revolution that broke the cycle of agricultural involution through mechanization and rural industrialization.

Notes

1. *Jimo xianzhi, Jimo dashi ji (Chronology of Events in Jimo County)* 73.
2. Interview with former county revolutionary committee leaders, summer, 1997.
3. Interview with former production team leaders, summer, 1989.
4. see Kate Zhou, *How the Farmers Changed China* (Boulder: Westview Press, 1996)
5. Interview with villagers in Jimo, summer, 1997.
6. After the Cultural Revolution, the Deng Xiaoping government charged that the campaign to criticize Lin Biao and Confucius was intended by the "Gang of Four" as an allegorical attack on the late Chinese premier Zhou Enlai. It was part of the government's efforts to discredit the "gang of four" and the Cultural Revolution. This study is mainly concerned with what the villagers felt at the time of the campaign, not with the post-cultural-revolution analysis of the goals of the campaign.
7. Interview with villagers in Jimo, summer, 1997.
8. Interview with villagers in Jimo, summer, 1997.
9. Interview with villagers in Jimo, summer, 1989.
10. Interview with former schoolteachers, 1995.
11. Interview with former village school students, 1990.
12. There were two kinds of teachers in rural China. Some teachers were on government payroll. Others were hired by the village and therefore were paid by the village with a fixed amount of work points, apart from a small monthly cash bonus. The former had no

financial connection with the village, the later did, because the value of the work points they got from the village depended on the economic performance of the village. Government employees and schoolteachers who were on the government payroll did not participate in the distribution of the village's grain production.

13. Interviews with former village school students in Jimo, Summer, 1997.
14. Interview with villagers in Jimo, summer 1997.
15. Angry farmers in North Jimo told municipal and provincial investigators in 1960 that they would refuse to work for the collective in protest of its leadership. *Jimo xianzhi,* 34:53.
16. Interview with villagers in Jimo, summer, 1997.
17. Anthropologist Yunxiang Yan called leaders in the village he studied "white hands" *(bai zhua zi)* because "they were able to avoid tanning their hands by farm work." See, Yan," The Impact of Rural Reform on Economic and Social Stratification in a Chinese Village," *The Australian journal of Chinese Affairs,* No. 27, January 1992, 6.
18. Interview with villagers in Jimo, summer 1990.
19. Interview with villagers in Jimo, summer 1997.
20. Interview with villagers in Jimo, summer, 1990.
21. Interview with villagers in Jimo, summer, 1990.
22. Interview with villagers in Jimo, Summer, 1990.
23. Interview with villagers in Jimo, summer, 1997.
24. Interview with villagers in Jimo, summer, 1990.
25. Interview with villagers, summer 1990.
26. *Jimo xianzhi,* 28:4.
27. *Jimo xianzhi,* 5:42.
28. This method was used for two years. It was discontinued because it was very time consuming, though effective.
29. *Jimo xianzhi,* 5:43.
30. *Jimo xianzhi,* 5:38.
31. *Jimo xianzhi,* 6:20.
32. *Jimo xianzhi,* 6:23.
33. *Jimo xianzhi, Jimo dashiji (Chronology of Events in Jimo),* 77.
34. *Jimo xianzhi,* 6:27.
35. *Jimo xianzhi,* 6:27.
36. *Jimo xianzhi,* 6:27.
37. Commune leaders and teachers all belonged to the category of state cadres. They were all on government payroll. They did not have any material interest in the production of villages.
38. Interview with villagers in Jimo, summer, 1990.
39. *Jimo xianzhi,* 6:27.
40. Spring festival is the most important Chinese festival. *Jiao zi,* Chinese dumplings, is the main dish for this festival. In normal time, villagers would stop working in the fields around this festival for at least one month.
41. *Jimo xianzhi,* 5:16.
42. *Jimo xianzhi,* 5:16.

43. *Jimo xianzhi,* 5:16.
44. *Jimo xianzhi* 9:6.
45. Interview with villagers in Jimo, summer, 1990.
46. *Jimo xianzhi,* 319.
47. *Jimo xianzhi,* 320.
48. *Jimo xianzhi,* 5:30.
49. *Jimo xianzhi,* 5:30.
50. *Jimo xianzhi,* 2:16.
51. *Jimo xianzhi,* 2:63-75.
52. See, for instance, Zhou (1996), page 29.
53. Interview with villagers in Jimo, summer, 1990.
54. Interview with villagers in Jimo, summer, 1990.
55. Interview with villagers in Jimo, summer, 1990.
56. Tsung Chao, *An Account of the Cultural Revolution,* 188.
57. This policy encouraged farmers to take advantage of local conditions to develop various enterprises to improve people's lives. For example, if there were ponds, the local people were encouraged to develop fish culture. If there were wood supplies farmers were encouraged to develop enterprises connected with that resource.
58. Interview with villagers in Jimo, summer, 1997.
59. Interview with villagers in Jimo, summer, 1997.
60. *Jimo xianzhi,* 5:34.
61. *Jimo xianzhi,* 5:49.
62. *Jimo xianzhi,* 5:51.
63. *Jimo xianzhi,* 5:50.
64. *Jimo xianzhi,* 9:2.
65. *Jimo xianzhi,* 9:6.
66. *Jimo xianzhi,* 9:3.
67. *Jimo xianzhi,* 9:3.
68. *Jimo xianzhi,* 28:5.
69. *Jimo xianzhi, Jimo dashiji (Chronology of Events in Jimo County)* 77.
70. *Jimo xianzhi,* 28:5.
71. Interview with villagers in Jimo, summer, 1997.
72. Interview with villagers in Jimo, summer, 1997.
73. Interview with villagers in Jimo, summer, 1990.
74. Interview with villagers, summer, 1990.
75. *Jimo xianzhi,* 3:27.
76. Interview with villagers in Jimo, summer, 1990.
77. Interview with villagers in Jimo, summer, 1990.
78. Interview with villagers in Jimo, summer, 1990.
79. Oreg Leary in his "Current Trends of China's Agricultural Strategy: A Survey of Communes in Hebei and Shandong," stated that farmers often deliberately under-reported their incomes. See Oreg Leary and Andrew Watson, "Current Trend of China's Agricultural Strategy: A Survey of Communes in Hebei and Shandong," *The Australian Journal of Chinese Affairs,* No. 4, 1980, 137.
80. *Jimo xianzhi,* 3:21.
81. Interview with villagers in Jimo, summer, 1990.

82. *Jimo xianzhi*, 756.
83. Interview with villagers, 1997.
84. Interview with villagers in Jimo, summer, 1990.
85. Interview with villagers in Jimo, summer, 1997.
86. Interview with villagers in Jimo, summer, 1997.
87. Interview with villagers in Jimo, Summer, 1997.
88. *Jimo Xianzhi*, 9.
89. Other third world countries, of course, achieved similar results with "green revolution" techniques. But there is a difference here that should not be overlooked. In other countries green revolution techniques were applied in the countryside with systematic help from the United States and other technologically advanced nations. Chinese farmers in Jimo and elsewhere, on the other hand, tried new methods and carried out experiments without help from foreign experts. In this situation, the educational reforms of the Cultural Revolution were critical to the modernization of agriculture.
90. Philip Huang, *The Peasant Family and Rural Development in the Yangzi Delta, 1350-1988*, (Stanford: Stanford University Press, 1990).
91. Huang documents the rapid growth of production and employment in commune and production brigade factories in the areas he studied during the Cultural Revolution decade. Philip Huang, *The Peasant Family and Rural Development in the Yangzi Delta, 1350-1988*, pp. 245, 279, 318, 347-353, 355.

CHAPTER 7

Negating the Cultural Revolution

Political empowerment is a long process. In China, where officialdom had been dominant for thousand of years, this process will not only be long but tortuous. The Cultural Revolution was one of the first attempts to empower ordinary rural Chinese against officialdom. It only succeeded to a limited extent. The complete negation of the Cultural Revolution following Deng Xiaoping's return to power in 1978 was like a quick deep frost on tender spring crops. It rolled back and in many respects destroyed the process of political empowerment in China—at least this seems to be the case for rural Jimo.

THE NEW HUAN XIANGTUAN

When Deng Xiaoping and former government officials who were thrown out during the Cultural Revolution returned to power in the late 1970s, former rebel leaders compared them to the *huan xiangtuan,* the vengeful regiments led by returning landlords during the Civil War (see Chapter 1). To Jimo residents with some knowledge of the Cultural Revolution and the land reform, the parallel between the *huan xiangtuan* during the Civil War and the returning CCP officials after the Cultural Revolution was obvious.

Many former CCP bosses were treated roughly during the initial period of the Cultural Revolution by the rebels, just as Jimo landlords had been treated very badly by the poor and landless during the land reform. Some former CCP officials had abused their power and offended ordinary people during the Great Leap Forward, thus incurring hatred of villagers they governed. Just as poor farmers had taken advantage of the opportunities provided by the land reform to take vengeance against landlords, at the beginning of the Cultural Revolution, rebels made CCP officials pay for their abuse of power. The CCP bosses who were subjected to mass criticism and physical attack during the Cultural Revolution had good reason to resent their treatment at the hands of the rebels. To the rebels, some CCP bosses had gone out of bounds during the Great Leap Forward when they forced people to work like slaves and built luxurious hotels while some farmers were starving.[1] But the CCP bosses felt that they were simply doing what officials had been doing for thousands of years—enjoying the privileges of power. Officials were officials after all, and should and would have more privileges than ordinary people, or so some former CCP bosses rationalized. Among a dozen former CCP officials I have interviewed, few believed that they had done anything wrong before the Cultural Revolution and they did not think they deserved the rough treatment they had received at the hands of the rebels. They all blamed the "Gang of Four"[2] and the rebels for the personal suffering they sustained during the Cultural Revolution.[3]

The emerging democratic culture of *da ming, da fang, da bianlun* and *dazibao* (great airing of opinions, great freedom, great debate and big character posters) of the Cultural Revolution empowered the rebels and ordinary people. They began to challenge aspects of China's traditional culture of officialdom, demanding that party leaders conform to the ascetic Maoist code of official conduct. As the rebels become dominant during the Cultural Revolution, this political culture had begun to prevail. Consequently, many former local CCP bosses and officials had begun to reconcile themselves to the new expectations. That was the only way to be accepted into the new power structure. In Jimo, all the former county party officials were eventually incorporated into the new power structure of the revolutionary committees, despite the humiliation to which they had been subjected during the initial period of the Cultural Revolution. They were working with the rebels inside the new power structure at the time Mao Zedong died in 1976.[4]

The political situation in China changed rapidly following Mao's death. Following the arrest of the Gang of Four at the center, old party officials at different levels of government around the country rounded up former rebel leaders. In Luoyang, an industrial city in Henan Province, for instance, hundreds of former rebel leaders were arrested and paraded in public and then disappeared.[5] In Jimo, the rehabilitated former party bosses retaliated against their former challengers. They targeted all the rebel leaders in Jimo who held significant official positions. A number of the important rebel leaders were incarcerated in May, 1977. Wang Sibo, a former rebel Red Guard leader and deputy head of the Jimo County Revolutionary Committee, was arrested and imprisoned for more than one year without specific charges. He was finally released after the authorities was unable to substantiate charges against him. Liu Shixing, former rebel leader and deputy manager of Jimo Hardware Factory, and Ge Dexin, former rebel leader and deputy head of Chengguan Commune, were both dismissed from office in May 1977, and arrested in November, 1977. Jiao Chuanfa, former rebel leader at Jimo Farm Machine Factory committed suicide in protest of the large-scale arrests of rebel leaders. From November 1977 to Spring 1979, the reconstructed Jimo Party Committee conducted its first large-scale purge of former rebel leaders.[6] Few rebel leaders survived the purge.

In the early 1980s, the Deng Xiaoping government mounted an

even larger and more extensive campaign of retaliation against the former rebels. Government departments, factories, schools, universities, research institutions all set up special offices to investigate charges against former rebels. A large number of people lost their jobs, housing, and many were imprisoned for their "crimes" during the Cultural Revolution. The Jimo CCP Committee started its second purge on December 11, 1983. Every government office, school, factory and village was ordered to purge former rank-and-file rebels.[7] Officials who had lost their positions at the beginning of the Cultural Revolution brought charges against individual rebels against whom they held grudges.[8]

The nationwide frenzy of retaliation against former rebels created an atmosphere of vindication among former party leaders. When *huan xiangtuan* landlords returned to the villages, they boasted that the weak could not defeat the strong. In the 1980s, rehabilitated former party leaders said the same words to former rebels. "The river changes courses; east of the river may become west of the river in time," they said. "You did not think that you would be under my control again in the end, did you?" After being rehabilitated in 1978, former Xiapo Commune Party Secretary Sun Sian went out of his way to look for a former challenger, Zhao Xianan from Mashan village, to tell him that while he now could ride in a jeep, Zhao still had to push a wheelbarrow.[9]

With the change in political climate, the rehabilitated former party leaders used regained official privileges for self-promotion. Rehabilitated former deputy secretary of Jimo County Party Committee Li Sili said: *"you quan bu shi, guoqi zuo fei"*(Use your power while you can).[10] This kind of political orientation was the prelude to the binge of "official gouge" which has prevailed in rural China during the 1980s and 1990s.[11] Officials soon discarded the ascetic principles they had been compelled to adopt during the Cultural Revolution years. Sun Xibao, former head of Jimo Grain Bureau, had accepted the Cultural Revolution's anti-elitist political culture. Four of his six children went to work in rural areas. When his youngest son, Sun Yingjin, graduated from rural high school in 1976, Sun Xibao asked him to take up the dirtiest and hardest job in the Third Production Team in South River Village, collecting night soil and applying it to fields as fertilizers. When his son showed some reluctance, Sun told him: "Other people can do it, why can't you? If you cannot do it by yourself in the beginning, I will help you." [12] However, in 1980 with the change of political climate, he found nice jobs in the government and factories for all of his children.[13]

Guo Yunlong, Party Secretary of South River Village, had worked with villagers three hundred days a year during the

Cultural Revolution decade. He ate in the fields with other villagers. Villagers noticed that his foods were often inferior to theirs because he had a big family.[14] His son also worked like everybody else in the fields. He had hesitated even to accept villagers' invitations to eat at wedding banquets, fearing that he might become the target of villagers' big character posters. When villagers had invited Guo to join them for drinks, his wife and children reminded him of the early criticisms of the rebels and warned him that those who invited him might have dishonest intentions. Guo's wife refused to allow Guo into the house at night if he drank at someone else's house.[15] But as the political climate changed in late 1970s, Guo changed too. When Deng Xiaoping promised that there would be no political campaigns in the future, Guo became bolder. After 1982, he began openly accepted bribes. He sold most of the village land to new development without consulting villagers, turning villagers into landless peddlers. He gave permission to more than one hundred outsiders, many of them relatives of upper government officials, to build new homes on village land. At the same time, he refused to allow many fellow villagers to build new homes on village land unless they gave him gifts.[16] In 1984, he bought a Toyota Crown car with village funds and used it like his personal vehicle. He managed to get his son into a junior college in Qingdao City. The village car was used to pick up his son at the school on weekends and bring him back to school at the beginning of the week.

With the change of political climate, the right to use big character posters was removed from the Chinese Constitution. Ordinary people could no longer criticize their leaders through big character posters and great debate. Corruption and abuse of power grew. People were angry but dared not speak up (*gan nu bu gan yan*). Attempts to use big character posters could be labeled as "starting another Cultural Revolution", which could have dire consequences. In 1996, one factory manager misused public funds. Somebody wrote an anonymous big character poster to expose the details. The factory manager was furious, and threatened in public to sue the writer of the poster. He suspected that the factory accountant was the writer, because the accountant knew the details of his illegal deals. The manager arbitrarily relieved the accountant of his responsibilities and sent him to do manual work in a workshop.[17]

The crisis in state enterprises that began in the 1980s is, in part, a product of the changes that freed enterprise directors from political control from above or below. While many enterprises cannot even find funds to pay workers, managers are getting fatter and fatter with their control of state resources. Press accounts have dubbed this phenomenon: *"qing miao fu fangzhang"* (poor temples with wealthy abbots).[18] Deng Xiaoping promoted the *changzhang fuzezhi* (manager responsibility) system, which put all authority in the hands of the managers. Under the new system, managers decided how much they would get paid and how much workers would get paid. They could dispose of public assets without being accountable to anybody. Since then, many managers in Jimo began riding in luxurious foreign cars, living in fancy houses, enjoying sumptuous banquets, frequenting exclusive nightclubs, and spending public money on expensive foreign tours. At the same time they refused to pay workers decent salaries. In many places workers have been laid off without reasonable compensation. In the capitalist West, at least, managers have to answer to a board of trustees, representatives of the owners. But Deng Xiaoping's reforms turned managers of state-owned enterprises into dictators who do not need to answer to anyone, least of all the workers, who are the so-called owners of the socialist enterprises. Workers in Jimo said that they were at the mercy of a new class of managers.[19]

In this situation, workers in some places began to sabotage the factories to protest mismanagement by their managers. The Jimo Meat Processing Factory was forced to close down when angry workers began to collectively steal products of the factory to protest the managers' mismanagement and stealing of factory funds.[20]

DISMANTLING THE COLLECTIVE ORGANIZATION

China scholars debate whether Deng Xiaoping's rural reforms were initiated from the top or the bottom.[21] Whether rural reforms were a bottom up or a top down development differed from place to place. China's rural collective system did not develop evenly. In some places it did poorly, in other places it did moderately well, while in other places it did very well. In places where collectives fared poorly, farmers did not mind changes or actively pursued changes. In places where collective farming fared well, farmers were more reluctant to change. In these places, collective farming had become a dependable way of life, and farmers' expectations were built around the collective as an important institution in their communities.

My research suggests that Jimo County was one of the places where collective farming had been successful during the Cultural Revolution years, despite the setbacks of collective farming during the Great Leap Forward period. Here the "household responsibility system," which was promoted by the Central Government in the early 1980s, was considered by many to be a reactionary measure imposed on Jimo farmers. Villagers said: *"xinxin kuku sanshi nian, yi yie huidao jiefang qian"* (we worked hard for thirty years to build up the collectives, but overnight we returned to the *status quo* before the liberation).[22] Many farmers in Jimo did not want to change their way of life. In fact, they were shocked by the government decision to disband the collectives on which important rural social security measures, education, and medical care depended. Initially, many villagers took the division of land as a signal that the CCP wanted to abandon them *(gongchan dang bu guan women le)*.[23] But the Deng Xiaoping government did not tolerate any hesitation in implementing its policies. In 1982, Jimo's county government leaders, together with the leaders of other seventeen other counties in Yantai district, were removed from office for dragging their feet in imposing the household responsibility system. These lower level government leaders resisted the individual household farming because they had close ties with farmers and knew what was going on in the villages.[24]

The Chinese press portrayed the adoption of the household responsibility system as a popular movement.[25] As this is the only version the official press carried, many people have taken for granted that individual house hold farming is universally popular among farmers. Needless to say, there were different attitudes and opinions regarding the division of land in any given locality. Even in places where collective farming did poorly, there were people who favored collective farming because they benefited from it. Fang Zhiyuan, from a relatively poor village in Jimo, said that without the collective his five children would not have had enough food and would not have had an education. During the collective years, his family constantly got relief grain and cash from the collective.[26] At the same time, in places where collective farming did well, there was a minority who preferred individual farming because they felt that collective farming had held them back and that their neighbors got more out of the collective than they did. One capable farmer from South River Village who had two able brothers said that if his family were allowed to farm alone, they would have gotten rich much earlier.[27]

It is inaccurate to say all Chinese farmers wanted individual household farming, just as it would be inaccurate to say that all people in the United States oppose welfare, affirmative action or abortion. Every farmer and every politician in China knew where Deng Xiaoping stood regarding agricultural policies in late 1970s. He had, after all, promoted contracting land to individual families in 1961, following the failure of the Great Leap Forward. The Deng Xiaoping governments used the action of eighteen farmers in a village in Fengyang County, Anhui Province to justify imposing a national policy of dismantling collectives on all the farmers of China, whatever their views.[28] There was no state-sanctioned public debate about the merits or shortcomings of either collective farming or the household responsibility system.

Chinese government leaders have always used a small group's

action to start big nation-wide movements. Collective farming started that way in the 1950s. For any policy or political move, there will be people for it and against it. With a tightly controlled press and propaganda machine, China's leaders need only support the side they want to support and suppress the other side to make any political move look like a spontaneous action on the part of the people. This was true with the establishment of the collective system, and was also true with the process of de-collectivization.

PROBLEMS ENGENDERED BY DISMANTLING THE COLLECTIVES

The Chinese government has portrayed the household responsibility system in a completely positive light. They seldom mention the setbacks Chinese farmers suffered as result of dissolution of the collectives. But there are very real setbacks, both in the organization of production and in the provision of education, medical care and other social services. The state leaders who promoted and demanded the dissolution of collectives, did not have to bear the direct consequences of their policies. Government officials all enjoyed job security, medical insurance, and retirement pensions, and their children have easy access to education at the time. They take these things for granted. But they never put themselves in the farmers' shoes. Before they were disbanded, collectives had become an important institution in rural life. Job security, medical insurance, old age safeguards and education in rural areas had all been built around this one institution.

Mechanization and the infrastructure of irrigation depended on the collective organization and both have faltered since the collectives were dismantled. In 1983, when land was divided among farmers in Jimo, most Jimo production brigades had adequate machinery to do basic farm work. The use of machines had reduced labor intensity in agriculture. After the land was divided into tiny pieces to be farmed by individual families, however, the use of big farm machines became problematic. For one thing, it was inefficient to use big machines on tiny plots. Secondly, it was very difficult to coordinate convenient and equitable use of the collective machines among several hundred individual households. Frustrated by the inequitable use of the collectively-owned machinery, farmers in some villages dismantled the tractors and divided the parts. In some extreme cases, villagers broke up the machinery and divided the scrap metal. Consequently, farmers have to do farm work manually again. This was one reason why some Jimo farmers needed their children to quit school to help them out in the fields after the household responsibility system was introduced.[29]

During the collective era, particularly during the Cultural Revolution decade, Jimo farmers worked very hard to build up an extensive irrigation system. As a result, farmers were less dependent on nature for a good harvest. However, these irrigation systems were planned and built during the collective era with collective farming in mind. With the division of land, unexpected problems arose. Some families' lands were closer to the irrigation facilities and they had easy and better access to these collective facilities. Other people's lands were further away from these irrigation facilities. They often had difficulties getting access to them. Since the division of land was mostly decided by lottery, individual farmers could not blame anybody — just "bad luck"—for having to farm a bad piece of land. But feelings of anger, frustration, and jealousy were common among villagers.[30] With the dismantling of the collectives, there was no efficient mechanism to coordinate an equitable and convenient use of the irrigation facilities. Villagers had to stand in line day and night to use the irrigation facilities. Sometimes there were fistfights over the use of these facilities.[31] Out of frustration and jealousy, farmers whose land is further away from the collective irrigation facilities began to sabotage these facilities.[32] In some villages, some people jammed the wells with stones. In other villages, the collective irrigation facilities deteriorated for lack of maintenance. It takes tremendous efforts to use and maintain these irrigation facilities efficiently under the conditions of private farming.[33]

Before Deng Xiaoping's rural reforms, Jimo's rural industrial enterprises were all owned and operated by the collectives. Workers in these industrial enterprises were paid in work points, the same way as farmers working in the fields and profits from these enterprises were distributed among farmers the same way crops were distributed. Managers and village party secretaries were paid the same amount of work points for a day's work as ordinary villagers. It was a very equitable system.[34] But with the division of land, the collectives did not exist any more. Management of these industrial enterprises was left in the hands of village party secretaries and the managers of the collective industrial enterprises. Frequently, these collective enterprises were rented to their managers for fixed rents decided by village party secretaries and managers of the collective industrial enterprises themselves. South River village, for example, rented its collective enterprises to the managers, Zhao Licheng and Guan Dunxiao, after 1984 for a fixed amount. In some other villages, the enterprises were sold to the managers. Despite the strong resistance of villagers, Yaotou Village sold its village enterprise to its managers.[35]

This practice changed the nature of rural industrial enterprises. Whether through renting or outright buying, the managers took complete control of the formerly collective enterprises. They had the right to hire or fire workers and to decide how much to pay workers. Workers lost their job security, medical insurance and job-related injury compensation. The managers of South River Village enterprises gradually replaced most village workers with outside workers. These owners did not want to invest money in safety measures. As a result, the work environment became hazardous. During the ten years from 1966 to 1976 when South River village operated its industrial enterprises collectively, there had been no major accidents involving personal injuries. But since the factory was privatized, there had been several serious accidents. One worker lost a hand while operating a sixty ton-press. He was a temporary worker from another village. The factory management blamed him for not following operation procedures; they only paid his medical bill and then kicked him out.[36] While managers have made millions with machines bought by the collectives, workers are working in dangerous conditions.[37] Today, ninety percent of those who are hired to work in the village factories are from outside the village. There are few laws protecting rural workers' rights in China, and workers are largely at the mercy of the factory managers.

THE IMPACT OF DE-COLLECTIVIZATION ON VILLAGE POLITICS

The division of land has provided Jimo villagers more freedom and flexibility regarding their economic activities. Farmers now decide what to grow and how much to invest in the land and they can dispose of their harvest freely. However, politically, the dissolution of the collective disempowered villagers. The power relationship in the rural areas was reshuffled by the dissolution of the collective. Unlike during the collective years when villagers worked together and shared common bonds because of their collective interests, villagers are now fragmented by issues concerning their own families as they farm their land separately[38] Villagers had been bound together by their common interests in the collective. After the collectives — the institutional framework that linked them together — were disbanded, villagers could not present a strong and coordinated voice, largely because there was no longer a public arena in the village.

The village party secretaries have gained most from the changes in power relations resulting from the division of land. During the Cultural Revolution decade, village party secretaries had to share decision making power with a number of production team leaders, and their power was also checked by a cohesive village population bound together by common public interests. The division of land eliminated the production team leaders — the most important check on village party secretaries — and also fragmented the village population, concentrating power in the hands of the village party secretaries. As village party secretaries became the sole power holders in the villages (despite the nominal existence of villagers' committees), the upper government's dependency on party secretaries to implement state policies also increased, thus further strengthening the position of the village party secretary.[39]

Changes in power relationships in the villages led to relapses towards pre-Cultural Revolution work styles among village party secretaries. In many cases, village politics has become a one-man show. Some party secretaries have closed down the village office and moved the office into their own house. Village party secretaries' houses often also served as village store houses. Public grains is stored in their houses and village money is kept in their personal accounts.[40] Thus the distinction between public and private has disappeared.

THE DECLINE OF RURAL EDUCATION

Rural education was a major casualty of Deng's reforms. In the decade after Deng came to power, rural schools were closed on a large scale and school attendance dropped precipitously. The sharp contraction of rural education was due both to the new central education policy — it was decided to close "poor quality" rural middle schools — and to the dismantling of rural collectives, which were the main economic support of the rural school system.

After 1978, the Central Government denounced the educational reforms introduced during the Cultural Revolution. Key schools at various levels were again established and resources were channeled to these key schools, which cater largely to the advantaged segments of urban Chinese society. Many rural schools, especially middle schools and high schools, were eliminated in the name of streamlining and quality control.

Rural education had largely been supported by the collective structure. Village schoolteachers were paid in work points the same way as villagers working in the fields. The burden of financing rural education thus was born collectively by the community. With the dissolution of China's rural collectives, rural teachers had to be supported by tuition, and the costs of education are now born by those who go to school. Most villages have little resources to support village schools.

During the Cultural Revolution decade, 98.5 percent school-age children in Jimo were in primary school, 90 percent were in middle school and over 70 percent were in high school.[41] Despite continuing economic growth since Deng came to power, far fewer rural children now have the opportunity to go to school. The attendance rate at all levels has declined. Many village primary schools closed down and children were forced to go to school in other places.[42] Rising tuition, the remote location of the remaining schools and the demands of family farming caused many rural families to decline to send their children to school.

Rural middle and high school education suffered most as a result of the rural reforms. The number of middle schools in Jimo decreased from 256 in 1976 to 106 in 1987. Many joint village middle schools were eliminated, because villages no longer had the resources to support the schools. Even though the population increased from 913,032,000 in 1976 to 1,000,481,000 in 1987, the size of the middle school first year class dropped from 29,660 in 1976 to 15,734 in 1987. The number of high schools dropped from eighty-nine in 1977 to eight in 1987. The high school first year class declined from 12,186 in 1977 to 1,935 in 1987.[43] By 1993, the number of Jimo middle schools had been reduced to fifty-eight, and the number of high schools had dropped to seven.[44]

Jimo's experience is typical of much of rural China. It has become more and more difficult for rural children to get an education since the rural reform. Millions of rural children lost the opportunity to go to school, swelling the ranks of a new illiterate generation.

Declining financial support for rural schools has made it impossible to provide decent facilities for learning. In some cases, over eighty students crowd into one rural classroom because of lack of funds to hire an extra schoolteacher and build an extra classroom. Because of lack of school furniture, some students have to kneel on the dirt floor of the classroom.[45] While reducing funding, the Central Government imposed tighter control over rural schools. Workers' and farmers' participation in managing schools was discontinued. Textbooks once again became standardized nationally. The national standardized textbooks put rural children at a great disadvantage because these textbooks focused mostly on urban life. At the same time, skills and knowledge that are useful in rural life have been taken out of the curriculum.

In 1977, the national college entrance examination was reintroduced and since then it has once again systematically drained talent from China's rural areas, in the same manner as before the Cultural Revolution. Talented rural children leave home to go to college and few return. The educational reforms of the Cultural Revolution had made serious efforts to link education with the needs of rural Jimo. The reinstitution of the college entrance examination system once again fundamentally changed the nature of rural high schools. Instead of being oriented to serve rural development, schools became an avenue to joining the urban elite. A high school education once again was valued mainly as a *qiaomen zhuan* (a brick to open the door for college). The reinstitution of the national college entrance exam was widely acclaimed by young people, especially those in cities. But few people paid any attention to the social cost and its impact on rural development.

In December 1977, more than two thousand high school graduates from the fifty villages in Chengguan Commune in Jimo

County sat for the first national college entrance examinations held for ten years. In the end, only one student succeeded. The success of this one person became known in every village household and school. Parents wanted their children to emulate him and teachers used him as an example to spur their students to study hard for the exams. Although the success rate was exceedingly low, the reward was high. just as a few farmers' children had succeeded in becoming officials through the imperial civil service examinations, students in rural China hoped success in the college entrance exam would allow them to jump from a low position in society to an official position upon graduation.[46]

Many young people quit their jobs and concentrated on preparing for the next entrance examination. High schools opened special classes for these college aspirants. Some young people went to these special classes for several years. Chen Xuqi from South River village, who graduated from high school in 1974, failed the exams in 1977, 1978 and succeeded in 1979. He spent two years preparing for the entrance examinations. Liu Qiang, graduated from high school in 1977, and sat in the college entrance examination for five years but never succeeded. He spent five years in the special preparation classes. Since what he studied in these special classes had nothing to do with real life, he did not learn any useful skills and later considered that he had wasted five years of his life. In the end his uncle, who was the president of the traffic police training school, got him into that school through the "back door."[47] Of course, the important thing here is not how many years a person spent in these special preparation classes, but whether an individual succeeds in the end. Those who failed after many attempts were failures, and those failed at first but succeeded in the end were still considered a success.[48] The problem is that too many failed, and too much time and energy had been wasted in the process.

The reinstitution of the college entrance examination had ramifications in other areas of rural life. As soon as the national entrance examination resumed, textbooks had to be standardized nationally, since students had to sit for the same examination. Since national standard textbooks are compiled mostly by experts from urban areas, local knowledge relevant to agriculture and rural development were sacrificed. Yao Qiancun, a farmer, complained that the national standard textbooks were out of touch with reality in rural life. Even though he had a primary school education, he could not understand what the first grade textbook was talking about. His twin daughters have repeated the first grade for three years.[49]

The divorce of school curriculum from rural life has put rural children in a disadvantaged position because it is harder to study subjects that have no connection with their lives. This in turn has also contributed to the change of orientation of education for rural children. For each individual family, education is a big investment. The family has to pay for the children's tuition, books, and other costs. If the children do well in school and have the potential to succeed in the college entrance examination, then the investment is worthwhile from the standpoint of individual families. But if the children do not do well in school, and have little chance to succeed in the college entrance examination, the families do not have an incentive to invest in their children's education. Frequently children who do not do well in school drop out, and their parents are only too happy to have an extra pair of hands to work on the family farm or to find a job in construction sites in the urban areas to earn extra income for the family.[50]

In this social climate, primary and middle school education lost their intrinsic value. They are valuable only in that they can pave the way for a college education. Parents see them this way, and primary and middle school students see them in a similar way. Many children drop out of primary school because they do not do well. Many parents encourage their children to drop out of primary school when they feel their children have no chance of getting to college.[51] From the viewpoint of local educational officials and teachers whose performance is measured by the number of students who succeed in the college entrance examination, there is great pressure to pay more attention to only the brightest children who have the greatest potential to succeed in the examination. Thus in order to achieve high success rates on the college entrance examination, schools and teachers often devote their energy to preparing the better students for the college entrance examination while ignoring the needs of other students. These measures make good sense from the perspective of individual schools and teachers. They also make good sense from the local educational officials' perspective. But such *credentialism* does not make good educational sense overall. In the final analysis, the quality of education has to be measured by how much students have learned and how useful students' knowledge is for society, rather than by how many students succeed in getting into colleges. In many rural schools, this practice of favoring a small number of good students hurt morale among ordinary students.[52]

THE COLLAPSE OF THE RURAL MEDICAL CARE SYSTEM AND THE "FIVE GUARANTEES"

The rural medical care system has suffered a fate similar to that of rural education. In 1983, after the collectives were dissolved, barefoot doctors in rural Jimo were renamed "rural doctors". Their service was no longer free, since the collective organization that supported these doctors was no longer there and they could no longer be paid in work points.[53] Village clinics became private medical practices. Villagers who fell ill and used the services of rural doctors had to pay the bills. The community medical insurance that was part of the previous barefoot doctor system was eliminated, so each rural family was left on their own.

The "five guarantees"(wu bao)—food, clothes, fuel, education and a funeral)[54] the collective had provided for old villagers and others who had no other support also disappeared with the dissolution of the collective. The economic foundation for the five guarantees had disappeared. Jimo farmers had never had formal pensions, as urban workers did. When the collective disappeared in 1983, many farmers who had worked for the collective for 25 years during their prime years found themselves having to depend on themselves for everything in their old age.

Song Guocheng and his wife from Yaozhuang had no children; they had worked for the collective all their lives. Their assumption was that when they reached old age, the collective would take care of them. However, since 1983 they had to farm their own share of land and pay a full share of the tax burden. In 1997, at the age of 85, Song Guocheng wondered what would happen to him and his wife if one day they could no longer work. Zhang Wangshi, a childless old woman from Guo Jiaxiang found life at age 92 unbearably hard. During the collective era, the collective always gave her a full share of grain and fuel. On the Chinese New Year and other holidays, she got a share of meat and fish from the collective plus a small sum of cash. After the land was divided in 1982, Zhang had to ask a neighbor to farm her share of land. But the neighbor had to keep half of the grain as compensation for farming the land. As Zhang could hardly live on her half share of the grain, she was reduced to begging and to soliciting help from neighbors and relatives. For lack of fat and oil in her diet, she had tremendous pain in emptying her bowels. In order to reduce her pain, she now has to go to a restaurant to collect the fat left on people's plates.[55]

There are only a few cases of childless villagers in each of Jimo's village, but their difficulties serve as a warning for other villagers. Witnessing the plight of these childless old folks, some farmers have defied the government's one-child policy and continued to have two or three children. They want to have at least one, better two, male children, not just to continue the family line but as security for their old age. What if something happens to their only male child? Jimo farmers have learned from their experiences that nothing provides a better economic security for old age than their own flesh and blood, and the removal of collective guarantees has prompted them to accentuate this safeguard.

To be fair to the Central Government, it had to impose a tough population policy on the people. Given the grave population situation in China, it had no other option but to restrict population growth. But farmers need security for their old age. If the government does not provide farmers any security, farmers will have no other choice but to find their own security. This is why despite the extreme family planning measures in the rural areas, including cutting off supplies of electricity and water, dismantling houses, heavy fines and physical punishment, Chinese farmers continue to have more than one child. Farmers' desire to have more children under today's private farming is completely justified. Why should they obey a government policy that completely disregards their need for security in old age?

Farmers' tendencies to have more children will have long term dire consequences for China and for the world. Even though Chinese leaders claim that China will have sufficient food in the future, the claim is no more than wishful thinking. Already they are importing more grain. China has been blessed with favorable weather conditions for quite a number of years, and its agricultural performance has been good. But if weather conditions take a turn for the worse, food shortages are still a possibility. In 1997, Northern China had a very good wheat harvest. But Jimo farmers, like farmers in other parts of Shandong and Henan Provinces, were not able to plant the fall crops because of serious drought. Individual farmers' ability to deal with adverse weather conditions is very limited.[56]

Moreover, unlike during the collective era when tax burdens were born by the collective, individual farmers have to pay taxes. The new taxation system in rural China is very regressive. The tax burden is not based on farmers' income but on the amount of land they farm. Consequently, the bigger a farmer's income, the smaller the tax burden as a percentage of his income. Vice versa, the smaller a villager's income, the bigger the tax burden he has to pay as a percentage of his income.[57] For example, Farmer A and Farmer B farm the same amount of land. But because Farmer A has more people working in his family, some outside of agriculture, he has a diversified total income of 10,000 yuan. Farmer B has more dependents and fewer people working in his family. Even though he farms the same amount of land, his family income is only 5,000 yuan. As Farmer A and Farmer B both have to pay 1,000 yuan tax. Farmer A with his larger income is paying only ten percent of his income as tax, while Farmer B with his smaller income has to pay 20 percent of his total income as tax.

Tax policy, like other aspect of de-collectivization is promoting economic polarization in villages. This, of course, is the intended outcome. Deng Xiaoping himself expressed the view that a small segment of the population should get rich first, so that this small segment of the population could then lead the whole society towards progress. This was a good reflection of Deng Xiaoping's elitist mentality. The problem is that in many villages I have studied, this small segment of population happens to be people who had power and connections and that their self-enrichment often take places at the expense of the majority.

VESTIGES OF POLITICAL EMPOWERMENT

Despite his persecution in the period of political retaliation after Mao Zedong's death, Lan Chengwu, one of the middle school rebels who initiated the Cultural Revolution in Jimo, remains undaunted. In South River Village, Lan Chengwu, is still dreaded by the village officials because of his political skills. In fact, Lan continues to publicly denounce the village party secretary for accepting bribes, and warned him that one day he would go to the party secretary's door to intercept the bribes. One day in March 1996, at a village mass meeting called by county and township officials, Lan Chengwu embarrassed the village party secretary by exposing his practice of demanding bribes in allocating building lots. The county and township officials were forced to investigate the matter, and had to dismiss the party secretary in question when the allegation was confirmed by the investigation.[58]

Village leaders call people like Lan Chengwu a *"ding zihu"* (defiant household). By *ding zihu* they refer to people who pose obstacles to "normal official business."[59] It seems there are two kinds of *ding zihu* in rural China. One kind of *ding zihu* bully both their neighbors and defy village leaders because they have large and powerful families. This kind of *ding zihu* resorts to force rather than reason. Law enforcement is very weak in rural China today and they can usually have their way, because they have big families and strong clans behind them. This kind of *ding zihu is* dreaded by village leaders, but even more by ordinary people. These bullies know that the state is behind the village leaders and if they go too far in defying village leaders the state can intervene. But it is a different story with ordinary villagers. *Ding Zihu* can beat up villagers without serious consequences, because it is costly and time consuming for the victims to bring them to court, and arbitration frequently only requires that the bully pay the medical bills of the victim. The sad thing is that in some villages, these *ding zihu* bullies often have usurped village power.[60]

People like Lan Chengwu are a second kind of *ding zihu*. They do not have big or powerful families. But they have a daring spirit of popular resistance and effective political skills. They do not bully their neighbors, but they cause a lot of headaches for village party leaders. To local villagers they are an important political resource. They understand China's political process and operations. When it is necessary, they are not afraid to confront village leaders because they believe they have nothing to lose. They also have found that higher government leaders often cannot openly protect guilty village leaders.[61]

How much does the phenomenon of the second kind of *ding zihu* have to do with the political empowerment of villagers during the Cultural Revolution and with the educational reforms of that period? The second kind of *ding zihu* share a common background: they went to high school during the Cultural Revolution and were active participants in the movement. Lan Chengwu and Liu Zhiyuan, the two most prominent *ding zihu* in South River village, were both educated during the Cultural Revolution.[62] They acquired their political skills during this era, and they have a good grasp of the declared values, philosophies and codes of official conduct of the Communist Party.[63]

Liu Zhiyuan used his knowledge about government policies to challenge village authorities. Instead of bribing the village party secretary for a building lot like many others, he investigated the village party secretary's practice of accepting bribes in allocating building lots, and exposed it at the mass meeting when township officials were present. His fighting spirit won him a reputation among villagers. When a new village party branch committee was formed, the first thing the new party secretary did was to set up a villagers' representative committee. He invited both Liu Zhiyuan and Lan Chengwu to join this representative committee and asked the committee to express their opinions on policy issues.[64] In this way, he attempted to preempted challenges from people like Liu Zhiyuan and Lan Chengwu.

In the contemporary period, people like Liu Zhiyuan and Lan Chengwu are a democratic force in the rural areas, checking the power of village leaders. They represent a legacy of the political empowerment of ordinary villagers brought about by the Cultural Revolution.

Notes

1. Interview with villagers in Jimo, summer, 1997.
2. Interview with villagers in Jimo, summer, 1997.
3. Interview with former CCP officials in Jimo, summer, 1997.
4. Interview with former rebel leaders in Jimo, summer, 1997.
5. Interview with Xu Jiankang, summer, 1994. Xu is in the United States now. When the Gang of Four was arrested he was visiting

Beijing. He told one of the rebel leaders from Luoyang the news, later he was arrested because he passed the news to local rebels. Later he was released, but he was denied the opportunity to sit for the examinations for college entrance examination and graduate school.

6.   *Jimo xianzhi,* 54.
7.   *Jimo xianzhi,* 56,
8.   Interview with members of teams that investigated former rebel activists, summer 1995.
9.   In 1975 Zhao had challenged his village party secretary Sun Sian, who was then party secretary of the commune to which Zhao's village belonged, had called in police to arrest Zhao. While in prison, Mr. Zhao wrote to Jiang Qing for help. With Jiang Qing's help, an investigation team freed Zhao and removed Sun Sian from office for wantonly arresting Zhao. Interview with former rebel leaders in Jimo, summer, 1997.
10. Interview with Jimo residents, 1990.
11. *Guo qi zuo fei* (expires upon ....) is a phrase printed on many tickets and coupons in China. Here the person made a pun stretching the meaning of the term.
12. Interview with farmers in Jimo, summer, 1997.
13. Interview with villagers in Jimo, summer, 1990.
14. In order to save time, villagers often ate two to three meals in the fields, the breakfast, lunch and sometimes supper during the Cultural Revolution years. Each family was responsible for providing meals for their own workers, and production team provided boiled water and also brought the meals to the field where villagers were working.
15. Interview with villagers in Jimo, summer, 1997.
16. Interview with villagers in Jimo, summer, 1997.
17. Interview with workers in Jimo, summer, 1997.
18. Zhang Yan, " *Guan Yu 'Qing Miao Fu Fangzhang' Xianxiang de Pao Xi yu* Sikao," (An Analysis of the Phenomenon of Rich Managers but Poor Factories) *People's Daily,* March 21, 1997.
19. Interview with workers in Jimo, summer, 1997.
20. Interview with workers in Jimo, summer, 1997.
21. Kate Xiao Zhou in *How the Farmers Changed China* (Boulder: Westview Press, 1996), Daniel Kelliher in *Peasant Power in China* (New Haven: Yale University Press, 1992), and to a lesser degree Vivienne Shue in *The Reach of the State* (Stanford: Stanford University Press, 1988), emphasized the bottom up nature of the reforms. David Zweig, in *Freeing China's Farmers* (New York: M.E. Sharpe, 1997), and Thomas Bernstein, in his chapter in *Driven by Growth* (James Morley, ed., New York: M.E. Sharpe, 1993), see a more balanced development.
22. Interview with villagers, summer, 1990.
23. Interview with villagers, summer, 1990.
24. Interview with former rebel leaders, summer, 1997.

25. Chinese press and mass media were filled with government propaganda and elite reports about the popularity of the household responsibility system among rural people.
26. Interview with villagers, summer, 1997.
27. Interview with villagers in Jimo, 1997.
28. Su Qingli, "The Household Responsibility System," *China and the World*, October, 1997.
29. Interview with villagers in Jimo, summer, 1990.
30. Interview with villagers in Jimo, Summer, 1997.
31. Interview with villagers in Jimo, summer, 1990.
32. Interview with villagers in Jimo, summer, 1990.
33. Interview with villagers in Jimo, summer, 1997.
34. Interview with villagers in Jimo, summer, 1997.
35. Interview with villagers in Jimo, summer, 1997. The story of this worker was contrasted to that of a villager killed while working on a reservoir project in 1972. Zhang Zilin, a villager from South River, was killed by falling stones. The village paid for his funeral and continued to pay his wife and his baby daughter until his wife decided to leave the village to remarry. Such a scenario is not possible for the families of workers who encounter a similar fate today.
36. Interview with villagers in Jimo, summer, 1997.
37. Interview with villagers in Jimo, summer, 1997.
38. Interview with villagers in Jimo, summer, 1997.
39. As Kevin J. O'Brien and Lianjiang Li have shown, township government leaders tend to protect and support village party secretaries in the latter's disputes with ordinary villagers under the new conditions. Kevin O'Brien and Liangjiang Li, "The Politics of Lodging Complaints in Rural China," *China Quarterly*, September 1995, 772.
40. Interview with villagers in Jimo, summer, 1997.
41. This was the figure throughout the 1970s in Jimo County. See *Jimo xianzhi*, the Education Volume.
42. Interview with villagers in Jimo, summer, 1997.
43. *Jimo xianzhi*, 704-705.
44. *Jimo Tongji Nianjian*, 1994 (Jimo Year Book, 1994)
45. I saw this with my own eyes during my research trip in the rural areas.
46. See Wu Jingzi, *Yulin Waishi (Scholars)* (Beijing: People's Publishing House, 1991) 32-50.
47. Interview with villagers in Jimo, summer, 1997.
48. Interview with villagers in Jimo, summer, 1997
49. Interview with villagers in Jimo, summer, 1997.
50. Interview with schoolteachers in Jimo, summer, 1997.
51. Interview with villagers in Jimo, summer, 1997.
52. Interview with school teachers and students, 1990.
53. *Jimo xianzhi*, 54.
54. These five guarantees were stipulated by the "Guidelines for

Agricultural development 1956-1967."
55. Interview with villagers in Jimo, summer, 1997.
56. *"Huang He Di Yici Quan Nian Gan Ku,* (For the First Time, the Yellow Rive Is Dry all Year Around in Some Area)" *The World Journal,* November 6, 1997.
57. Interview with villagers in Jimo, summer, 1997.
58. Interview with villagers in Jimo, summer, 1997.
59. Interview with villagers in Jimo Summer, 1997.
60. Interview with villagers in Jimo, summer, 1997.
61. Interview with villagers in Jimo, summer, 1997.
62. Interview with Villagers in Jimo, summer, 1997.
63. Kevin O'Brien and Li Liangjiang refer to this aspect of the *ding zihu* phenomenon in "The Politics of Lodging Complaints Protest in Rural China," *China Quarterly,* September 1995, No. 143, 763.
64. Interview with villagers in Jimo, summer, 1997.

Conclusion

Standard Chinese government accounts maintain that rapid economic growth in rural China began with the political ascendancy of Deng Xiaoping in 1978 and the ensuing market reforms. In these accounts, Deng's reforms rescued China, including its rural population, from a decade of economic disaster caused by the Cultural Revolution. This disaster, the story goes, resulted from an overemphasis on the collective economy, vengeful political campaigns that persecuted party officials and intellectuals, contempt for educational standards and institutions, and an overzealous pursuit of egalitarian goals. This investigation of the history of Jimo County has challenged this official account. The take-off of the rural economy in Jimo began not with market reforms, I have shown, but rather during the Cultural Revolution decade. Agricultural production more than doubled and a network of rural factories were established which fundamentally transformed the county's rural economy in less than ten years.

Jimo's story is not unique. The years between 1966 and 1976 were ones of substantial economic development in most of rural China. Rural production statistics might persuade an observer to doubt the government account, while still believing that the Cultural Revolution itself was antithetical to economic development. The rural economy, one might be inclined to believe, developed *despite* the Cultural Revolution. Perhaps the turmoil of the Cultural Revolution simply did not have much impact on the countryside. This study comes to the opposite conclusion: economic development in the countryside was facilitated by political and cultural changes brought about by the Cultural Revolution. These changes included a change in political culture that allowed ordinary villagers to challenge party officials, promoted a collective work ethic that required cadre participation in manual labor and provided for local initiative and the participation of villagers in economic decision making. The Cultural Revolution also led to the reform of the elite-oriented education system that had denied most rural children a chance to finish school, while siphoning talent out of the countryside. The rapid construction of village schools during the Cultural Revolution decade gave all rural children a chance to learn to read and write as well as practical agricultural and industrial skills, facilitating economic development.

Rapid economic growth has continued in Jimo in the period after 1978. Market reforms — and the changes in incentive structures and economic flexibility that they brought — undoubtedly have been a part of this story, especially in Jimo, which enjoys geographic advantages in attracting capital and finding markets. But there is reason to doubt the official claim that market reforms are the entire explanation. The educational advances, infrastructure improvements, and rural industrial enterprises that made rapid economic growth possible during the Cultural Revolution decade clearly continued to have an impact. Once it has been established that the economic take-off began during the collective era, the claims of market reformers have to be put in perspective.

Market economies can be extraordinarily dynamic. The continued rapid growth of the Jimo economy in the market reform decades offers further proof of this truism of the modern age. The decline of mechanization and difficulties in maintaining collectively-developed irrigation systems, however, raise questions about the sustainability of agrarian development through small-scale farming organized increasingly through the market. Even more troubling is declining access to medical care and education in the wake of de-collectivization. The sharp contraction of the rural education system, in particular, cannot but present a serious long-term obstacle to development.

Jimo's experience during the Cultural Revolution decade shows that collectively-organized economies can also be dynamic and achieve rapid economic development. The factors that made agricultural modernization possible — irrigation, mechanization, experimentation and chemical fertilizer — were all developed through the concentration of resources brought about by collective organization. Collective organization also provided the initial foundations of rural industry. The long-term tendency towards agricultural involution in rural China, diagnosed by Philip Huang, was actually broken and true economic development began during the collective era. The fundamental turn was made during the Cultural Revolution decade.

Like market economies, collective economies also have internal contradictions, all of which were encountered in China during the collective era. Ambiguous incentive structures and lack of flexibility presented serious economic problems. This study has focused on the political and cultural problems encountered. One of my central arguments is that a collective economy cannot function well without a democratic political culture and institutions that empower ordinary farmers and workers. The Chinese Communist Party was able to transform the ownership of the land and other means of production in China in the course of a few years. The transformation of political culture proved to be a more intractable problem.

The Cultural Revolution was an attempt to address this problem. It was an intensive and extensive social revolution aimed at changing people's social consciousness, the parallel of which is hard to find in history. It attempted to enhance collective organization by challenging autocratic political authority within the collective. Big character posters widely used by villagers proved to be an important media of political communication between villagers and village leaders. The mass associations, public debate and mass meetings provided an important public forums to put matters of public interests onto the agenda. To a great extent, the political culture in the rural area had been significantly changed in the rural areas. Farmers were no longer timid, submissive as they used to be. They were empowered by the experience of the Cultural Revolution to constantly keep village leaders in line.

The consolidation of the collective institutions during the Cultural Revolution cultivated a very different public spirit in the rural life. Corruption among village leaders was greatly reduced. Village, commune and county leaders were required to work with farmers on a regular basis. By the end of the Cultural Revolution, both leaders and common people began to take that practice for granted. This practice in turn reinforced the public spirit of the time. The social vices like official corruption, prostitution, drug abuse, fake products and others that plague Chinese society today were completely absent at the end of the Cultural Revolution.

More importantly, the Cultural Revolution denounced the old educational philosophy that served to distinguish an educated elite from farmers and workers. Exclusive bookish learning that used mainly the rote method was opposed. During the educational reforms, the concept of education was greatly broadened to include productive labor and many other related activities. Education was no longer limited to reading books inside the classroom; learning could take place in the workshops and on the farms, and many other places. Teachers were not considered to have a monopoly on knowledge. Workers and farmers and soldiers could all impart experiential knowledge to students. In fact, even students might know something the teachers did not know. The Cultural Revolution in the countryside also denounced teachers' rigidity and tyranny in the classroom. It tried to place teachers and students on a more equal basis, encouraging teachers to treat students with affection and students to treat teachers with respect. But I realized during my research how hard old ways die.

As soon as Deng Xiaoping came back to power, he denounced the Cultural Revolution and reversed its reforms. Deng had the power to do whatever he wanted. But more important, he was supported by the persistence of traditional philosophies and practices that had been challenged during the Cultural Revolution, and by people who stood to benefit by the restoration of the old ways, or thought they would.

One of the first things Deng Xiaoping did was to outlaw the *sida* (big character posters, the great debate, the great airing and great political freedom). He also announced that there would be no more political campaigns, which was like to give the officials a guarantee that they would not be harassed by the masses even they were corrupt. Many officials slipped into their corrupt old ways very quickly. In Jimo many officials said that *you chuan bu shi guo qi zuofei* (use your power while you still have it. You won't be able to use it once you lose it).

During the Cultural Revolution years, government officials worked with farmers and workers, and sent their children to work with farmers and workers. Everybody regard it as normal practice. As soon as the political climate changes, officials ceased to work with farmers, and they began to look after their families. They found their children better jobs, and put them in important positions. That was how the official corruption started in China since the reform.

Deng revived the old education philosophy. Education reforms introduced during the Cultural Revolution were wiped out overnight. He was supported by an educated elite who clung to the old educational philosophy and practices. Many teachers began to feel that they were mistreated during the Cultural Revolution. In fact, the distance between teachers and the members of less educated social strata, including many of their students, was reduced. Confucian ideas that a good education should pave the way for an official career, and that schooling is above everything else have proven very resilient. Many old intellectuals did not like the idea that education should interact with society. Many farmers and workers also cherished the idea that their children might one day become members of the elite through education. Therefore, Deng's denunciation of the Cultural Revolution educational reform initially struck a responsive chord among these people.

It takes a perspective beyond the individual level and often takes some time before one can realize the social consequences of distinct political, economic and cultural policies. This book has tried to explore the policies promoted by proponents and opponents of the Chinese Cultural Revolution from such a perspective.

The Chinese government's official evaluation of the Cultural Revolution serves to underline the idea, currently very much in vogue around the world, that efforts to achieve development and efforts to attain social equality are contradictory. The remarkable currency of this idea in China and internationally is due, at least in part, to the fact that such an idea is so convenient to those threatened by efforts to attain social equality. This study of the history of Jimo County has challenged this idea. During the Cultural Revolution decade and in the two decades of market reform that followed, Jimo has experienced alternative paths, both of which have led to rural development. The difference in the paths was not between development and stagnation but rather between different kinds of development. The main conclusion I hope readers will draw from the experience of Jimo County during the Cultural Revolution decade is that measures to empower and educate people at the bottom of society can also serve the goal of economic development. It is not necessary to choose between pursuing social equality and pursuing economic development. The choice is whether or not to pursue social equality.

Bibliography

Sources in Chinese

Baxian Xianzhi Committee. *Baxian Xianzhi* (Baxian Local Records) Shijiazhuang: Hebei People's Press, 1989.

Chinese Communist Party Central Committee. "Resolution on Questions in the History of our Party since the Founding of People's Republic of China." *A Collection of CCPs Documents.* Beijing: People's Publishing House, 1983.

Chuansha Xianzhi Committee. *Chuansha Xianzhi* (Chuansha Local Records) Shanghai: Shanghai People's Press, 1992.

Fushan Quzhi Committee. *Fushan Quzhi* (Fushan Local Records) Jinan: Qilu Press 1989.

Haiyang Xianzhi Committee. *Haiyang Xianzhi* (Haiyang Local Records) Haiyang Haiyang Press, 1987.

Huanghua Xianzhi Committee. *Huanghua Xianzhi* (Huanghua Local Records)Huanghua: Haichao Publishing House, 1990.

Jimo County Records Committee (d*ifangzhi weiyunhui),* Jimo xianzhi. Jimo: Xinshuachang, 1987. (uncensured version) Volume *3, Ju Min,* (Population) Volume 5, *Nong* Ye, (Agriculture) Volume *6, Shui* Li, (Irrigation) Volume 71, Yu Ye, (Fishery) Volume 8, *Gong* Ye, (Industry) Volume 9, *Xiang Zhen Qi Ye,* (Rural Industry) Volume 19, *Dang Pai she tuan,* (Political Parties and organizations) Volume 20, *Zheng Quan Zheng Xie,* (Political Power and Political consultation) Volume 27, *Jiao Yu,* (Education) Volume 28, *Ke Ji,* (Science and Technology) Volume 34, *Zaji,* (The Miscellaneous) Volume 35, Buji, (Supplementary Materials)

Jimo County Records Committee *(difangzhi weiyunhui), Jimo xianzhi.* Beijing:Xinghua Publishing House, 1991.

Jimo Local Records' Committee (Difangzhi Weiyuanhui), *Jimo Da Shi Ji*(Chronology of Events in Jimo), Jimo: Xinhua Yinshuachang, 1987.

Jiuyu Gemin Wenxuan (A Collection of Articles on Educational Revolution(Internal Documents)

Linzi Quzhi Committee. *Linzi Quzhi* (Linzi Local Records) Beijing: International Cultural Press, 1988.

Liu Yingji. *Zhongguo guanwenbua de than jizhe yu pipanfia: Kongzi yu Mao Zedong* (The Founder and Critics of Chinese Culture of Officialdom—Confucius and Mao Zedong) Jinan: Shandong People's Press, 1994)

Mao, Zedong. *Mao Zedong Xuanzhi,* (Selected works of Mao Zedong). BeijingPeople Publishing House, 1964.

Meishan Xianzhi Committee. *Meishan Xianzhi* (Meishan Local Records) Chengdu:Sichuan People's Press, 1992.

Pingdu Xianzhi Committee. *Pingdu Xianzhi* (Pingdu Local Records) Qingdao:Baozhuang Press, 1987.

Pujiang Xianzhi Committee. *Pujiang Xianzhi* (Pujiang Local Records) Hangzhou:Zhejiang People's Publishing House, 1985.

Qihe Xianzhi Committee. *Qihe Xianzhi* (Qihe Local Records) Beijing: Zhenghua Press, 1988.

Qingzhou Shizhi Committee. *Qingzhou Shizhi* (Qingzhou City Records) Tianjing:Nankai University Press, 1988.

Qixia Xianzhi Committee. *Qixia Xianzhi* (Qixia Local Records) Jinan: ShandongPeople's Publishing House, 1990.

Sunxian Xianzhi Committee. *Sunxian Xianzhi* (Sun Xian Local Records) Zhengzhou: Zhongzhou Guji Press, 1990.

Tongxian Xianzhi Committee. *Tongxian Xianzhi* (Tongxian Local Records) Beijing: Zhenghua Press, 1989.

Wang, Nianyi. *Da Donglun De Nian Dai.* (The Era of Great Chaos) Henan: People's Publishing House, 1993.

Wuchanjiejie Wenhua Dagemin Shenli Wansui (Long Live the Victory Of Great Proletarian Cultural Revolution. (Internal Documents)

Wuchanjieji Wenhua Dagemin Zhengyao Shelun Wenzhang Huibian (A Collection of Important Editorials and Articles of Great Proletarian Cultural Revolution. (Internal Documents) Vol. I to Vol. 6.

Yan, Jiaqi and Gao Gao. *Wenhua Da Gemin Shinianshi.* (The Ten Year History of the Cultural Revolution) Tianjin: People's Publishing House, 1986.

Yanggu Xianzhi Committee. *Yanggu Xianzhi* (Yanggu Local Records) Beijing Zhanghua Press, 1990.

Yanshan Xianzhi Committee. *Yanshan Xianzhi* (Yanshan Local Records) Tianjing: Nankai University Press, 1991.

Zichuna Xianzhi Committee. *Zichuan Xianzhi* (Zichuan Local Records) Jinan: Qilu Press, 1990.

Sources in English

Ballantine, Jeanne H. *Schools and Society.* London: Mayfield Publishing Company, 1985.

Bannister, Judith. *China's Changing Population.* Stanford: Stanford University Press, 1987.

Barcata, Louis. *China in the Throes of the Cultural Revolution.* New York: Hart Publishing Company, Inc. 1968.

Barnett, A. Doak. *China After Mao.* Princeton: Princeton University Press, 1967.

Barnouin, Barbara and Yu Changgen. *Ten Years of Turbulence- Chinese Cultural Revolution.* London: Kegan Paul International, 1993.

Baum, Richard. *Prelude to Revolution.* New York: Columbia University Press, 1975.

Bennett, Gordon, and Ronald Montaperto, *Red Guard,* New York: Anchor Books, 1972.

Blecher, Marc. *China–Politics, Economics and Society.* London: Frances printer, 1986.

Borthwick, Sally. *Education and Social Change in China.* Stanford: Stanford University of Stanford Press, 1983.

Bramall, Chris. *In Praise of Maoist Economic Planning.* Oxford: Clarendon Press, 1993.

Carnoy, Martin and Joel Samoff. *Education and Social Transition in the Third World.* Princeton: Princeton University Press, 1990.

Chao, Tsung. *An Account of the Cultural Revolution.* Hong Kong: Union Press, 1971.

Chen, Jerome. *Mao and the Chinese Revolution.* London: Oxford University Press, 1965.

Chesneaux, jean. "My Forty Years of Chinese History." *The Australian Journal of Chinese Affairs,* No.22, July 1989.

Chung, Hua-min and Arthur C. Miller. *Madame Mao.* Hong Kong: Union Research Institute, 1968.

Dietrich, Craig. *People's China.* Oxford: Oxford University Press,1986.

Dittmer, Lowell. *Liu Shao-chi and the Chinese Cultural Revolution–The. Politics of Mass Criticism.* Berkeley: University of California Press, 1974.

Du, Ruqing. *Chinese Higher Education: A Decade of Reform and Development (1978-1988)* London, 1992.

Epstein, Irving. "Class and Inequality in Chinese Education," *Compare, Vol.* 23, No. 2 1993. pp131-147.

—*Chinese Education: Problems, Policies and Prospects*. New York: Garland Publishing, Inc. 1991.

Fan, K. H. and K. T. Fan. *From the Other Side of the River.* New York: Anchor Books, 1975.

—*The Chinese Cultural Revolution: Selected Documents*. New York: MR Press, 1968.

Foley, Griff. "A 'democratic moment': Political Education in the Chinese Liberation Struggle," *International Journal of Lifelong Education. Vol* 12, No. 4 1995 pp323-342.

Friedman, Edward, Paul G. Pickowicz, and Mark Selden. *Chinese Village, Socialist State,* New Haven: Yale University Press, 1991.

—"The Flaws and Failure of Mao Zedong's Communist Fundamentalism," *The Australian Journal of Chinese Affairs*. No. 18, Jul 1987.

—"(Mao) The Innovator." in Dick Wilson Ed. *Mao Tsetung in the Scale of History.* London: Cambridge University Press, 1977.

Gao, Yuan. *Born Red.* Stanford: Stanford University Press, 1987.

Hayhoe, Ruth. *Education and Modernization——Chinese Experience.* New York Pergamon Press, 1992.

Hsu, Immanuel C.Y.. *China without Mao,* Oxford: Oxford University press,1982.

Huang, Philip C. C. "Rural Class Struggle in the Chinese Revolution— Representational and Objective Realities from the Land Reform to The Cultural Revolution." *Modern China. Vol.* 2 1, No. 1, January 1995. 105-143.

—*The Peasant Family and Rural Development in the Yangzi Delta, 1350-1988.* Stanford: Stanford University Press, 1990.

Karsnow, Stanley. *Mao and China,* New York: The Viking Press, 1972.

Kelliher, Daniel. *Peasant Power in China.* New Haven: Yale University Press, 1992.

Kwong, Julia. "In Pursuit of Efficiency," *Modern China, Vol.* 13, No. 2, April 1987 226-256.

-*Chinese Education in Transition.* Montreal: McGill-Queens University

Press, 1979.

-*Cultural Revolution in China's Schools, May 1966-April 1969.* Stanford: Hoover Institution Press, 1988.

Lampton, David. Policy *Implementation in Post-Mao China.* Berkeley: University of California Press, 1987.

Leary, Oreg and Andrew Watson. "Current Trend of China's Agricultural Strategy." *The Australian Journal of Chinese Affairs.* No.4 (1988): 119-166.

Leys, Simon. *The Burning Forest.* New York: Henry Holt and company, 1986.

—*Broken Images.* New York: St. Martin's Press, 1979.

—*The Chairman's New Clothes—Mao and The Cultural Revolution.* New York: Allison and Busby, 1981.

Liang, Heng and Judith Shaprio. *Son of Revolution.* New York: Afred A Knopf, 1983.

Lieberthal, Kenneth. *Governing China: From Revolution Through Reform.* New York: W.W. Norton & Company, Inc. 1995.

Lifton, Robert Jay. *Revolutionary Immortality—Mao Tse-Tung And the Chinese Cultural Revolution.* New York: Random House, 1968.

—*Thought Reform and the Psychology of Totalism.* New York: W. W. Norton & Company. Inc. 1961.

Liu, T. C. and Wei-ming Tu. *Traditional China.* Englewood Cliffs: Prentice-Hall, 1970.

Madsen, Richard. *Morality and Power in a Chinese Village,* Berkeley: University of California Press, 1984.

MacFarquhar, Roderick. *Origins of the Cultural Revolution, Vol. 2: The Great Leap Forward 1958-1960,* New York: Columbia University Press, 1983.

Mauger, Peter. "Changing Policy and Practice in Chinese Rural Education." *China Quarterly vol.* 93 No. 2. 139-148.

Meisner, Maurice. *'Mao' China,* New York: The Free Press, 1979.

Mosher, Steven W. *Broken Earth—The Rural China.* New York: The Free Press, 1983.

Munro, Donald. *The Concept of Man in Contemporary China.* An Arbor: the University of Michigan Press, 1977.

Nathan, Andrew. *China's Crisis—Dilemmas of Reform and Prospects for*

Democracy. New York: Columbia University Press, 1990.

Ng, Pedro Pak-Tao. "Open-Door Education in Chinese Communes—Rationale, Problems, and Recent Changes," *Modern China. Vol.* 6 No. 3, July 327-356.

Nie, Cheng. *Life and Death in Shanghai.* New York: Grove Press, 1987.

Obrien, Kevin and Liangjiang Li. "Politics of Lodging Complaints in Rural China, *China Quarterly,* No. 143; September, 1995.

Pepper, Suzanne. *Radicalism and Education Reform in 20th Century China.* Oxford:Cambridge University Press, 1996

Pye, Lucian. *The Spirit of Chinese Politics.* Cambridge: Harvard University Press, 1992.

—"An Introductory Profile: Deng Xiaoping and China's Political Culture" *China Quarterly,* No. 135, September, 1993. 412-443.

—"Rethinkingthe Man in the Leader," *The China journal,* January 1996.107-113.

Rafferty, Max. *Suffer, Little Children.* New York: Signet Books, 1963,

Reed, Gay Garland. "Looking in the Chinese Mirror: Reflecting on Moral-Political Education in the United States," *Educational Policy Vol.* 9, No. 3 Sept. 1995 pp.244-259.

Rosen, Stanley. "Obstacles to Educational Reform in China, *"Modern China, Vol.* 8 No. 1 January 1982, 3-40.

—"Recentralization, Decentralization and Rationalization—Deng Xiaoping's Bifurcated Educational Policy." *Modern China Vol. 11* No.3 July 1985, 301-346.

—"Restoring Key Secondary Schools," David M. Lampton Ed. Policy *Implementation in Post-Mao China.* Berkeley: University of California Press, 1987, 321-354.

Rousseau, Jean-Jacques. *Emile or On Education.* New York: Basic Books, 1979.

Rozman, Gibert. Ed. *The Modernization of China,* New York: The Free Press 1981.

School Boys of Barbiana. *Letter to A Teacher.* New York: Vintage Books, 1971.

Shue, Vivienne. *The Reach of the State: Sketch of the Chinese Body Politic,* Stanford: Stanford University Press, 1988.

Solomon, Richard H. *Mao's Revolution and the Chinese Political Culture.*

Berkeley: University of California Press, 1971.

Stevenson, Harld and James W. Stigler. *The Learning Gap: Why our Schools are Failing and What We can Learn from Japanese and Chinese Education.* New York: Summit Books, 1992.

Su, Zhixin. "A Critical Evaluation of John Dewey's Influence on Chinese Education." *American Journal of Education.* 103, May 1995. 302-325.

—"Science Education Goals and Curriculum Designs in American And Chinese High Schools." *International Review of Education. Vol. 41,* No. 5 pp 371-388.

Terrill, Ross. *China Profile.* New York: Friendship Press, 1969.

—Ed. *The China Difference,* New York: Harper and Row, Publishers, 1972.

Thurston, Anne. *Enemies of the People.* New York: Alfred Knopf, 1987.

Walder, Andrew. "Actually Existing Maoism." *The Australian Journal of Chinese Affairs* No. 19, July 1988. pp 155-166.

White, Lynn. T. *Policies of Chaos.* Princeton: Princeton University Press, 1989.

Wielemans, Willy and Pauline Choi-Ping Chan. *Education and Culture in Industrial Asia.* Leuven University Press, 1992.

Xu, Xiu. "Reflections on the Reform of Admission to Colleges andUniversities and the job Assignment System for Their Graduates." *Studies in Chinese Higher Education.* No.4, 1992. 44-48.

Yan, Yunxiang. "The Impact of Rural Reform on Economic and Social Stratificationin a Chinese Village," *The Australian Journal of Chinese Affairs,* No. 27, January 1992.

Yin, Dalu. "Reforming Chinese Education: Context, Structure and Attitudes in the1980s," *Compare. Vol.* 23, No. 2 1993 115-130.

Yue, Daiyun. *To the Storm.* Berkeley: University of California Press, 1987.

Zhelokhovtsev, A. *The Cultural Revolution, A Close up.* Moscow: Progress Publishers, 1975.

Zhou, Kate Xiao. *How the Farmers Changed China.* Boulder: Westview Press,1996.

Index

Printed in the United States
134782LV00001B/29/P